This is the story of how a who   ns-
plant — A young man on his lifelong dream of a Mormon... ...on,
his siblings, a father deeply enmeshed in LDS priesthood, and the
author, Lynn Wilder, a tenured professor at Brigham Young University. One by one they plucked the lifeless, works-driven core of
Mormonism from their breasts and replaced it with the vibrant grace
of Jesus Christ. A remarkable, tender account.

> — Latayne C. Scott, former Latter-day Saint;
> author, *The Mormon Mirage*

Unveiling Grace is the inspiring account of one Mormon family's journey from error to truth, from relying on priesthood authority to
faith, from trusting in temple ordinances to trusting Christ alone.
The Wilders' story demonstrates the love of the Shepherd as he
seeks his lost sheep.

> — Sandra Tanner, great-great-granddaughter of Brigham Young;
> president, Utah Lighthouse Ministry

With velvet articulation and a heart for the Latter-day Saint, Lynn
Wilder weaves an impressive narrative that proves that leaving Mormonism for Christ is not the end of abundant living but only the
beginning. Praise God for this warm and inviting work.

> — Shawn McCraney, former Latter-day Saint;
> host, *Heart of the Matter*; president, Alathea Ministries

Lynn Wilder does a wonderful job of describing from the inside both
why Mormonism makes sense and is so appealing to its followers,
and why so many Mormons today are coming to the conclusion that
the LDS religion is not the one true church it claims to be. Personally
engaging as well as theologically informed, *Unveiling Grace* goes beyond
explaining the problems with Mormonism and presents a sound, liber-
ating alternative in the gospel of grace. Highly recommended!

> — Robert M. Bowman Jr., director of research, Institute for
> Religious Research; author, *What Mormons Believe*

UNVEILING
GRACE

Lynn K. Wilder

UNVEILING
GRACE

THE STORY OF
HOW WE FOUND OUR WAY OUT
OF THE MORMON CHURCH

ZONDERVAN

Unveiling Grace
Copyright © 2013 by Lynn K. Wilder

This title is also available as a Zondervan ebook.
Visit www.zondervan.com/ebooks.

Requests for information should be addressed to:
Zondervan, *Grand Rapids, Michigan* 49530

Library of Congress Cataloging-in-Publication Data
Wilder, Lynn K., 1952-
    Unveiling grace : the story of how we found our way out of the Mormon Church /
Lynn K. Wilder.
      pages cm
    Includes bibliographical references.
    ISBN 978-0-310-33112-4 (softcover)
      1. Wilder, Lynn K., 1952- 2. Church of Jesus Christ of Latter-day Saints —
Biography. 3. Mormon Church — Biography. 4. Ex-church members — Church of
Jesus Christ of Latter-day Saints — Biography. 5. Ex-church members — Mormon
Church — Biography. 6. Church of Jesus Christ of Latter-day Saints — Controversial
literature. 7. Mormon Church — Controversial literature. I. Title.
BX8695.W5443A3 2013
289.3092 — dc23
    [B]   2013016772

Cover design: Michelle Lenger
Cover Image: Masterfile / Bill Frymire
Interior design: Katherine Lloyd, The DESK

Printed in the United States of America

13 14 15 16 17 18 /DCI/ 21 20 19 18 17 16 15 14 13 12 11 10 9 8 7 6 5 4 3 2

To the Lord, Jesus Christ

CONTENTS

Part One
MORMON BLISS

Part Two
CRACKS IN THE FACADE

Part Three

STARTING OVER

FOREWORD

When I first met Lynn Wilder and her husband, Michael, and heard their story of converting from the Mormon Church to biblical Christianity, I recognized that they have a perspective on Mormonism that few have ever heard. I invited them to share their story on my television program and quickly discovered that many others were interested in their journey as well.

One of the most common criticisms I receive from Mormons is, "You've never been a Mormon. You don't really know what we believe. Why should anyone listen to what you say?" But Lynn *has* been a Mormon, and her story describes the impact the Mormon Church's doctrines had on her real-life journey as a Brigham Young University professor who came to faith in the biblical Jesus. When she did, her life was transformed, as well as the lives of her family. Today, whenever a Mormon asks me about the differences between their beliefs and biblical Christianity, I tell Lynn's story.

Those who read about her journey need to know two things.

First, Lynn is relatively new to biblical Christianity. For thirty years, rather than experiencing the traditions of the evangelical church, Lynn participated in a set of cultural and spiritual traditions unique to Mormon teachings. As a result, she is sensitive to the needs and concerns of Mormons and their family members and is able to communicate the biblical gospel to them in a relevant, beneficial way. Her heart and message are exactly the same as mine in teaching the truth of the risen Savior, Jesus Christ, and the love and forgiveness he offers by grace through faith alone.

Second, Lynn's life is a testimony to the many differences that continue to exist between Mormon teachings and biblical Christianity. While those who claim "I am Mormon" strive to fit in with everyday Americans and even evangelical Christians, Mormon doctrine is quite distinct in many areas. Mormon doctrine does not believe in the Christian teaching of the Trinity, adds additional inspired writing to the Bible with the Book of Mormon, holds to many different views of Jesus than are found in the New Testament, and offers a different gospel message that includes a variety of works. As Lynn has grown in her faith in the Christ of the Bible, she has had to come to a new understanding in each of these areas in ways that help her to communicate the true gospel of the Bible to Mormons, ex-Mormons, and many others.

Remember, this book is not simply the words of some person who converted from Mormonism to the teachings found in the New Testament; Lynn is a walking testimony of God's grace poured out in the life of a person seeking to find true purpose and meaning in life. She has found it in the biblical Jesus Christ and now serves him by communicating his story through her life. May God bless you as you learn from her life how to better grow in the knowledge of our Lord Jesus Christ and serve him.

— Dr. John Ankerberg, president and
host of *The John Ankerberg Show*

Part One

———◆———

MORMON
BLISS

CHAPTER 1

OUR BELOVED FAITH

⚜

I know what happiness is, for I have done good work.

— ROBERT LOUIS STEVENSON

The three of us, dressed up and laughing, raced down the sidewalk and around the corner from our mountain home in Utah to the church building.

"Hurry, we'll be late," Micah called. The organ was playing the prelude for the opening hymn when Katie (fifteen), Micah (eighteen), and I stepped through the foyer, past the couch and the painting of Christ in a red robe, and into the chapel.

My husband, Michael, was sitting behind the podium in his dark suit and tie. He'd been at church since early morning, in meetings related to his responsibilities as one of three members of the bishopric. (This is similar to being an assistant pastor.) I was accustomed to sitting alone with the kids and was proud of Michael for his calling and his commitment to the Mormon Church—also known as the Church of Jesus Christ of Latter-day Saints, or the LDS Church.

The opening hymn began as we slid into seats in the back. It was fast-and-testimony Sunday, a once-a-month church service. Members fasted for twenty-four hours prior to the service and then filed up to the podium during the service to bear testimony of their love for the Mormon gospel. (Our son Micah hated to be late on these days, because the only seats left were way in the back. He preferred to sit up front, in ready position to bear his testimony.)

Mormon hymns are not all that rousing compared with, say, the gospel songs of the Brooklyn Tabernacle Choir, but most people in the congregation knew this one by heart. We obediently joined in the singing about Joseph Smith, the founder of the Mormon faith.

> *Praise to the man who communed with Jehovah!*
> *Jesus anointed that Prophet and Seer.*
> *Blessed to open the last dispensation,*
> *Kings will extol him and nations revere.*
>
> *Great is his glory and endless his priesthood.*
> *Ever and ever the keys he will hold.*
> *Faithful and true, he will enter his kingdom,*
> *Crowned in the midst of the prophets of old.*
>
> *Hail to the Prophet, ascended to heaven!*
> *Traitors and tyrants now fight him in vain.*
> *Mingling with Gods, he can plan for his brethren;*
> *Death cannot conquer the hero again.*[1]

When the testimonies began, Micah strode up the long aisle to the front of the plain chapel (we had pews but no cross, windows, or artwork) and up the steps. The bishop gave Mike a you're-doing-a-great-job-as-a-father wink.

Micah leaned down to speak into the microphone.

"I've had a very spiritual week. Every morning this week at

5:00 a.m., my girlfriend and I went to the Mount Timpanogos Temple before school to perform baptisms for the dead. It was so amazing. The Spirit was so strong. Friday night we went to Temple Square to see the movie *The Testaments of One Fold and One Shepherd*. The Book of Mormon and the Bible are two sticks—two testaments—together in Christ's hand. I couldn't help but cry, because I love my Savior so much." He looked out at the hundreds in the audience. "I want you to know that I *know* that Joseph Smith was a prophet of God. I *know* that the Father and the Son appeared to him in the Sacred Grove. I know that Heavenly Father chose him to bring forth the Book of Mormon and to restore the true church of Jesus Christ to the earth in these, the latter days. I can't wait to serve a mission and bring others into the fold. I love my family, and I love each of you. In the name of Jesus Christ, amen."

It was February of 2003, Micah's senior year in high school. He was a year from turning nineteen, when he could follow his two older brothers and serve his long-awaited two-year mission.[2] Micah made this podium pilgrimage monthly to bear witness to the truth of Mormonism. It was something he wanted to do to prepare himself spiritually for his mission. He often wept as he expressed his love for his church and for Christ.

After the seventy-minute church service, several priesthood brethren approached Micah to shake his hand, pound him on the shoulder, and congratulate him for his faith. Katie and I stood by smiling, but we all needed to get moving. We had two more meetings before the three-hour block was over.

Next hour, Mike and I taught the "Strengthening Your Marriage" Sunday school class while the kids went to their Sunday school classes. The third hour, Katie and Micah attended their respective youth organizations—Mia Maids, part of the Young Women organization, and priest's quorum, part of the Young Men organization—of which they both were officers. That hour,

Mike presided over the Primary organization (ages birth through eleven), assisting the workers with some rowdy boys. I was a leader in Young Women.

It was another ordinary Sunday.

Missionary Sons

Wilder family life in Utah was a desert whirlwind of Mormon bliss. My husband of thirty years was busy with his church callings and his home-based business. I loved teaching at Brigham Young University (BYU), which is owned and operated by the Mormon Church. And of course there were our children, whom we adored.

Mike and I had had four children within a nine-year period. Along with our two youngest children, Katie and Micah, we had two other sons: Josh was twenty-three and Matt was twenty. The kids seemed grounded in our religion and content with school, friends, and activities. With the two older boys gone on their missions, I had a hard time getting used to the idea that there were only four of us at home.

Entering the house after church, I imagined seeing our oldest son, tall and dark-haired Josh, looking hungry for Sunday dinner. Before his mission, he'd been a student—a social soul majoring in communications—first at Indiana University and then at the University of Utah, located forty-five minutes to the north of us in Salt Lake. At the U of U, he worked as a manager for Rick Majerus' Utes basketball team. Josh completed three years of college before deciding to serve a mission. Because he was older than many missionaries in his mission, he had an advantage. He was called to serve as a branch president (pastor of a very small Mormon congregation). Currently he was in Russia, soon to be transferred to Belarus, nearing the end of his LDS mission. He planned to finish college at the University of Utah when he returned.

Our second son, tall and Nordic Matt, powerful yet kind-hearted, was in Denmark preaching the Mormon gospel to the Danes, where he had some opportunity to write and perform sacred music. Before his mission, Matt had completed his freshman year at BYU, located forty-five minutes to the south of us in Provo, and was contemplating a piano performance major. He spent long hours at the piano every day. Soon after he left on his mission, he was accepted by the College of Fine Arts and Communications. When he was back in the country, he planned to return to BYU with both music and academic scholarships.

Since the boys' missions overlapped, Josh and Matt went almost three years without seeing each other; later Matt and Micah went nearly four years. We did not have a family photo with all of us present from September 2001 until April 2006. But we were proud of our Mormon missionary sons. First Josh, then Matt, and soon Micah — all bearing testimony to the truth of our beloved LDS faith. What could be better?

An Exemplary Mormon Youth

Micah is about six feet three inches tall with an easy magnetic smile, and characteristically tilts his head to his left. With his black, curly hair, he could easily grow a 1970s Afro, but he has always kept his hair conservatively short. He has his dad's Roman nose, my dark eyes and serious ways, and a curiosity that asks probing questions.

Never much of an eater, Micah was leaner than his brothers, a quick athlete who enjoyed basketball, soccer, and track. But mostly his interests tended toward his Mormon faith and the band he and friends had formed. He was an exemplary son who caused us little pain, a kind young man who tried his best to do what his parents and our solid Mormon faith expected of him. His faith in the Mormon Church was the center of his life. Ours too.

When Micah was in high school, we lived a mile high in an area of Utah that had the highest percentage of active Mormons in the world. At the time, I was so proud of Micah and the choices he made; just thinking about him made me grin.

This was a typical conversation between Micah and me his senior year:

Me: "Hi. You were up early again."

Micah: "Yeah, Leash [Alicia, his girlfriend] and I went to the temple again to do baptisms for the dead before school. I really like her, Mom. She's strong in the church, like me."

Me: "Alicia's a very spiritual young woman with a good head on her shoulders, Micah. You hungry?"

Micah: "No, I'm good. Mom, do you think when I'm a missionary, I'll convert a lot of people to the church?"

He wanted to be "good" and to do what would please Heavenly Father, as Mormons call him.

Me: "I'm sure you will be a great missionary, Micah. Your heart is in the right place."

Micah: "Is there anything I can do for you, Mom? Do you need me to run to the store or something?"

Now, what mother would not love this?

Me: "Well, you could go pick up Katie from dance lessons."

Micah: "No problem."

And out the door he went. He jumped into his dad's red Mitsubishi 3000GT twin turbo, the one Micah kept spit-shined, and rolled past our manicured lawn, the one he mowed in perfect golf course stripes. Even though the car's engine thundered with 320 horses, Micah always drove a little like an old lady. I liked that about him too.

Micah was eager to convert the corner of the world to which the living Mormon prophet would send him on his mission. He was ready to serve as a representative of the Church of Jesus

Christ of Latter-day Saints. It was exciting for the entire family to imagine where he might go.

Preparing for a Mission

On his eighteenth birthday, a week prior to the ordinary fast-and-testimony Sunday, Micah met with his Mormon bishop (pastor) in our church building, whose parking lot was across the grapevine-laden fence from our home, to design a plan to prepare himself during the ensuing year to be an effective missionary. The plan suggested he get up at 6:00 a.m., read his Mormon scriptures in the early morning, and practice throughout the day doing all the good deeds he had been taught by the Mormon Church and his parents over the years. Micah decided to add to this list that he would bear his testimony once a month every fast-and-testimony Sunday. He executed his plan as faithfully as an eighteen-year-old young man could. All he could think about was his mission. All he talked about was his mission.

After high school graduation, he worked a construction job. Then in the fall of 2003, he began his first semester as a physics major at Brigham Young University. In LDS culture, parents expect their sons to obtain at least a four-year degree after their mission, and Micah intended to follow suit. But he could barely concentrate on his studies. By late October, he had submitted his mission papers.

One morning, about the time Micah got up, the post office called to tell us that the 8 ½ x 11 white envelope with Micah's mission call from the first presidency of the Church of Jesus Christ of Latter-day Saints had arrived and that we did not have to wait for the postman to deliver it. The close Mormon community was delightfully friendly. We could pick the envelope up, which we did, before the sun rose.

In front of the gas fireplace in the living room, Michael,

Katie, and I pulled up chairs around Micah as he sat alone on the living room couch, wide-eyed, eagerly fingering the envelope. The anticipation was brutal. Open it! The Mormon prophet had heard from Heavenly Father, and Micah's mission call (see the glossary for the Mormon meanings of religious words) was to Mexico City. Wow.

I immediately put his revered call in a picture frame and nailed it to his bedroom wall. Missionary sons in Russia, Denmark, and now Mexico! It was something to be proud of. In Mormon culture, it was whispered that the worthiest missionaries received international assignments.

Before he could serve as a missionary, Micah was required to attend the temple proper for the first time. He'd been attending the basement of the temple since the age of twelve to do baptisms for the dead; now he could finally go upstairs to receive his washings and anointings and his endowment.

In November 2003, the Mount Timpanogos Temple, close to our home, was closed for the annual cleaning, so Micah chose to receive his ordinances in the historic Salt Lake Temple. Since Mike and I held temple recommends (which meant our church leaders deemed us worthy to enter), we showed our recommend cards to the couple standing as sentinels at the entrance, then accompanied our son inside.

First, the men went to the initiatory so Micah could receive his washings and anointings. Both Michael and Micah were washed symbolically with water, anointed with oil, and dressed in the garment of the holy priesthood. Once Micah received his garments, he was given a new name to be used later in the endowment, and the men met me in the hallway. We proceeded to a small chapel to await the endowment ceremony in a room down the hall, where we were instructed, with approximately thirty people, in what we needed to know to live with Heavenly Father in the next life. We entered into six specific covenants and then imitated passing through the veil to enter the Lord's presence at the end of this life. The three of us felt greatly blessed and emotionally weakened by this three-hour experience in the temple.

Soon afterward Micah earned the privilege of becoming the youngest full-time temple worker in the modern age of the Mormon Church. We lived no more than fifteen minutes from the Mount Timpanogos Temple, located at the base of the majestic Timpanogos Mountain, and he wanted to serve as a full-time temple worker in the two months before his mission began. This was unheard of. I admit we were somewhat disappointed he had chosen not to get a paying job to contribute financially toward his mission but instead to work in a Mormon temple gratis, assisting attendees with carrying out the saving ordinances for people who were already dead, a righteous act to convert the dead to Mormonism. But that was Micah. How could we object to such honorable desires to serve the Mormon Lord?

The Torture Room

When the treasured moment — on February 10, 2004 — finally arrived, everyone in the family dressed in their Sunday best and accompanied Micah to the Missionary Training Center (MTC) on the campus of BYU. The LDS Church is very organized. We had to park in a certain spot, enter through a certain door, and stay in a certain foyer while Micah checked in and took his luggage down the hall to a designated room. He seemed a bit tense but was raring to go.

Families and future missionaries were ushered into a large convention-like hall — the torture room, my husband called it. This was our third experience in the same room being ripped from a son with whom we would have very limited contact for the next two years. Essentially, we were giving up our parental rights to Micah's mission president. After we all watched a video about being called to serve a mission, heard two brief talks by MTC leaders, and sang a couple of LDS hymns, Micah said his goodbyes to his father and me individually.

He held my shoulders, pierced me with his eyes, and told me he loved me but was excited to begin his mission. I didn't know what to say. He hugged and kissed me one last time, then embraced his cherished younger sister and his dad. Then he turned to exit the door for missionaries, which was opposite the door for families. As he reached the door, he spun and gave us a two-fingered salute. It was more than I could bear. While my husband stood in shock, I bawled silently. We exited the family door in emotional agony. The torture room had lived up to its name once again.

Micah was called to a leadership position in the MTC, his letters to us said. Since he was headed to Mexico City to proselytize, he was scheduled to spend about six weeks at the MTC learning how to teach the basics of the Mormon gospel in Spanish. From his letters home, he sounded exhilarated.

Each of the three times I had a son in the Mission Training Center, it was agonizingly difficult to work just a few blocks away at my office at BYU during their training. Even if I drove by the training center, I could see nothing because of the high walls surrounding the complex. The church had the missionaries well isolated.

But then something occurred that later proved to be instrumental in shifting the trajectory of our lives. After about two weeks in the MTC, Micah's left lung collapsed while he was playing basketball. We were allowed to spend two glorious days by his side in the hospital in Provo. Still dedicated to his mission, Micah pinned his missionary badge to his hospital gown.

This medical emergency necessitated that church prophet,

seer, and revelator Gordon B. Hinckley reassign Micah "stateside," as Mormons say, because living in Mexico City posed health risks for a person with a lung problem. We worried that this glitch would shake Micah's testimony regarding the prophet's direction for his life, but Micah told us in the hospital that he knew all along he was destined for a Spanish-speaking mission in Florida. Heavenly Father had a plan.

Micah was called to Orlando, the happiest place on earth. We adjusted to his absence as best we could, just as we had twice before with his brothers, setting a place at the table for him on holidays. Occasionally I went to his bedroom to pray and cry, mourning his absence, pleading with Heavenly Father for Micah's success in spreading the Mormon gospel. Our relationship with Micah became distant, but in the two years he was gone on his mission, life went on.

A Phone Call

On a Friday in January 2006, three weeks before Micah was scheduled to return, I was writing a professional paper in my home office and Mike was making calls in his home office next to mine—a routine and enjoyable Friday in the Wilder home. But the apple cart of Mormon bliss was about to overturn, flinging apples in every direction.

At 11:30 a.m. the phone rang. It was Vanesa, a former coworker at BYU and one of my best friends; she sometimes had interesting premonitions. She simply asked how Micah was.

"Okay," I answered, "as far as I know. Thanks for your concern."

At 11:57 a.m. the phone rang again.

"Hello," I said cheerily.

Pause. "It's over." It was Micah's solemn voice. He was still on his mission in Florida.

"Okay ...," I said, my heart pounding. I decided right then

and there to be fine with whatever was happening, even if I did not understand it yet. After all, this was Micah, one of our precious children, whom I had cradled and so dearly loved. But from the tone of his voice, I knew right away what he meant. The mission. His belief in the Mormon faith. It was over.

It would take many long months—years—of excruciating truth-seeking and acts of God before my own belief in the Mormon faith was over. The grace of the true God did not blaze in blinding Damascus glory. Instead, like a veiled Dancer, God allured me, drew me, unveiled portions of his grace at crucial moments, blessed me only with tantalizing glimpses of him.

Looking back, I can remember having such glimpses of God's grace as early as age five. Had God been revealing himself to me throughout my life? Then why did it take a trial so harrowing to finally get my attention?

Only now, looking back, can I begin to piece together God's plan.

CHAPTER 2

GROWING UP CHRISTIAN

"No one can come to me unless the Father who sent me draws them."

—JOHN 6:44

Like many of our neighbors on the south side of Indianapolis in the 1960s, I grew up nominally Christian. Each week, my parents took the four of us children to a Methodist church and later to a Presbyterian church. But what did I really know about faith in Jesus? Not much.

What I remember about church is this. A former marine, my dad was a stickler for punctuality. On Sunday morning, we hurried to get dressed for church and ran to the car. My mother was usually late, probably because she had to get the little ones dressed before she could get ready herself. Meanwhile Dad sat impatiently in the car and called to her to hurry or he would leave. If she did not come, he honked the horn. If she still did not come, we left without her. Tension was in the air, but we had no real fear of my dad, just anxiety over his sharp bark. In public,

Dad was a loud, friendly, in-charge guy — a typical father of the time who didn't do diapers. We loved him.

The oldest child, I was serious, quiet, and studious, always anxious to avoid trouble. I attended kindergarten in a church. There I learned about God and assumed he existed, believing in him enough to pray a sincere prayer at about the age of five. I remember standing next to the Steinway grand piano that had belonged to my grandmother and asking Jesus if he would please let me create music for him. Today I play very little piano and sing rather poorly. I would not by any stretch of the imagination be considered a good musician. But I remember this prayer.

Every day, we children had to be in bed before my dad got home for dinner at seven. I remember lying in the still-light bedroom at the top of the stairs, looking at the slanted pine ceiling and listening to mice run in the attic. Sometimes I was afraid of being alone, especially if we had a booming Indiana thunderstorm. I talked to God often, as if he were an imaginary friend.

Fear of Fire

In the third grade, I had a stern red-haired teacher. Even though she was teaching in a public school in Indianapolis, this teacher used to tell us we would burn in hell if we were not good. I believed her, and she scared me to death because I knew I wasn't good. During that school year, I developed an irrational fear of fire. Every night when I got into bed, I pulled the edges of the comforter off the floor and up onto the bed so that when the fire came, it wouldn't creep up to where I was sleeping.

For the next four years, I had recurring nightmares of being roused in the middle of the night by fire, trying to find my way outside, and then searching for my family and my cat. In the last scene of the dream, I was always watching the house burn.

One freezing winter weekend when I was twelve, our family went to the tiny Amish town of Berne, Indiana, to visit my parents' good friends. That night while we were sleeping, the downtown drugstore burned down. The next morning, the news spread, and the entire town, including us, went to see it.

At first I was too nervous to look, but soon I was mesmerized by the heaps of smoldering ruins. Except for one wall. One drugstore wall, painted off-white, remained standing, while the other brick walls had tumbled down and their paint had melted away. In the middle of that wall was a framed painting of Jesus, untouched by the fire.

It couldn't be. It just was not reasonable — at least I'd never seen anything like it in my short life. Could Jesus do that? Keep his picture from being touched when everything else was destroyed? I realize now that this, like the friendship of One who comforted me when I lay in bed alone at night, was a glimpse of grace from a God who loved me personally. After that, my nightmares of fire disappeared forever. But I stopped talking to Jesus at night. My favorite grandmother had died, and talking to her when I needed a friend replaced talking to Jesus.

Glimpses of Faith

That summer, we vacationed in Biloxi, Mississippi. While Dad checked into the hotel, the TV was on in the lobby. Spellbound, I watched Billy Graham preach Jesus to tens of thousands of people in an arena somewhere. Although I yearned to stay and listen, I had to straggle along behind the family.

We must have continued to attend church and probably Sunday school every week, but I have little recollection of it. At age twelve, I memorized the Twenty-Third Psalm and the Lord's Prayer for my Presbyterian catechism. I had a male Sunday school teacher in junior high, whom I remember mostly because he was cute. On Saturdays, we rehearsed for the youth choir at church: *"Dona, nobis pa-a-cem, pacem."*

My memories of Bible reading are similarly scanty. I received a Bible from our church when I was eight, but it has no markings in it, no dog-eared pages. I never read it. At school, I received a Gideon New Testament with Psalms that I placed by my bed and looked at occasionally. I liked this verse in 2 Timothy: "Study to shew thyself approved unto God" (2:15 KJV). I thought that meant to study in school, so I did that to the best of my ability and was an A student.

Once, just once, after Sunday dinner, Dad asked the family to stay at the table while he read from our huge, gold family Bible. The atmosphere was solemn. Now a senior in high school, I loved having the family together like that, but I was unprepared for what I was about to hear.

After Dad finished reading, Mom announced to us that when she was eleven, her physician-surgeon father had committed suicide, and she had found him. He and her concert pianist mother had been caught in the sucking hellhole of drug addiction. The two intellectuals had married in 1926 with great hopes. They belonged to Greenpeace, spoke Esperanto — the international language — and rejected faith in God. My grandfather perpetrated abuse on his family for more than a decade, tried in vain to free himself, and finally took his life.

After the funeral, my grandmother was admitted to an institution for rehab, where she remained until Mom was a senior in high school. My uncle and mother were taken to separate foster homes in the same small town a stone's throw away from their house. Mom said, "We remained in foster care for several years; I lived with an old maid. No one talked to me about what had happened to my family."

When Mom was twelve, someone invited her to the little white clapboard church barely a block from the home where her family had shared their nightmare. Mom told us, "There I found someone — God — who cared whether I lived or died. I clung to my relationship with him. I became a good student, went on to a Christian college, and met your father." A devoted mother, Mom was determined that her children would have the unconditional love that she had been denied.[3]

The family Scripture reading never happened again, that I recall. It was Dad's way of doing what he could to help Mom feel comforted. Although I don't recall what they were, the words he read from the Bible that day left me with a sense of well-being that I remembered down through the years.

God or No God?

In high school, I nannied for a Catholic family of eight, so for a time I was curious about Catholicism. Their eight-year-old daughter used to get on her knees and pray for the injured each time she heard an ambulance, and her faith impressed me. I loved her and her siblings a lot. As I was making post-high-school decisions, I even visited a local convent to ask a nun about her sequestered life. She told me she had taken three vows: poverty, chastity, and obedience. Not understanding how poverty and chastity would get me close to God, I dismissed the cloistered life as an option.

One day in our high school library, I was pondering what to do with my life. The library, with its dark wood shelves and musty smell, was one of my favorite places. That day, a beam of late-afternoon sunlight touched a book on the bottom shelf near my seat at the wooden table. When I opened it, I read about a woman who started an orphanage for unwanted children in New York City. *This is it!* I thought. *This is what I want to do with the rest of my life — rescue people no one else cares about so that those like Mom will never want for love.* I decided to major in special education.

Two of the three top universities in the nation for special education were within five hours of my home. The top-ranked program was in California. That seemed too far away, so I went to the second-ranked program, which was in Michigan. During my first year of college, I attended a weekly Bible study at the Catholic Newman Center, but my motives were mostly social. I didn't pray. By the end of that first year, I wasn't sure I even believed in God. What did it matter? I learned in my comparative economics course that social justice could right the world's wrongs, so God seemed irrelevant.

About the time I decided to dismiss God, a weird thing happened. It was summer vacation, and I was in my parent's house in Indiana. One night I was awakened abruptly from a deep sleep, feeling as though an elephant were standing on my chest. I was frantic, panicking, gasping for breath. Someone or something was suffocating me. I could get no air. Something heavy was overpowering me, squeezing the very life from me. If I couldn't get air soon, I knew I would die.

Unable to utter a word, I called out to Jesus in my head. Then I mentally sang the words of the only hymn I could think of.

What a friend we have in Jesus,
all our sins and griefs to bear.

I then said in my head, "I choose Jesus."

I had no idea what that statement meant, except to protect myself from the immediate danger of suffocation. And it seemed to work, for gradually the heaviness lifted so I could breathe.

I thought, *If there is a God and if this experience is real, then I would choose Jesus and life. I don't want Satan sitting on my chest.* But I was not ready to accept that the experience was real or what a serious decision for Christ might mean. Like most young people, I was content to be god of my own life. I had plans, and as far as I was concerned, Jesus played no part in them. I dismissed the experience and avoided thinking about it.

Philosophies of Men

The fall of my sophomore year, I transferred to the university in Indiana that had the third-ranked program in special education, partly because of a boyfriend and partly because in-state tuition was cheaper. Life went on as usual. The only time I was inside a church that year was to work with intellectually disabled adults on a midweek morning. At the university, I was exposed to the world's philosophers, scholars, and poets. I read Sigmund Freud, B. F. Skinner, and Charles Darwin and learned about socialism and Marxism. Good student that I was, I read pretty much every assigned word, took notes, studied, and made these teachings part of my academic self.

On my own, I read popular spiritual books like Khalil Gibran's *The Prophet*, Richard Bach's *Jonathon Livingston Seagull*, and Shel Silverstein's *The Giving Tree*. In German class, we read Goethe's *Faust*, about Dr. Faust selling his soul to the Devil. The Dalai Lama was popular among my peers, as were Buddha, chakras, and yoga, although I was never into Eastern religions. Jesus wasn't on the reading lists or my spiritual radar. Once, a street preacher came to campus and yelled that we were going to hell, but the shouting approach didn't work for me. Back home, my parents and youngest sister joined a community church and found renewed faith in Jesus, but I do not remember them sharing their experience with me. Perhaps they assumed I knew Jesus from my years of church attendance growing up. My mother, a peacemaker, tended to avoid any uncomfortable direct communication.

Mom went to work teaching weekday release-time religious

education classes in Christian churches next to public elementary schools, where she influenced untold lives of fourth- and fifth-grade children. When she was in her fifties, she and Dad went through eight years of Bible Study Fellowship. Her kitchen table was forever strewn with Bible study materials. Later she was instrumental in bringing Bible Study Fellowship to the south side of Indianapolis, and she grew to be a local mentor and leader in that organization. Mom also led a women's Bible study in her home. She obviously knew the importance of studying God's Word, but I did not.

The woman my mom morphed into during those years spent in God's Word, while I was in college, bordered on saintly. But at the time, I didn't connect her developing character with her study of the Bible or her faith in Jesus. Nor did I realize she was probably praying for my soul — or soon would be.

Michael Dean Wilder

A confident, career-bound young woman, I met Michael Dean Wilder in a folk dance class we were required to take as a physical education credit our junior year in college. Mike was tall and lanky, dark, curly-haired, and somewhat shy. He'd grown up with humble older parents on a farm in Indiana and was unpretentious, relaxed, and hardworking. He laughed easily and took life matter-of-factly. In contrast, I was so serious. We were a great complementary pair from the very beginning.

We danced together occasionally in class. Reticent, he waited until the very last day of class to try to ask me out. But he turned away for a moment at the end of class, and I was gone. He dashed out into the hall by one of the gyms, and there I was, cooling my head under the stream of water at the drinking fountain. When I looked up, he was grinning at me with that characteristic twinkle in his eye. His carefully chosen first words to me were, "Gee, you sweat a lot."

Jerk, I thought.

I had not gone to college to find a husband, as many of my peers seemed to have done. I was excited about changing the world, and I wasn't sure I wanted a husband and a family to interfere. Besides, these were the days of dedication to population control (in part because of Paul Ehrlich's book *The Population Bomb*), and college and my parents had indoctrinated me with the idea that having too many children was selfish and irresponsible.

But I accepted Mike's invitation for a first date, and at the end of it, he bent down (not too far; I was fairly tall too) and gave me a peck. That peck stirred in me a fire for more of his kindness, his gentleness, his humor. It was all over. After that first date, we could barely go a day apart. We talked late into the nights, although neither of us had been chatty people. Okay, so I was in love, but that did not mean I had to have a family. Maybe we would just do life together.

On one date, we drove to Fort Wayne, Indiana, to go folk dancing. Michael worked two jobs and attended college full-time. I studied endless hours, so time together was priceless. We rode in his tiny green MG Midget convertible, which was so hard to start that he had to run beside it holding the door, jump into the driver's seat, and pop the clutch to engage the engine. As I got out of the car in Fort Wayne, something spoke to my mind and said very clearly, "Marry that man." I stared at Michael, who was several paces in front of me, and thought, *I could imagine that.* Another instance of grace?

Michael and I wanted whatever the other one wanted, and life was good. When his parents met me, his father told him not to let that one get away. His mother was less impressed and found me plain because I didn't wear makeup. Meanwhile my well-educated parents were concerned that Michael's grammar was less than perfect. But in the end, they approved of the relationship, and we all got along remarkably well.

Soon enough I just wanted to marry Michael and wake up beside him every morning—*plus* save the unwanted children of the world. We had our first date February 9, got engaged the end of July, and were married December 28. We danced an Israeli love dance to each other at the wedding, and our two hundred guests were treated to some hilariously joyful line dancing.

Mike was raised in a hellfire-and-damnation Baptist church, but he never caught the vision. His parents read the Bible to the children at home. In fact, his father read it quite a bit and discussed it with Mike. Michael did believe in Jesus, and after our marriage, we tried to find a church, but none seemed to fit. They were all distant, formal, and out of touch.

Despite our lack of a church home, I decided I wanted to know more about the Bible. In my typical academic way of seeking, I signed up for a correspondence course to learn the Old Testament. I read the assigned passages, completed the materials, sent them in, and received the next set. At the end of the course, I was convinced that, because modern Israel had finally returned to her homeland as prophesied in the Old Testament, we were living in the "latter days" spoken of by the prophets Jeremiah, Ezekiel, Daniel, Hosea, and others. I felt an urgency to know more about this. The pastors in the churches we visited never talked about the latter days. But soon two young men in dark suits who knocked at our door did.

The veiled Dancer of truth had been alluring me, but I was oblivious, and I was about to embark on a major tangent.

CHAPTER 3

MORMONS COME CALLING

I know the church is true. I know Joseph Smith was a prophet of God . . .

— ANY MORMON'S TESTIMONY

Michael and I had been married without children for almost three years. Together we had bought a little four-room, red-brick home just off the campus of Ball State University in Muncie, Indiana. I gardened and read. Mike did some woodworking and built us a cozy fireplace in the living room. Instead of children, we nurtured plants and our dog Troika, a Samoyed. I was teaching special education to children living in abject rural poverty. Plus, I was in school again evenings and summers to earn a master's degree. Meanwhile Michael was completing his graduate degree in accounting and had been offered a full-time teaching position at the university. He was working to complete the pesky master's thesis by fall semester.

Michael was home alone, working on his thesis, that August day in 1977 when the missionaries knocked. His thesis was titled

Using the Beta Coefficient to Measure Changes in Stock Volatility. We laugh now that had he mastered the topic, we might be wealthy.

"Come on In"

Mike was a bit crazy from too much time with the subject matter, so as a diversion he let the missionaries in. He got the diversion. They got respite from the heat, a cool drink, and a chance to teach the Mormon gospel to an intelligent twenty-five-year-old.

"Have you heard of prophets?" they began.

"Yeah, I've heard of prophets," he answered.

"Do you know about apostles?"

"Yeah, Jesus had apostles."

"Don't you think God loves us enough to send prophets and apostles to speak to us like he did the Israelites in times of old?"

"Sounds reasonable."

With their flip charts, characteristic of the time, the missionaries taught Michael the first discussion.

"Joseph Smith was only fourteen when he went to the grove to ask Heavenly Father which of the churches he should join. Heavenly Father and Jesus appeared to Joseph in a pillar of light — after the Enemy had kept him bound for a time — and told him not to join any of them."

The young missionaries were just so nice and sincere. They'd left their families, their education, and their friends to serve their church for two years. Mike listened intently that first visit and was excited to tell me about it when I got home from teaching.

I was upset with Michael at first for letting them in, and even more annoyed at him for inviting them to come back when I got home. The idea of strangers teaching us in our own living room seemed invasive. When I thought of Mormons, I pictured the Amish. I envisioned long dark skirts on the women and maybe pioneer bonnets. Weren't they polygamists?

When the clean-cut missionary pair in dark suits with badges came back, I immediately noticed that the title of their church—the Church of Jesus Christ of Latter-day Saints—addressed my concern about latter days from the Old Testament correspondence course. Just when I became convinced that these were the latter days—but no pastor we knew was talking about them—the missionaries knocked on our door. Right on cue.

One of my character traits was to scrutinize everything and then be highly critical of it. The academic world had also taught me to question. My analytical brain never slept peacefully back then. The problem was that in this case, I was so ignorant about Christianity, I didn't even know intelligent questions to ask the Mormon missionaries. The questions I conjured up came from what they had just presented to us. How could I tell if any of it was true? At first, not knowing about this Book of Mormon thing, we bade them stick to the Bible. But they persisted in interjecting Book of Mormon scriptures with the Bible ones and asking us to read specific assignments in the Book of Mormon as homework.

Despite my correspondence course and interest in spiritual things, Mike and I rarely read the Bible. We had no foundational knowledge of truth with which to recognize falsehood. Could the missionaries' Book of Mormon really be the absolute standard of truth?

Perhaps getting wind of what was happening, someone placed anti-Mormon/pro-Christian literature in Michael's mailbox at the university. When we told the missionaries about it, they said, "You can expect that kind of opposition to Mormon teachings. The opposition is how you know it is the truth."

Really? I wondered. *Opposition is evidence that the Devil has reared up against it, so it has to be true? Maybe, maybe not.*

Mike was genuinely interested in the missionaries' stories. So

I acquiesced, agreeing to let them return on a regular basis twice a week. Even though we laughed at the canned presentations and the leading questions they were required to use, we listened. The missionaries kept returning to our home with new official men in tow each time to persuade us that all was well in the Zion of Mormonism. They soon ran out of their artificial discussions, but they kept coming back to convince us to join the Mormon Church.

Then someone got smart. They sent a Mormon professor from Mike's department at the university, and the professor's wife, to mentor us and to love on us like parents. We were invited to dinners at their home and to church activities, gaining status in the university and in the church community in one fell swoop. This join-the-family technique was the most effective of all in getting us to stay with them. Mormons understand the role that relationships play in potential converts' willingness to accept new ideas and the LDS culture. Establishing relationships and loving people works. Mormons do it well.

This family's acceptance and love meant so much to us that we endured even our first awkward visit to the LDS Church. Although Mormon women always wear dresses to church, I wore pants. Men are clean-shaven and wear dark suits, white shirts, and ties to church, but Michael had a beard and dressed casually. Still, the professor and his wife sat beside us, fussing over us. When the silver sacrament tray passed by with the leavened bread, Mike reached out to take a piece, thinking it was just like the Communion he'd taken as a Baptist. The professor's wife smacked his hand away, telling him we were unworthy to take the sacrament because we were not yet members of the church. Besides, I had pants on. Despite this classic display of legalism (we would have seen red flags if we had read the New Testament), we really did love the missionaries and the professor's family.

Testing Truth with Feelings

Now the closer. We were challenged to pray about whether the Book of Mormon was true. This challenge comes from Moroni 10:4 in the Book of Mormon: "When ye shall receive these things, I would exhort you that ye would ask God, the Eternal Father, in the name of Christ, if these things are not true; and if ye shall ask with a sincere heart, with real intent, having faith in Christ, he will manifest the truth of it unto you, by the power of the Holy Ghost."

The Holy Ghost would tell us that the Book of Mormon was true if we just asked Heavenly Father in the name of Christ with a sincere heart.

I don't recall ever praying this prayer; perhaps I didn't want to know. The only reasons why I considered Mormonism were: (1) Mormons seemed to know that these were latter days, and (2) Joseph Smith's experience with Satan during his First Vision was similar to the experience I had in the middle of the night.[4]

Mike, however, dutifully prayed to ask if the Book of Mormon was true. Then he had a stark dream in which he vehemently defended the Mormon people from their attackers. This seemed to him like his answer: the Book of Mormon must be true, and he should join the Mormon Church and defend its doctrines. I was still skeptical, but I knew he felt he *had* to do this.

Our first big conundrum. Mike offered not to join Mormonism for me. I offered to try it for him. We made a pact then and there that throughout our life together, whatever we did in the area of faith we would do together. So we decided to try Mormonism together.

The Mormons were ecstatic to hear we'd finally folded. The next step was to be baptized by immersion and to become members of the Church of Jesus Christ of Latter-day Saints by having people in authority lay hands on us. It was about ten weeks from the missionaries' first visit to our baptism.

My mother and youngest sister, Cindy, both Christians, refused to attend the Saturday evening baptism on October 28, 1977. They never told me why. My father did come, and members of the local Mormon congregation came out in droves. I guess it was a big deal to win converts. The baptism required a worthy priesthood holder with proper authority, in this case one of our missionaries, to enter the water and perform the baptism in a certain way, with just the right words. It required two other priesthood holders as witnesses to make sure not one hair of our heads was left undunked; otherwise we would have to be rebaptized. The baptism took place in an oblong vat in a basement room of the church, where all could see. The missionary baptized Mike and then me.

The next morning, during the sacrament service (the normal church service), in front of the congregation, we were confirmed members of the Church of Jesus Christ of Latter-day Saints. The priesthood men stood in a circle with their hands on my head and declared, "Receive the Holy Ghost!" Nothing discernable happened. But a lot was about to change.

A New Family

Within six months I was fully indoctrinated into the faith family, weeping like the rest of the Mormons when I bore testimony of "the only true and living church upon the face of the whole earth, with which I, the Lord, am well pleased" (Mormon scripture, the Doctrine and Covenants [D&C] 1:30). With other Mormons during the often-emotional monthly fast-and-testimony meeting, I declared the standard LDS testimony: "I know the church is true. I know Joseph Smith was a prophet of God and that he restored the *true* church. I know Heavenly Father and Jesus appeared to him in the sacred grove ..."

The Mormon Church had a powerful grip that pulled me in.

Church relationships began to supplant biological family relationships as we dove into a life of active participation with our new religious family. They made sure we were busy and involved with church callings.

One of Mike's first callings in the Mormon Church was as ward clerk. In this capacity, he served the bishop and his two counselors clerically as a layperson for no pay. In Protestantism, this would be roughly equivalent to an administrative assistant serving the pastor and two assistant pastors.

At the time Mike started in this position, the stake leaders (regional) were in town to split the local ward (congregation) into two wards. (Mormonism keeps its congregations at about five hundred members, small enough so everyone can hold a calling and so most members know most other members.) This second congregation would share the existing church building.

After a prayer, Michael's interview with a member of the stake presidency went something like this:

"Good morning, Brother Wilder."

"Good morning, President."

"As you know, the ward has split. We have felt inspired to call you as the ward clerk for the new ward. There's just one problem. The beard has to go."

"Why would I have to shave my beard?" His beard was neatly trimmed.

"We follow the example of the living prophet. We want our leadership to be clean-shaven so we are not in any way associated with the hippies of the 1960s or do not validate any other negative association people may have with beards. Appearance is very important. Keeping your beard is not optional, Brother Wilder. If you choose to keep a moustache, it must remain neatly trimmed and cannot hang below the corners of your mouth."

"Okay, President. Whatever it takes to serve."

Mike made the decision on the spot. He was not characteristically a pushover, but priesthood brethren were training him well to obey his leaders. My input carried no weight with priesthood leadership. (I rather liked the beard.)

When the ward split, I was called to be the Young Women (YW) president for the new ward. I was responsible for administering, with the oversight of my priesthood leader, the weeknight activities and the Sunday teaching of young Mormon women ages twelve to eighteen.

After we had served several months in the church, church leaders began to talk to us about preparing to go to the temple. This is a big deal in Mormonism. Most LDS Church members are not considered worthy to attend the temple, but everyone is encouraged to become worthy. We trusted that they knew what Christ wanted for faithful members of his church, so we agreed to prepare.

The Temple and a Baby

I had a compelling reason to want to visit the temple: I longed for a baby. Although I hadn't thought I wanted children, after a year or so of marriage, I unexpectedly got pregnant. During my pregnancy, I kept touching my belly. It was a glorious, spiritual experience to carry that little life. I moved gently, gingerly. Nonetheless, at four months we miscarried. I was bewildered and in terrible mourning for that tiny baby.

Now, among Mormons, children are everywhere. Some families have six or eight or even ten kids. In the world outside Mormonism, having too many children is often seen as irresponsible. But the Mormons taught us just the opposite. We *must* have children, and we *must* have as many as we could physically and emotionally support.

The reason behind this mandate is a peculiar LDS doctrine

of pre-existent spirits. The LDS Church teaches that before the creation of the world, Heavenly Father had sired and Heavenly Mother had borne millions of their spirit children. After the world was created, these spirits eagerly waited to come to earth to receive physical bodies. Only the righteous spirits who had followed Jesus (not Satan) in the pre-existence war in heaven were allowed by Heavenly Father to come to earth. They longed to be born into a "righteous" family (Mormon), in which they could learn the "true gospel of Jesus Christ" (Mormonism).

Behavior in the pre-existence could determine a spirit's lot here on earth. Coming to earth and gaining a body was a necessary part of their "eternal progression." If we didn't provide bodies for these spirits, they might have to come to a less desirable home on earth.

This doctrine sounds bizarre now. But since Mike and I knew little about biblical teaching, we had no warning signs, no reasons to doubt what the Mormons told us. The Mormon families we saw in our ward seemed—and many were—so close, so devoted to each other. They seemed happy. The ward itself functioned as one big family. Everyone had a role (calling). We came to love our new church family, and we were with them at least three hours each Sunday and again a couple of days during the week. We wanted all that the church had to offer. So toward the end of our first year, we prepared to go to the holy temple. But first we got our patriarchal blessings.

Dangerous Ground

As a part of our progression in the church, we were asked to travel to West Lafayette, Indiana, to meet with an ordained church patriarch who held a higher calling in the Mormon hierarchy. Mormons talked to us about this experience with reverent anticipation, because a patriarch receives the blessing for a worthy member directly from the Mormon Lord after the fasting and spiritual preparation of both the patriarch and the member.

One patriarchal blessing suffices for a lifetime. The official church website explains, "Patriarchal blessings include a declaration of a person's lineage in the house of Israel [which tribe of Israel members are from or adopted into] and contain personal counsel from the Lord. As a person studies his or her patriarchal blessing and follows the counsel it contains, it will provide guidance, comfort, and protection."[5]

When we arrived in West Lafayette, the patriarch got acquainted with us and then placed his hands on my head first to deliver the blessing. This moment is expected to be a spiritual experience. The promises of the blessing come to pass only if one remains faithful to the church, of course, and the blessing is shown only to people who will not scoff at it. During the blessing, electricity coursed from the patriarch's hands through my body. It was like nothing I had experienced before.

The words of our blessings were recorded, typed up onto two legal-sized pages each, and mailed to us. Mike's blessing said, "The blood of Ephraim flows in your veins." Wow, he had a Jewish heritage? Later I searched his genealogy, since we were encouraged to find the names of dead ancestors to take with us to the temple for their saving ordinances, but I didn't find any Jewish ancestry.

Mine said, "I bless you with children." I held those words sacred and often read the blessing at bedtime. My patriarchal blessing became my guiding star.

Now we were nearly ready to go to the temple, the next step in my quest to have a child. What does going to the temple have to do with having babies? In the temple, our marriage could be sealed for time and all eternity—Michael and I would be married for this life and the next. An eternal marriage was what Heavenly

Father wanted for us, we were told, and we would be blessed if we did what was right. If we were sealed in the temple, we would have children born under the covenant. Heavenly Father was waiting for us to do what was right. And we were willing and eager to please him.

Our first pregnancy ended in miscarriage, but after I had experienced the sensation of life within me, we developed a robust craving for a baby, which increased once we joined the church. We got pregnant four more times, and each time, the baby miscarried at about sixteen weeks.

In the end, we took fertility drugs and finally kept a child in utero past sixteen weeks. We became pregnant with this child at the same time we attended the Washington D.C. Temple to receive our endowments and to be sealed as a couple. The pregnancy occurred just as the Mormons had promised us. Right on cue. However, this pregnancy was not without its challenges.

Early in the pregnancy, I flew to Denver to present at a national Head Start convention for a grant I was working on at the university. The second morning of the conference, I woke up in a downtown Denver hotel room soaked in blood. Alone and nearly hysterical, I did not know where to turn or what to do. We had been members of the Mormon Church about a year and a half at that point and were already thoroughly integrated. I had been taught to call on the Mormon elders to pray in case of an emergency, so I found the number of an LDS ward in the phone book and called the bishop. He sent two men to the hotel room to pray for me. Assuming I had lost the baby, the bishop's wife talked to me on the phone about her own miscarriage.

When I flew back to Indianapolis, my mother picked me up at the airport and took me immediately to the hospital. Michael couldn't come, because he was in Connecticut baptizing his only sister into the LDS Church. Back then, a blood test was required to determine pregnancy status. Miracle of miracles, I was still pregnant.

We began to look at such incidences through the lens of Mormonism. We believed that God supernaturally saved this child because we had joined the Lord's true church and because we had been found worthy, had received our endowments, and had been sealed in the temple a couple of months earlier. We were being blessed.

Although I continued to bleed from time to time, Michael and I decided to travel the twelve hours by car to attend the D.C. Temple again to demonstrate to Heavenly Father our gratitude for this imminent birth. We believed we were closer to Heavenly Father in the celestial room of a Mormon temple than anywhere else on earth, and the D.C. Temple was the closest temple to us, our assigned temple. There, we were taught, we could shut out the world and hear answers to prayer.

The Washington D.C. Temple is a large white edifice with spires towering over the trees. As you round a bend on the beltway, it rises suddenly into view. Someone had written on the beltway overpass, "Surrender, Dorothy!" I suppose it does look like the Emerald City from *The Wizard of Oz*. But we reverently took part in a two-hour endowment ritual for people who were dead, to redeem them to the Mormon Church, thus showing our devotion and perhaps ensuring the baby's health.

But to our horror, while in the temple I went into labor — not at all what we had expected after our lengthy trip to the Mormon mecca. Cramps bent me double. I was in my fifth month of pregnancy, and again I was gripped by fear. Irrationally, I refused to let anyone call an ambulance. I had such faith in the LDS Church, in the people and the procedures, that I asked Michael and two missionaries at the temple to pray for the baby. Then one of the temple workers, a woman, drove us to her house. A nurse who lived there seemed to help get the labor stopped, or maybe several hours of bed rest just made it stop. We returned to our hotel room and the next day made the long trek home.

I was diagnosed with a placenta previa, and my doctor ordered me to bed for the remainder of the pregnancy. In my bed or on the couch, I read and embroidered cross-stitch after cross-stitch after cross-stitch. In my head, I was convinced that Mormonism had somehow saved my baby.

What was the result of our precarious pregnancy? The doctor told us he would take the baby by C-section six weeks early, but for some reason, even though I was bleeding daily now, he allowed the baby to stay a little longer. At the first childbirth class—just in case I could deliver normally—Mike told the other couples this child was a gift from God. Indeed. The baby was due on Christmas Day. Ten days early, my water broke in the middle of the night. Joshua Michael Wilder was born naturally in Ball Memorial Hospital about four hours later. He was perfectly healthy and so was I. We thanked the God of Mormonism for his great blessing.

In 1979, I didn't see the spiritual danger we had put Joshua in. This kind of misguided faith in Mormonism would prove to be dangerous more than once.

CHAPTER 4

FOREVER
FAMILY

\i/

*You created my inmost being; you knit me together in my
mother's womb.*

— PSALM 139:13

A fter Joshua's birth, I overflowed with joy and gratitude. Both
my husband and I did. We believed that because of our
faith in the Mormon Lord, he blessed us. With Joshua's birth, we
were well on the way to building our forever family. Mormonism
seemed oh so good.

In order to introduce Michael to some of my extended family—
the polka-dancing, brats-eating, beer-drinking clan—we traveled
to Wisconsin with little Joshie. While we stayed on my aunt and
uncle's farm with the greenhouses and beehives, my uncle told
us a joke that insulted Mormons as well as people with intel-
lectual disabilities, something about a Tab-and-apple choir. I was
extremely offended. I asked him if he knew that I taught intellectually disabled children and that we were Mormon. He said
no and apologized.

Mormonism bred in us an antenna for persecution. We were told that Satan and others would attack us at every angle because we had the truth, and this teaching gave me a suspicion of the outside world. I was sensitive to anything that smelled like opposition to the Mormon gospel, even a joke.

A Book of Mormon scripture states that contention (argument, discord) is of the Devil.[6] So anything that seemed to belittle or contradict the Mormon gospel was deemed satanic — a double bind that would one day tie me in knots.

Farmland, Indiana

Anticipating the need for more room for our family, we moved into a two-story home with four bedrooms. We had to move forty-five minutes away from Muncie to the rural community of Farmland, Indiana, in order to find a house big enough that we could afford. We couldn't afford the electric heat, though, so we bought a wood burner and Mike chopped wood. Josh and the dog loved the large fenced-in back yard with jungle gym and pine trees, and I loved my side-yard garden.

When we bought the house, I needed to return to teaching full-time for one year. This time, I had students whose disabilities were more severe. I dealt with tantrums, escape artists, and great physical needs. Yet I loved my kids. Mike's mom stayed with Josh at the house during the week and went home to Rushville on the weekends.

Every Sunday, we drove to Muncie for church, a challenging trip for a one-year-old. Mike was now Young Men president (responsible for teenaged males) and financial ward clerk. Plus, he had a list of families to home teach once a month. As a result, he spent another one to two nights a week at church. Typically, Mike left the house at 7:00 a.m. and did not return until Josh's bedtime. Time with Daddy was rare.

I was teaching the "Gospel Essentials" Sunday school class for individuals investigating whether to join the Mormon Church. Teaching was perhaps the only gift, I decided, that Heavenly Father had blessed me with. The class was popular, with sometimes fifteen people attending. I was excited to sell the church and share my faith, because to me, Mormonism was everything. As converts ourselves, Mike and I had a heart for Mormon evangelism. Whenever a new face entered the church, we welcomed that person right into our Wilder family, starting with Sunday dinner. We had a great time, and a few people even joined us as members of the church.

I also taught monthly in Relief Society, a women's organization that was auxiliary to the priesthood. For women, Sunday meetings included the seventy-minute sacrament (church) meeting, fifty minutes of Sunday school, and fifty minutes of Relief Society. We were proud that Relief Society, the charity arm of the church, was one of the oldest and largest women's organizations in the world, with every Mormon woman eighteen and older as a member. Its purpose was to prepare women for the "blessings of eternal life by helping them increase faith and personal righteousness, strengthen families and homes, and help those in need."[7]

The Relief Society met each Sunday and once a month in the evening for homemaking meetings (now called enrichment meetings). I taught directly from a scripted lesson manual, which contained the full text of all the scripture quotes so I didn't even need to open my scriptures to read them. With my full-time job, I was glad to trek into the ward building only on Sundays and once a month for homemaking meetings. In addition, I was required to call on several women monthly as a visiting teacher, to see if they had any needs or if they had questions about the church.

We tried to live the Mormon life to please Heavenly Father. I grew and canned vegetables, stored water, and did genealogy. I also fulfilled my church callings and taught my son the Mormon gospel through stories and song. Mike worked hard to provide for us, preside over us, and protect us, as the church charged a man to do. He progressed in the LDS priesthood and fulfilled his church callings and responsibilities to the best of his ability. We visited the temple about twice a year—a financial sacrifice for us—in order to redeem the dead. Sometimes we did baptisms for the dead, sometimes washings and anointings, sometimes endowments, sometimes sealings. In all this, we believed we were pleasing the Lord.

When Josh was about two, we had another miscarriage at sixteen weeks. My fellow teachers sent flowers until the whole house smelled like a funeral. Although the loss was difficult, we did not give up hope. After all, our church patriarch had promised that the Lord would bless us with *children*, not just one child. Plus, the Mormon faith taught us that we would see our dead children again and would be privileged to rear them during the millennium, that thousand-year reign of Christ. They belonged to us "under the covenant." We believed we now knew how to please Heavenly Father with our callings and our works. As a result of our honorable behavior and righteous life, he would bless us. And with our next pregnancy, that thinking appeared to prove correct.

Blond and Funny Matt

Again, we got pregnant, and this time there were few troubles during the pregnancy. But one incident stands out to me from those months of expectation—what I see now as another glimpse of God's grace.

When I was two months pregnant, I went to the Farmland post office to buy stamps. While walking toward the building on a beautiful fall day, I was stung by a bee. I was severely allergic to bee stings and previously had almost died convulsing from a reaction to bee venom. I quickly drove home and pounded on my neighbor's door. Her mother took Josh, and she drove me the forty-five minutes to the hospital to get my shot of Benadryl. But the doctor in the emergency room did not want to give it to me for fear of the consequences to my unborn child. At this time, we had only one living child and had had six miscarriages.

Of course I did not want to do anything to risk the health of my baby. But not getting the Benadryl might mean I would have a toxic reaction to the sting that also could harm that baby. What to do? Benadryl or allow the reaction? The doctor did not want to make the decision, so he left it up to me. I had no idea which to choose.

This was before cell phones. Mike was out visiting a client and couldn't be located. I was forced to make the decision alone, and time was running out. They admitted me and gave me a hospital room. It was afternoon, but the shades were drawn and the room was dark. In my bed, I called out to Heavenly Father.

The next thing I knew, I felt the presence of Jesus sitting next to me on the bed, his arm around my shoulder. I sat still, stunned, and then melted into his embrace. He talked with me like a mentor to a trusted friend. He told me not to let them give me the Benadryl. *Thank you, Jesus. Thank you.* I informed the doctor of my decision.

Even without the antidote, I had no reaction to the bee sting. Nothing. In a few hours, I was released from the hospital. Amazed, I couldn't wait to tell Mike. He was the only one I trusted with my strange spiritual happenings. He was the one who always believed me.

Seven months later, Matthias Daniel Wilder was born. Whereas Josh had a dark complexion like both Mike and me, Matt was blond and blue-eyed — a bouncy, cheery child with his dad's twinkle in the eye. Our righteousness seemed confirmed.

Then I had another demonic encounter in the middle of the night. As I recorded in my journal, it was early Friday morning, October 28, 1983, and Matt was seven months old. I awakened a little before 4:00 a.m., shivering from a frightening dream. In my dream, an emissary from Satan had briefly possessed my body as I struggled to save Matt and myself. I clung to Mike's leg, desperately hoping for some warmth. I was so cold. Mike held Matt high, struggling to get away. Confusion. Loud noise. Fear. Despair.

As I awoke, I felt warmth return to my frame. It probably took ten minutes before I was aware that the heating pad was too hot against my aching lumbar. That dull ache in my back, yes, a sure sign I was back. Yet the evil spirit hung close. I sternly told him to leave. He went to the door to Josh and Matt's bedroom and spoke just one word, "Matthias." Clearly, he wanted Matt.

The spirit world is very real to Mormons, although the legitimacy of any personal spiritual experience was determined by a priesthood authority with stewardship over me. I decided I would not share the story of my experience with anyone, except Mike. As Mormons, we believed in (1) a pre-existent spirit world and (2) an everywhere-present spirit world of demons looking for bodies to inhabit. However, so no one would ask why *I* had experiences with demons, I resolved to remain silent. We Mormons whispered that sometimes dead individuals, especially relatives, manifested themselves to communicate their desire for someone to perform their LDS temple ordinances to save them. That was a good thing. But I knew that what I encountered was not a dead ancestor waiting for me to complete their temple work, or one of my future children waiting to come down from the spirit world. It was clearly a demon cast to the earth.

As Mormons, we were taught that before the world was created, there was a war in heaven between Satan and Jesus. As sons of Heavenly Father and Heavenly Mother, Satan and Jesus both proposed plans of salvation to the council in heaven. Satan wanted to force everyone to be saved, while Jesus wanted people to have free will to choose. Heavenly Father accepted Jesus' plan, angering Satan, who began a war. When Satan lost, he and the spirits who followed him were cast to the earth. Banished to roam, they sought bodies to inhabit, like mine or Matt's.

Believing I needed the power of the Mormon priesthood to remove the offending spirit because Mike and I had seen the righthand raise — arm in a perfect right angle — demonstrated in the temple endowment ceremony against Satan (who, by the way, had in his employ a Christian minister), I woke Mike and described my experience. Rare tears came to his eyes at my words. Raising his right arm to the square as the apostle Peter had done in the endowment ceremony to declare his priesthood authority over Satan in order to get him to leave, Mike demanded, "In the name of Jesus Christ and by the power of the holy Melchizedek priesthood which I hold, I command you to go!" We checked Matt. He was breathing regularly, peacefully asleep.

Back in our bed, it came to me: *Today is the sixth anniversary of our baptism into the Mormon Church.* I told Mike, and he was quiet, humbled. We talked a few more minutes before we finally fell asleep. Perhaps this experience, applying these truths, would teach us more about the gospel and enhance our testimony of the Mormon Church.

After the encounter with the demon, I bought a baby monitor so I could hear Matt's every breath throughout the night. At the time, we never suspected that this encounter had anything to do with our worshiping at the altar of the Mormon faith and the Mormon temple. Mormons had taught us to expect opposition. Instead of taking the attack as a warning, we took the opposition as a sign that we were on the right track.

Fire!

After Christmas a year later, Josh and Matt had the stomach flu. Then I caught it. Lying in a quilt by the wood burner with my boys, I raised up only to have dry heaves. Once again I'd hit the bottom of the pit. Depression because of hormones ("baby blues") had dogged me for more than a year, ever since Matt was young. When Mike returned in the evening (he said he'd be home at noon), I was exhausted. "I don't care if I live or die," I told him. Physically and mentally defeated, I went to bed.

At 2:00 a.m. I was awakened by a fearful smell. *Hot. Something's hot.* Dragging my body downstairs, I found the wood-burning stove red-hot like I'd never seen it, with a horrible metallic smell. Although the drafts were not open very far, they were open far enough to feed a searing fire in the flue. Several articles near the stove were hot — burnt-plastic-smelling moon boots, pieces of wood, paper. A fire was imminent, had my keen nose not intervened. Or was it the Spirit? I quickly moved to save our lives.

Just as in my childhood nightmare, we all could have lost our lives in a fire. At the time, I connected this instance of grace with the physical protection of my temple garments (underwear) and our faith in the power of the Mormon priesthood. Now I interpret it differently. We were in a dangerous place spiritually. The God of the Bible, no doubt, intervened to save us.

A God-Ordained Child

After Matt was born and the baby blues vexed me, we decided on birth control to space the next child. The God I know now has such a sense of humor. We were on birth control, I was still nursing Matt, and lo and behold, I got pregnant. In a works-based faith like Mormonism, I was taught that I was in charge of my decisions, I determined my destiny, I was the god of my life. But in this case, I had no control. God ordained the next child. And as soon as I was expecting, the depression suddenly lifted.

I wrote in my journal, "When the lab technician told me 'positive' over the phone, I was in shock. SHOCK ... Waited until I saw Mike face-to-face to tell him. He was pretty shocked too ... but as I had heard the news, I felt a warm spirit go from my head to my feet. I was happy, peaceful, joyful. Glad to welcome a new life to this earth."

As Mormons, we were taught to trust our feelings. They were the Holy Ghost's message to us to indicate what was true. The more emotional we felt, or the more we felt a "burning in the bosom," the more we could be sure that the Holy Ghost was confirming that what we were experiencing was true (D&C 9:8). I felt peace, so I knew this baby needed to come to our family from the spirit world.

Full of anticipation, I went to my first doctor's appointment at the end of June to see the same nice doctor who had delivered our two boys. My doctor combined his knowledge of Eastern Ayurveda and chakras with traditional Western medicine. Each time I went to see him, he grabbed my wrist and felt my blood flow, then told me where in my body the problem seemed to be.

We trusted our doctor because he was kind, and Mormonism gave me no reason to doubt he was good. I measured "Christian" or "goodness" by how well someone represented the "actions" of Christ. We simply thought the doctor needed Mormon truth added to his knowledge. So we sent the Mormon missionaries to his office, and he took the first discussion or two. He knew about our Mormon garments and told me he thought it was a great idea to wear day and night something that reminds you of your faith.

That day I went with my most recent pregnancy, my doctor took out his stethoscope and pressed it to my belly. "Today we should be able to hear the heartbeat," he said. He tried for what seemed a very, very long time to find it. Two or three times he excused himself and left the room. Later his receptionist, who was a member of our Mormon ward, told me she saw him go into the hallway to pray. He seemed quite upset, she said. But each time he reentered the room, he showed me only calm. After several attempts, he finally said, "Just come back next month. Maybe you're not as far along as we thought."

As I left the office, my panic mounted. How could there not be a heartbeat? Would this be baby-lost number seven and the earliest one yet? Back home, I was so distraught that I begged Mike for a priesthood blessing. Mike called a fellow priesthood brother, and about ten o'clock that night, he and his wife came. He and Mike put their hands on my head and gave me a blessing: "Lord, this baby's life is in Lynn's hands. If she unleashes her faith—and it will take much faith—the child will live. If not, it will die. Only her faith can save this child."

At first I was overwhelmed with the responsibility. It was up to me whether this child lived or died! Of course, I was feeling guilty that I had questioned whether I could mother a third child so soon and had taken one month of birth control. The first two children seemed a handful, with my responsibilities in the home and yard, the gardening and canning, and the various church callings. Now Heavenly Father might be punishing me for being so weak. It was a couple's privilege to have as many children as they could support, our church leaders taught us. *How do I conjure up enough faith to save a child's life?* I wondered. *And in what do I have faith, exactly?*

Despite my wandering in the false faith of Mormonism, God's grace again raised me up. This is the entry from my journal two days later: "But now I feel better, stronger, confident. I began to feel confident the baby would be okay. I stopped worrying."

I knew I had done nothing to warrant this confidence or to deserve this peace. I had not been to the temple, had not prayed enough, had hardly had sufficient time to do anything to demonstrate my faith. But I accepted this strength without questioning. Only years later did I realize that God's grace had not only given me this third child but also saved me from offering works to a false Mormon god. From the very first, God put his mark upon Micah. This child would be a product of grace, not works. An Isaac, not an Ishmael.

At sixteen weeks, I had my second doctor's appointment. This time he found a strong heartbeat when I told him where to listen—right on my hip. A few days later, I felt movement and began to show a protruding belly. All six of our miscarriages had been at sixteen weeks, but I did not worry. I had a spiritual assurance for this baby—a glimpse of grace.

A Beautiful Baby

Micah Andrew Wilder was born three weeks past his due date, during a snow emergency. In our rural county, three moms went into labor that day. One delivered in the back of a 4 x 4. The second was taken by snowmobile to a train, and then to an ambulance. Mike got me through the snow all the way to the hospital in time. My hero.

The delivery had complications, one of them being that the umbilical cord was wrapped around Micah's neck. When I delivered the rest of his lanky, thin body, he was blue and needed help breathing. It was several horrible moments before we saw that he would be all right. The fear in the frenzied doctor's eyes caused Michael to panic; he nearly passed out.

On the way home from the hospital during better weather, I had Mike extend the drive through the countryside a little longer. I was still apprehensive about whether I could mother three little boys, and I felt guilty about it. God bless my own sweet Christian mother, who with each child helped out for the first ten days I was home from the hospital.

Josh had been an active baby. Matt too had been active, plus colicky and jaundiced, and on top of that had a hernia and chronic earaches. After the initial birth scare, however, Micah was calm and quiet. The doctor said he ran across a good baby like Micah only now and then. His word for him was, "Beautiful."

Having a third child, this third, turned out to be wonderful. That is, until Micah made that fateful decision. Twenty-one years later, God would use Micah to wield a sledgehammer to demolish everything we were painstakingly building. Our "forever family" was more finite and fragile than we could possibly know.

CHAPTER 5

THE PERFECT MORMON LIFE

‰

I love Mother. She loves me. We love Daddy, yessiree.
He loves us and so you see, we are a happy family!
— MORMON PRIMARY CHILDREN'S SONG

If there is anything Mormonism is known for, it is having happy families. I sang the Mormon children's song "Happy Family" to my precious boys several times a day when they were little. Michael and I believed in the principle of eternal families; since we'd been sealed in the temple, we could be a married couple in the next life and have our children with us forever. Family was everything. We attended church each week and taught our children the Mormon gospel.

To remain active in the Mormon Church, we decided we needed to move closer to the ward building. It was just too hard on me to have Mike gone all day and then gone several nights a week as well with church work. Living closer should at least get him home earlier, more involved in his sons' lives.

So we bought a home fifteen minutes away from the LDS

ward building — a home that isolated the children from the world. The rustic stone-and-cedar home built into the side of a hill was at the end of a gravel lane on seven acres of woods along White River.

Our new home had office space for Michael and an apartment upstairs for his parents, who moved in with us. Michael's father had developed diabetes, and his mom did not drive.

Damon and Gertie were delighted to be invited into the lives of their grandsons. They joined the local Baptist church. Grandma made us cookies, fed Matt lasagna, baked and decorated the family birthday cakes, and asked me often if the boys didn't need sweaters.

One day their pastor visited them and told them that Mormons believe in sex in heaven. Damon asked us if this was true and we laughed. "What would be so wrong with that?" we asked. We did believe that righteous, temple-attending Mormons who were sealed together would be married in the next life. That was us.

Heaven on Earth

The boys were in heaven on earth, climbing trees, swinging on vines, jumping into leaf piles, and feeding and watching various creatures, including snakes, salamanders, fish, raccoons, beaver, and mink. They had a sandbox, a swing set, a basketball hoop, a rabbit, and a dog. They played T-ball in the summer, played Pop Warner football in the fall, and went sledding on the hill by our house in the winter. They rollerbladed and biked in the nearby high school parking lot when school was out, and later did basketball, track, cross-country, and soccer. As they got older, they were allowed to fish with a buddy at the river. We had a dinner bell to call them across the acres to come home for meals.

Josh went to first grade in the public schools. The first day of school, he carried a very lucky cat home from the bus stop. He named her Fluffy, and she lived with us another twenty-one years.

Matt and Micah attended preschool and then kindergarten at their grandparents' Baptist church school a mile from the house. This school's academics were so challenging that the boys could read even the Bible by the end of first grade, so we kept them there for the early elementary years.

Michael and I were all about good schools, music lessons, and sports for the boys. We moved Matt and Micah to public school only after Micah's classmates taunted him on the playground: "You're not a Christian. You're not a Christian!" We wanted them to have a supreme education, but we would not tolerate such unkindness from Christian schoolmates.

Michael and his business partner moved their office into our new home, so he too was available to the kids, at least in theory, whenever I was at my part-time work. This was the best thing ever for our family. In years past, the boys had been largely my responsibility, since I was home with them and Michael was away working. When Mike came home to work, he started to pay more attention to his sons. He began to notice when they got home from school, what they were interested in, what they ate, and how they interacted. He occasionally came downstairs from the office just to see them, tickle them, be their dad.

I remember one night when Matt came down with the stomach flu. I had always been the one to get up with the kids if they were sick. This night Mike said he wanted to get up. Who was I to argue with that kind of wisdom? As I watched from the doorway, I marveled at how tenderly he embraced his sick son, held his head when he vomited, cleaned up after him. Being with them more was changing Michael and the boys' dependence on him. Father and sons. I loved to watch them together. Of all the good things about the move to this new house, that was the best.

New Arrival

Prayerfully, Michael and I decided to try for a daughter. We loved our three sons, and four would be a blessing, but it would be nice to have just one girl. Plus, there was that Mormon obligation to have as many children as we felt we could. So in our later thirties, we got pregnant one last time.

While eight months pregnant during the hottest summer in fifty years, I was walking barefoot around the yard. We had recently reroofed. With forty additional pounds weighing me down, I stepped on a long nail that went clear through my foot. I could not sit down, or I wouldn't be able to get up again by myself. The phone was in the house. I was too big to scoot to the house. I couldn't hop on one foot. I also couldn't reach my foot to pull the nail out. My belly was in the way. Fortunately, Mike was upstairs in his office, so I began screaming. I screamed for a while before he heard, but he did come running to rescue me, roaring with laughter.

This time, labor was long. I was older and feeling it. Was it a girl or a boy? The doctor kept telling us to expect a boy, judging by the heartbeat. Then I heard shouting.

"It's a girl! It's a girl!" the doctor shouted.

"It's a girl! It's a girl!" Michael echoed.

"I didn't think it was in the cards for the Wilders to have a girl," Doc said.

Kathryn Michelle Wilder. I was so thrilled, I cried with joy for two days. I hadn't even realized I wanted a girl that badly. The boys came to visit. Daddy was excited. Josh was excited. Matt was excited. But Micah's sour face in the pictures taken sitting on my hospital bed said it all. He'd been the baby for four years and was loath to relinquish his status.

Full House

When Katie was about a year old, a friend spotted her dragging one of the boys' gym bags down the hall. "Get that girl a purse!" my friend said. Since I'm not a girlie girl myself, the idea of getting her a purse had never occurred to me.

Katie was cheerful and extremely articulate. Her first sentence was to the clerk at Target: "I like clothes." She used to speak in rhyming sentences and in song. At age five, her drama career began when she got the part of Gretl in the community theater's production of *The Sound of Music*.

Unlike her brothers, Katie never liked school or organized athletics. Besides drama and singing, she danced, took piano lessons, and loved animals. She took horseback riding lessons and hung out at the barn. People learned to dump unwanted cats on our property, and she, Josh, and her dad nurtured them all. And like all of us, Katie was very active in the Mormon Church.

Meanwhile Josh played sports and was a good student. When he was in fifth grade, the girls started calling the house, and his active social life continued through high school. He had a paper route, earned his Eagle Scout award, and governed his younger brothers.

At age five, Matt begged me for piano lessons. By six he was transposing little melodies, by eight he was composing, and at twelve he had his first copyrighted piece of music, a piece about the Holocaust. Matt was a quiet, humorous, hardworking, and obedient child. His other love was basketball. Every Saturday morning, way too early, all we heard from the driveway was, *Bump, bump, bump, swish. Bump, bump, bump, swish.* When Matt was thirteen, he asked me if he could do chores around the house for pay. When he'd accumulated one hundred dollars, he asked his father to drive him to Home Depot. There he picked out lumber, nails, and a hammer. Then Matt spent hours deep in the woods building himself an A-frame open to the air. Matt and a friend lived in the A-frame that whole summer.

Micah was a much more cautious child and stayed indoors more than Josh or Matt, perhaps as a safety measure against his two older brothers. Bright and articulate, he spoke in full sentences at a year and a half but rarely spoke. When he was a little older, Micah liked to fish. (He took Katie with him to put the bait on the hook and remove the fish after he caught it.) When the White River overflowed and then receded, it left pools of water filled with carp in the lower levels of our property. Micah had a fish net that he used to rescue the trapped carp. He didn't want the puddles to dry up and the fish to die. He spent hours hauling these huge bottom-dwelling fish from the pools back to the river. This boyhood gesture was a foreshadow of what he would one day become — a fisher of men.

Church and Temple Life

Although Josh struggled to like church from about the age of twelve, and Matt simply accepted it, Micah loved everything about it. Micah's greatest desire was always to be good and please God. He believed, like we did, that only Mormonism offered the true way.

Sunday attendance alone was not sufficient for an active Mormon family. Before age twelve, the children had once-a-quarter Primary activities on a Saturday. When they were twelve, they met in church youth organizations that included sports teams, road shows (drama and singing shows), summer camps, and service projects in addition to their weekly meetings. At fourteen, they attended 6:00 a.m. seminary classes. At sixteen, they could attend stake dances and date in groups. Adding this to school, sports practices and games, homework, weekends with friends, and music lessons made their young lives, and our lives, very Mormon-busy.

Mike had quarterly priesthood meetings; I had monthly Relief Society homemaking meetings. We went to baptisms. The missionaries came for dinner. Callings required training meetings. Biannually we went to Fishers, Indiana, for stake conference, and biannually we watched the General Conference of the Church of Jesus Christ of Latter-day Saints via satellite to hear from the general authorities in Salt Lake.

Temple visits were also a crucial piece of the LDS activity puzzle. One could visit the temple only with a temple recommend, earned from a worthiness interview with a member of the bishopric. (Adults also had to pass a second worthiness interview — same questions — with a member of the stake presidency.) Temple recommend questions for adults include whether one sustains the Mormon prophet as the prophet, seer, and revelator and as the only person on the earth who possesses and is authorized to exercise all priesthood keys. The leaders ask whether one is a full-tithe payer, keeps the Word of Wisdom (the LDS health code), and attends sacrament and other meetings. They ask if one supports, is affiliated with, or agrees with any group or individual whose teachings or practices are contrary to or oppose those accepted by the Church of Jesus Christ of Latter-day Saints. The three members of the bishopric and also of the stake presidency can give or refuse to give the temple recommend, based on one's answers to the temple recommend questions or just because they feel it is Heavenly Father's will.[8]

Priesthood leaders challenged families with a temple recommend to attend the temple twice a year, so Mike and I traveled to the Washington D.C. Temple until the Chicago Temple opened in 1985. The many church members who were *not* temple worthy understood that they would be relegated to the middle of three heavens, the place where the Christians also live after this life, the terrestrial kingdom. Here Jesus would visit but the Father would never go (D&C 76). For many, this sufficed. Attending the temple, however, could allow one to attain the highest celestial kingdom. And if parents were sealed together in the temple, they could go to the highest rung of that kingdom, living as families (with at least one wife) and procreating spirit children forever, even reaching godhood.

We had made our first temple visit back in March of 1979, when we received the ordinances for our own exaltation and eternal progression. That experience was quite disturbing. After entry and examination of our recommends, Mike and I were ushered to a counter where we paid to rent temple clothes. Next we were accompanied to gender-separate locker rooms. I was instructed to remove all of my clothes in an individual curtained booth and to put on the shield. The shield is like a thick white hospital gown that has a circular cutout for the head and is open on both sides under the arms.

I proceeded to the location where the ordinances would take place and entered an area partitioned into four parts approximately four feet by four feet, separated by white curtains. The first was a holding area, the second the washing area, the third the anointing area, and the fourth the area where I was to be dressed in the undergarment of the holy priesthood from my shoulders to my knees.

A female temple worker invited me from the holding area into the second partitioned area, where she touched various parts of my body with her index finger dipped in water for the washing, and then sealed the washing when she, now joined by a second female worker, placed hands on my head, repeating memorized words to seal the washing.

In the third area, the second worker dipped her finger in oil for the anointing and touched various body parts (forehead, ears, eyes, nose, mouth, neck, shoulders, back, breast, sides, stomach, arms, hands, vitals and bowels, legs, and feet) as she repeated the scripted ordinance. (The frequent touching of body parts—which I found unsettling—was removed from the washing and anointing in 2005.) Then the anointing with oil was sealed by the second worker and a new worker who had just appeared, repeating scripted words.

Finally, I was moved by the third temple worker to the last partitioned area and told to step into the undergarment of the holy priesthood, which, if I were true to my temple covenants, would be a physical and spiritual "shield and a protection," the ordinance proclaimed, "until my work on earth was finished." Of course, I hadn't received the covenants yet. They came in the ensuing endowment ceremony, so I didn't know yet what I needed to be faithful to.

I returned to the dressing area and removed the shield but kept the garments on. Then I dressed in a long slip and a white to-the-ankle and to-the-wrist dress, socks, and slippers from my rented packet and took the rest of the packet with me for the endowment ceremony. Everything was white except for the green fig-leaf apron I would don during the endowment ceremony.

Next I moved to a booth at the edge of the locker room to receive my worker-whispered new name, the one my righteous priesthood-holder husband would have to remember so he could call me up during the resurrection of my dead body in the future. I exited to a hallway and walked to a chapel room to await the endowment ceremony. Here Mike and I sat together, waiting along with others, listening as the organist played LDS hymns.

At the appointed time, a group of about thirty of us was escorted to one of the several endowment rooms with theater-like seats. Men sat on the right side as we entered the room, women on the left. We were invited to withdraw if we did not wish to make the covenants in the endowment. The problem was we didn't know what they were yet! Then an instructional movie was started and stopped by a male officiator and his female counterpart. We added pieces of clothing from our packets, as we were instructed, and the women veiled their faces as we learned the true order of prayer. We agreed to "suffer our lives to be taken" if we revealed the Masonic-like tokens with their accompanying names, signs, and penalties. Verbal acknowledgment of ensuing death penalties for revealing aspects of the tokens were removed by the LDS first presidency (the prophet and his two counselors) from the temple ceremony in 1990, but every time we went to the temple after 1990, we remembered them at the appropriate place in the ceremony.

The instruction included several covenants and clothing additions from the packet. With the white robe of the holy priesthood on my right shoulder on top of my white dress, with my green fig-leaf apron and white sash around my waist on top of the robe, and with a veil on my head but not over my face except during the true order of prayer, I was ready for the final covenant, called the law of consecration. A man represented the apostle Peter.

Peter: "You and each of you covenant and promise before God, angels, and these witnesses at this altar, that you do accept the Law of Consecration as contained in this [the officiator holds up a copy], the Book of Doctrine and Covenants, in that you do consecrate yourselves, your time, talents, and everything with which the Lord has blessed you, or with which he may bless you, to the Church of Jesus Christ of Latter-day Saints, for the building up of the Kingdom of God on the earth and for the establishment of Zion. Each of you bow your head and say 'yes.'"[9]

I did not realize it at the time, but I had just dedicated myself, my time, my money, my future children, and everything I had or would have to the earthly organization of the Church of Jesus

Christ of Latter-day Saints. The Mormon Church held my life in its hands. Like the medieval feudal system, in which the master owned even one's excrement for fertilizer, I belonged to the Mormon Church. Any good works I might do would be credited to what I believed was the Lord's true church.

During the endowment ceremony the character playing Lucifer in the movie (in the Salt Lake Temple, the players are live) looked right at us and warned, "If they do not walk up to every covenant they make at these altars in this temple this day, they will be in my power!" I did not want that.

After the endowment ceremony, during which I had a terrible headache, Michael and I went upstairs to a small, carpeted sealing room with a kneeling altar and wall mirrors. There we knelt across from each other and held hands in a special grip we had just learned in the endowment. In a simple ceremony led by a male temple sealer, we were sealed together for time and all eternity. We believed that this sealing allowed us to be married in the celestial kingdom after this life, procreating spirit children and ruling our own world with our earthly children — forever families. [10]

Michael and I did love each other, and I had to smile as tears welled up in his eyes when we were sealed.

Each time we returned to the temple after that initial visit, we received the same ordinances by proxy for someone who was dead. In other words, we went through the temple ordinances in place of a person who was dead, in their name, so he or she could accept or reject the ordinances of baptism, washing and anointing, the endowment, and marriage sealing wherever they were in the afterlife (paradise or spirit prison). This was their chance to hear and accept the Mormon gospel, in case they had not heard it while alive, so they could progress to the highest rung of the celestial kingdom. I could bring names of my dead ancestors who needed their work done, or the temple would provide me with names from lists submitted by people doing genealogy.

A few years later, Mike and I were called to serve as ordinance workers in the Chicago Temple. We did not work there full-time, but we served in whatever capacity they needed us to serve in when our local ward and others traveled to Chicago. In this capacity, I memorized the words of every temple ordinance and rotated through every role someone could play in the temple.

The full-time temple workers told us stories to inspire us, about dead ancestors appearing in the temple. One worker told me a female spirit once manifested to her when she was alone in the endowment room, to thank her for the ordinance work done for her that day. Jesus was said to have appeared in the Salt Lake Temple to Lorenzo Snow in 1898, prior to Snow's call as prophet.[11] We assumed that Jesus appears to the current prophet as well. We adjusted to the strangeness of the temple and figured we were too ignorant to know the mind of Heavenly Father. Having gone through so much to bear our four children, we ached to keep them forever. And so we led the perfect Mormon life, attending services, volunteering for the church in a myriad of ways, and visiting the temple at least twice a year.

Ready for the Temple

Once our children turned twelve, we encouraged them to apply for a temple recommend. If Mormon youths passed the temple interview, they could enter the bottom level of the temple to perform baptisms for the dead.

The first time each of our children went to the temple, Mike and I accompanied them. When Josh entered the bottom level of the Chicago Temple for the first time, a smiling, elderly temple worker dressed completely in white checked his temple recommend for worthiness. The worker whispered, "Good morning,

Brother Wilder. Welcome to the House of the Lord." The worker instructed Josh and the other youths to speak in a reverent whisper, then ushered them to a sterile, colorless locker room, where they changed into white baptismal jumpsuits. Next they emerged into a humid room that contained the large, circular, warm-water baptismal font. The font sat on the backs of a statue of twelve oxen in a circle, facing outward.

A male temple worker guided Josh into the water as Mike and I sat watching. The temple worker then entered the water and dunked Josh over and over by proxy for a list of dead people who were being baptized into the Mormon Church. After the baptisms, Josh went to the locker room to change back into his Sunday clothes. Then he was led to a small side room where male temple workers laid hands on his head and declared one by one a list of dead persons to be members of the Church of Jesus Christ of Latter-day Saints. At the end, the workers said, "Receive the Holy Ghost."

Worthy youth twelve and up, if they remain worthy, attend the basement of the temple to perform baptisms for the dead for several years. Prior to a mission (about age eighteen for a young man), or prior to marriage for men or women who did not serve a mission, worthy members enter the upper level of the temple to receive the ordinance of washings and anointings and the endowment. The ultimate ordinance is the marriage sealing—unless one is specially chosen by the prophet to obtain the second anointing, a rare ceremony in which one's calling and election to the highest level of the celestial kingdom is made sure. The brother receiving the second anointing is assured he will become a god and his wife a queen or priestess to him.[12]

A Good Woman

And so I strived to be a good Mormon wife and mother, celebrating as each of my children made their first visit to the temple, encouraging them in their faith, serving as the co-ringleader for our many church activities. Among the numerous expectations for a righteous Mormon woman, homemaking was an area that did not come naturally to me, so I tried to make it up in other ways. And in most ways, I felt successful during those years. Except in one area. I worked outside the home.

CHAPTER 6

A WORKING MORMON MOTHER?

✦

*By divine design, fathers are to preside over their
families in love and righteousness and are responsible
to provide the necessities of life and protection for their
families. Mothers are primarily responsible for the
nurture of their children.*

— THE FIRST PRESIDENCY AND COUNCIL OF THE
TWELVE APOSTLES OF THE CHURCH OF JESUS
CHRIST OF LATTER-DAY SAINTS

Passionate about my life's calling with the world's "throw-
aways," I worked outside the home off and on over the years.
Before we had our own children, I taught public school. At the
university, I taught a demonstration preschool class for students
with physical disabilities. There I supervised Ball State University
practicum students and co-taught the college class. Later I was the
assistant director for a federal Head Start grant and worked with
low-income families in their homes. These things I did to keep
busy, since I didn't have my own kids yet, but also because I loved

the work. After I had children, *they* were preeminent. But family and work together accorded me a useful, rich existence.

Michael had decided not to get a doctorate, which he needed to keep teaching full-time at the university. Instead he started his own business, and as a result, our income was up and down. We had good years and not-so-good years, depending on the economy and a hundred other things. Rather than have him work long hours to support us and have me raise the kids as the Mormon Church suggested, we chose to have him home some while I worked part-time. It worked for us.

It's not that we were doing something contrary to what the LDS Church allowed. Members had free will to make choices, and Michael and I liked the choices we made. We understood each other better when we stepped into each other's world for a time. After all, Mormon pioneer families had worked side by side. Indiana farm families, such as Michael's parents, worked side by side too.

Largely, though, I was the children's caregiver. When Josh was born, I was home with him. When we moved to Farmland, I taught one year. When Matt was born, I was home with both boys. After Micah was born, I taught GED classes one day and one night a week for more than a decade. The grandparents watched the boys if I was working, and Michael watched them that evening. We were an extended family helping each other. That seemed right.

As a GED teacher, I had the privilege of helping high school dropouts pass their high school equivalency exam. Once again, I loved my students, the ones no one else cared much about. Most were unemployed. Some had taken detours into juvenile detention, jail, homelessness, teen pregnancy, drug addiction, prostitution, cutting, mental illness, or gangs. Now they were ready to finish school and get on with a healthy life and financially support themselves. I saw many people turn their lives in a positive direction. Some even went on to a trade school or to college.

Not only did I love my work; I felt I was a better mom for the brief time I spent away from my kids. I was energized to come back to the family. Besides, I felt I was teaching my own children to serve others as Christ had.

But the Mormon Church really did not recommend that LDS women work outside the home. The church depends on its members for lay labor. Women put untold hours into church service, and working outside the home limits what women can do for the church.

The debate carried over into politics. In 1972, the Equal Rights Amendment (ERA), designed to guarantee equal rights for women, passed both houses of Congress. Within ten years, it had to be ratified by enough states to become an amendment to the U.S. Constitution.

The Mormon Church stood publically opposed to the ERA. A Mormon woman, Sonia Johnson, was deeply involved in the feminist movement to ratify the ERA, speaking out against the Mormon Church's stance. Her LDS husband subsequently divorced her, and the LDS Church excommunicated her. She was a bit of a legend. Quietly, Mike and I paid attention.

In 1980, when Josh was a baby, Michael, Josh, and I traveled to Ann Arbor, Michigan, to hear the LDS prophet Spencer W. Kimball speak to about fourteen thousand Mormons in an area conference. Outside Crisler Arena were hordes of ERA supporters picketing the Mormon Church. I hugged little Josh to my chest as we passed their signs and shouting on the narrowed sidewalk. Though somewhat sympathetic to their cause, I was still dedicated to my family first.

Torn

So I continued trying to do it all — work and family and church.

The year Katie was born, I was the Indianapolis North Stake Primary president. It was my job to visit each of the twelve wards (congregations) in our stake (region) to make sure they were properly trained and implementing the Primary program according to the Mormon Church Primary handbook. Because I lived in a far corner of the stake, I needed to travel as far as an hour and a half to visit some wards.

A typical Sunday went like this: On Saturday, I prepared the children's Sunday clothes and communicated Sunday's plans with their Mormon teen babysitter, who would watch them and take them to church. The babysitter would arrive by 6:00 a.m. Sunday, and Mike and I would leave the house by 6:15, go different directions, and not return home for twelve hours.

Mormon leadership is many-layered and highly regimented. Mike drove to his assigned ward in the stake. He was one of the stake president's twelve high counselors, in charge of one of the twelve wards. He visited his ward often and delivered special messages from the stake president to the congregation during the sacrament meeting. He called priesthood brethren to leadership positions, trained them, and acted as the stake president's eyes and ears for that ward. He loved his people and visited them sometimes during the week.

In October of 1988, I took six-week-old Katie and drove the hour and a half to the first of that day's assigned wards. I attended all three hours of meetings, which began at eight o'clock that morning, spoke during sacrament meeting as the stake Primary president, then attended the two hours of Primary — visiting classes, the nursery, observing the children's music, and so on. After church, my stake Primary board members, who had met me there and were also observing, met with the ward Primary leaders to give them feedback, direction, and training. Then we had to meet as a board and write a report for the stake president on this particular ward's Primary organization and their reaction to our feedback.

By 2:00 p.m. we arrived at a second ward and went through the same procedure again, starting with the 2:00–5:00 p.m. meeting block. We met afterward with that ward's Primary leaders, and then met together as a board to solidify this ward Primary's report to the stake president.

This particular day, Katie began crying, and I could not soothe my sweet daughter. I returned home exhausted. It seemed a lot to ask of a mother and her four young children for her to be on the road every Sunday. Shouldn't Sundays be for family? But in Mormonism, Monday night—family home evening—was the one time a week reserved for families to be together. Sundays were often filled with church-related responsibilities.

Two days later, Katie was running a fever of 104 degrees. We took her to the hospital, and she was put on an IV. She had a severe ear infection, and I stayed in the hospital with her for several days. About that time, I was responsible for a meeting of multiple stake Primaries and their ward Primaries. The Mormon Church general Primary secretary flew in from Salt Lake to stay in our home and be escorted to the meetings I had arranged. We were an hour away from these meetings.

As we dealt with the pressures of raising four children, helping to care for aging parents, working, and fulfilling our church callings, Mike and I discussed the impact of all this on our family. We decided I would talk to my superior in the stake presidency the next time I drove the fifty minutes to Fishers, Indiana, for Thursday night meetings. Mike had stake meetings there Thursday nights too, almost every week, but mine was coming up next. I arranged an appointment through his secretary.

At the meeting with my superior, I laid out a characteristic Sunday at our house and asked him if Heavenly Father intended for parents to be absent from their children almost every Sunday. I questioned whether a babysitter should have to get the kids up, dressed, to church, and fed and then entertain them all day. I asked him to please pray about it.

His reaction was the standard LDS mantra.

"Sister Wilder, you know you will be blessed if you obey and serve. Your Father knows your needs, and he will bless you if you magnify the calling he has given you."

Then he softened and did agree to think and pray about it. Next he thought to tell me something more. "You realize that priesthood leadership is critical in a stake. There are few leadership roles for women and so many women who can fill them. We want the stake to split, and we will need to train reliable male priesthood brethren for leadership. Your husband is one of these. Do you understand?" He was insinuating that if I asked him to pray about releasing one of us, it would likely be me, since I was more expendable.

"Whatever the Lord wants, President," I said. (Even though he was a counselor to the stake president, we still addressed him as "President" out of respect.)

Time went by and nothing happened. I kept serving. One day, six-year-old Matt was with me at a copy store off campus while I was copying materials for my church calling. Mormons are not supposed to smoke according to the Word of Wisdom, and Matt had never seen anyone smoke. The door to the store was off its hinges, and a repairman was leaning against the doorjamb, smoking. He inhaled and blew out smoke time and again. Watching him, Matt got hysterical and began shouting, "Mommy, that man is on fire! Smoke is coming out of his mouth! Mommy, do something! Mommy, he's on fire! Put it out!" The store was full of people. Everyone in the place broke up laughing. I realized we LDS parents were raising our kids pretty isolated from the real world.

Months later, I received a phone call from a member of the stake presidency who told me the stake president wanted his auxiliary leaders (that's what I was) to stay in their callings at least three years. Okay. That seemed to be our answer.

But the next week, I was called in and questioned by two priesthood leaders. I asked them, "Can you promise me my little ones will be fine when I am out serving the Lord? I know the stake president says this is the case."

"No, Sister Wilder, I can't promise you that ... I release you." Then they called in Michael, who was sitting outside, and told him they had released me. I was officially released at the next Indianapolis North Stake conference, with all twelve wards in attendance. I wanted to please Heavenly Father but, honestly, the release was a great relief.

Michael continued to serve as one of the stake president's twelve high counselors. He had to sit up front during stake conferences with the members of the stake presidency and the other eleven high counselors. Stake conferences began with Thursday or Friday meetings for local leaders with visiting church authorities, including a Saturday priesthood meeting and an adults-only evening session. The Sunday morning session, which ran two hours, was much like an extended sacrament meeting for everyone, except that leaders added the business of biannual reports, votes to sustain church leaders, and multiple lay speakers. We drove to Fishers for each meeting. I sat in the audience Sunday morning, struggling to manage four young children who were disinterested in the service. Although I was released from the calling of North Stake Primary president, I was never without several callings at the same time, including visiting teacher, Primary pianist, and homemaking leader in Relief Society. Not every member chose to fulfill church callings.

"Come Home from the Typewriter"

It was around this time, on February 22, 1987, that LDS prophet Ezra Taft Benson asked Mormon women to stay home and have children. In his fireside talk, Prophet Benson admonished, "Do not curtail the number of your children for personal or selfish reasons. Material possessions, social convenience, and so-called professional advantages are nothing compared to a righteous posterity. In the eternal perspective, children — not possessions, not position, not prestige — are our greatest jewels." He also quoted from former prophet Spencer W. Kimball's famous "come home from the typewriter" speech: "I beg of you, you who could and should be bearing and rearing a family: Wives, come home from the typewriter, the laundry, the nursing, come home from the factory, the cafe. No career approaches in importance that of wife, homemaker, mother — cooking meals, washing dishes, making beds for one's precious husband and children. Come home, wives, to your husbands. Make home a heaven for them. Come home, wives, to your children, born and unborn. Wrap the motherly cloak about you and, unembarrassed, help in a major role to create the bodies for the immortal souls who anxiously await."[13]

One woman in my ward took this speech so seriously that she stopped teaching piano in her living room, as a sign of her faithfulness to the Mormon Church. After all, we were taught that when the prophet speaks, the discussion is over. The prophet of the Mormon Church is revered as a prophet, seer, and revelator for God in contemporary times. In other words, he speaks for God. So when he tells the sisters to come home from their typewriters and have multitudes of children, they are to obey. If one questions him or does anything contrary to his direction, one might be in danger of disciplinary action. Or worse — losing testimony in the Mormon faith. Or even worse — excommunication. When the prophet speaks, the debate is over.

Even so, Mike and I tried to continue quietly doing what worked for us. At the time, I was working two days a week as the director of education programs in five different homeless shelters.

Michael and I saw this as valuable community service and felt that it enhanced rather than interfered with our family life. And, of course, I was earning money.

Then our new bishop came to our door by 2:00 p.m. on the Sunday that he was called to be the bishop. Michael ushered him in to wait to see me. I went to the bedroom, crying. I knew that a new bishop would come to visit for one reason only—to find an auxiliary president—and I didn't want to be one again. Nor did I want to face the inevitable conflict over my working. Mike tried to console me, but he also offered this stern warning: "You have to come out eventually."

The bishop was calling me to be the Relief Society (RS) president over the women of the ward ages eighteen and older until death. As the RS president, I would dress the dead bodies of several LDS sisters under my stewardship in their temple clothes before their burials. Serving as Relief Society president meant I was to be an example. The RS president works closely with the bishop to teach the women and to provide for the poor members in the ward.

"No, Lord," I pleaded. "No! You don't want *me*."

But the bishop kept encouraging me. I so strongly believed that any calling offered came from Heavenly Father himself that I knew I could not in good conscience say no.

Although I agreed to *consider* the calling, I talked Mike into going on vacation, and then to the City of Joseph Pageant, an annual summer pageant honoring Joseph Smith's legacy in Nauvoo, Illinois. I managed to avoid church for three weeks.

I was frantic about the Relief Society calling. I did not want to open myself up to opposition to my work outside the home. I did not want the responsibility of the role. I did not want my settled life disturbed. Yet I believed callings came from the Lord Jesus Christ to my priesthood leaders to me. How could I refuse?

When I could avoid it no more, I went to my knees by our bed in desperation and pleaded with Heavenly Father not to make me do this. I knew I could be judged for disobeying the prophet. Then, in my despair, I felt the presence of Jesus.

It had been eleven years since Jesus came to me in that hospital room when I was pregnant with Matt. There he was, with me again. I just *knew*. I sensed his hands on my bowed head. He spoke, saying, "Be patient. I need for you to be calm and not overwrought or nervous." I did not dare look up.

He blessed me and told me what to do for the women eighteen and older in our ward. He told me which sisters to trust. He told me whom to call to work beside me as I served as Relief Society president. He told me to call one of the women who would oppose me to work closely beside me. He gave me insight into each of the women's lives. I felt his overwhelming love for me, and this gave me an overflowing love and understanding for them. Then he was gone, and I was calm and resolute. The Dancer of grace had answered me in my anguish. I *knew* Jesus was real and living; I had felt his presence. At the time, I connected any association with him to membership in the Mormon Church.

I accepted the calling, and then the dam broke. Several women and a priesthood brother in our ward decided I could not possibly lead the women because I worked outside the home. Given my bedside experience, I had insight that helped me withstand, and even understand, the opposition. I assume that this group tried to change the bishop's mind first, but I have no evidence of it. I do know, however, that the priesthood brother went to see the stake president on behalf of a group of women to complain. In the end, both the bishop and the stake president upheld "the Lord's" decision to call me.

The first year in that position was very difficult. But one by one, the women who opposed me were removed from Relief Society, either because they were called to work in other church aux-iliary organizations or because they moved away. I was amazed at what Christ had done to support and love me through this. Surely, Brother Jesus who cared for me was in the Mormon Church.

Back to School Again

Imagine how people who had opposed me felt when a year later I decided to go back to school for my doctorate. This necessitated my working even more hours. Why did I go to doctoral school? Well, one night I was awakened at about two in the morning and sat bolt upright, as if someone had called my name. Because I could not go back to sleep, I quietly got up to read my Mormon scriptures and try to bore myself back to sleep. I tiptoed into the living room and sat on the couch across from the stone hearth.

After a couple of hours of reading the Book of Mormon, I knelt and prayed. What else could I do? It was the middle of the night, and the family was asleep around me. I was up all night.

The next night, the same thing happened. Bolt upright at 2:00 a.m. Did someone call my name? Third night, same. Fourth night, same. Fifth night, same. Busy with family, part-time work, and my church callings, I had no time to catch up on any sleep during the day. After fourteen consecutive nights of waking at 2:00 a.m. and being in LDS scriptures and then in prayer, I was physically exhausted and spiritually frustrated, reaching for answers.

I finally told Heavenly Father in defeat, "If you want me to do something, just tell me. I can't stay up another night."

I was shocked to receive a clear answer: "You need to go back to school."

It certainly was not normal for Heavenly Father to speak to me. I'd had the experience of a sure encounter with Deity only a few times in my adult life. But that answer was surprisingly sure.

I already had a master's degree. What good Mormon woman needed more than that?

Still, I wanted to obey, so I tried one doctoral course in educational leadership at Ball State University. I really didn't like it. The professor, a socialist, told me I was the most radical individualist he had ever met. Of course. I had worked with special education kids and high school dropouts, and reaching them was all about the individual, their needs, and exclusively designed solutions. So I didn't take a second course and just went on with my contented Mormon life.

Then, a couple of years later, I was in two automobile accidents, two months apart to the day. The first time I was sitting at a stoplight on a major street in early December. The gentleman in the blocky, navy-blue van behind me, with the lit miniature Christmas tree between the front seats, was blaring Christmas music. He hadn't noticed that the traffic light had changed to red, he said, when he rear-ended me. He never applied his brakes. He was watching the ambulance on the scene of an accident off to our left.

As I gingerly stepped out of the car, the pain burned from my head to my toes, but it was accompanied by a strange, supernatural calm. As if Someone were telling me that this accident had happened for a reason and that it would be all right in the end. Was Heavenly Father reaching out to me? As LDS, I imagined Jesus as a brother I could talk to, but I had a hard time wrapping my mind around who Heavenly Father—the one with the physical body who'd worked his way to godhood—was, besides a punitive lawgiver. I sustained severe whiplash from my head snapping back and then forward. The pain and stiffness increased greatly in the first twenty-four hours.

Then the second accident. It had rained, and the temperature turned the rain into black ice. This time, someone came sliding across an intersection on ice, and I was T-boned just behind the driver's seat and thrown into a ditch, where I hit a second vehicle already in the ditch. This time the whiplash was side to side.

For the next year and a half, I went to therapy a couple of times a week with horrible pain in my neck and right hip, pain that kept me from sleeping soundly for nine years. While lying on the therapy table, I was finally still enough to think around the pain. The LDS life was incredibly harrowing, and I rarely if ever stopped to just think. As I lay there, I contemplated how I had been asked to return to school. I'd been awakened fourteen nights in a row, and God answered my prayer and told me he wanted me to go to school. I knew it had been real. I had to do it.

This time I enrolled in a doctoral program in earnest and never looked back. At the time, there was no field of study for what I did in GED, so I chose to get a doctorate in emotional/ behavioral disorders, an area closest to the area of passion I had committed to that day in the high school library. To this day, if I feel pain in my body, I am reminded not to tempt God to take drastic measures to reach me; I try to be still and to listen the first thing every morning. Now I believe that the true God used this experience to again reach out to me when I called to him, to show me he is real, but I was not yet prepared to accept what I would come to know as truth. Little by little, the Dancer was enticing me, knowing me intimately.

When my joyful little Katie entered first grade, I took a part-time job teaching at the university to cover my tuition expenses so I could go back to school. Eventually, Katie and Micah attended the lab school a block from my office on campus. Having them close helped me feel less guilty about working. I was still the Relief Society president. I served one bishop, and when he was released, I served a second. The lay church work, which really was not volunteer because my temple recommend depended on it, could be overwhelming. The only time I was unavailable to the sisters in the ward was on Saturday mornings, when I turned off my phone until 10:00 a.m.

Super Mom

Mormon women endure great pressure to conform to LDS Church standards, to have everything look great on the outside, and to do everything well. Mormon scholars have tried to refute the idea that pressure for women to be perfect impacts their emotional life. But in my church work, I met many hurting and discouraged women. One struggled to get seven small children to church on time. One fretted that she didn't have time to read her scriptures. Others worried that their homes were not clean enough or that their children were not faithful enough, smart enough, or talented enough to stand out in the outside world. Some were anxious because they did not hold temple recommends or did not have husbands to get them to the top of the celestial kingdom or were not spreading the Mormon gospel or did not have time for their callings. Some felt a burden to complete their family genealogy to save their dead family members through temple work; the research and the temple work could take years of effort. If others were going to look to us for answers and want to join Mormonism, we needed to have it all together. There was a lot to worry about.

When I was LDS, I certainly felt the weight of super-mom-hood. I tried to be the best latter-day saint I could, which meant spending time with each of my children and my husband every day, fixing a nutritious dinner, attending all of my kids' activities, having family scripture study and prayer, keeping the house clean, growing flowers and canning vegetables, being involved in the kids' schools, helping with my in-laws, and performing as Relief Society president to the best of my ability. And now I was back at school working on a doctorate. When I was released as Relief

Society president, I taught seminary at 6:00 a.m. every day before high school. Mike helped out. I did feel the pressure.

Eventually, I graduated with the Dean's Citation for Academic Excellence and was offered a job at the school where I had received my doctorate. Mike and I had always wanted to move west to Utah, though, because we loved the mountains and the Mormon people. Brigham Young University had a position open in my field. So I applied there and was thrilled when they invited me for an interview.

Even so, I was fully aware that this interview had come about only because I had followed a personal revelation that conflicted with the prophet's own revelation that women were to stay home. How would this strange scenario play itself out?

I was soon to find out.

CHAPTER 7

MOVING TO GOD'S COUNTRY

✣

*The glory of God is intelligence, or, in other words, light
and truth.*

— DOCTRINE AND COVENANTS 93:36

I sat dressed in a proper navy-blue pinstriped suit with shin-length skirt, nervously rubbing the black heels of my conservative pumps together. I glanced around at the exquisitely carved wood environment of the old office building of the Church of Jesus Christ of Latter-day Saints in downtown Salt Lake City. Across the plaza, the high-spired Salt Lake Temple gleamed in the spring sunlight.

It was May 12, 1999. I was awaiting my interview with a general authority (GA), a man with administrative authority under the prophet and twelve apostles of the Mormon Church. In other words, one of the top leaders in the church.

Starched security guards working for the church followed me around from the moment I entered the building, even when I went to the restroom, where they stood outside. I was mildly amused; how odd that men of God would need bodyguards to protect them.

In order to be hired as full-time professorial faculty at Brigham Young University (BYU, or the Y, as some affectionately call it), I had to be interviewed not only by a search team of future colleagues from BYU but also by a GA for ecclesiastical approval. Faculty must maintain ecclesiastical clearance at all times to keep a job there.

The Mormon Church owns, finances, and administers the thirty-four-thousand-student university, one of the largest private universities in the United States. Liberty University is the only religious institution in the United States with more students, but most of them are online — not so at BYU. There is also a BYU Idaho, BYU Hawaii, and Southern Virginia University for Mormon students. BYU Provo, located forty-five miles south of Salt Lake, is the premier research institution. BYU students must abide by the standards of the honor code, including appropriate dress, no drinking, no smoking, and no premarital sex.

The school is difficult to get into. Standards are high. Students are very bright. This Mormon scripture from the Doctrine and Covenants instructs Mormon youth to pay attention to academic pursuits: "The glory of God is intelligence, or, in other words, light and truth" (D&C 93:36).

When I was finally ushered into the ornate Salt Lake office, the clean-cut, graying GA, wearing a dark suit, welcomed me with a firm handshake. The GA was at the time a member of the first quorum of the seventy. The Mormon hierarchy consists of the prophet and his two counselors, the twelve apostles, and several quorums of the seventy. These leaders administer the affairs of the church. As a GA, this elder had assisted the first Mormon missionaries entering a part of the world previously closed to Mormon missionaries. He, like most general authorities, holds an advanced degree from a reputable university.

During the interview, I asked the elder the long-awaited question — the one thing that might cause Michael and me not to accept the position.

"How would a working woman be treated at BYU and in Utah? Would I be accepted?" I assumed that in the midst of Mormon territory, I might be shunned as a woman who worked.

He answered slowly, carefully choosing his words. "General authorities now recognize that some women can raise successful LDS families and still have a professional career."

I was relieved to hear this from a GA — and stunned as well. A few short years ago, as a mother working less than two days a week, I had met with major resistance in my home ward. BYU, in contrast, would require full-time employment.

He suggested that there was general revelation for the church as a whole that works for the majority of people. And then there was personal revelation for an individual. He admitted that rarely, but sometimes, personal revelation conflicted with general revelation. Even though I had not shared my personal revelation with him, he told me Heavenly Father needed me at BYU. "Besides," he added, "fifty percent of BYU students are women who deserve good female role models and mentors. You have been called as a role model for them."

I took it all in and sat up a little taller. *Wow, Heavenly Father needs me?* Later I learned the Y needed female faculty for accreditation. So the political powers-that-be needed me even more.

Before the interview ended, the elder made a curious remark. He said, "I've been interviewing faculty for BYU for many years, and I've never come upon someone like you."

"How's that?" I asked.

He replied, "You've never lived in Utah, you've never attended BYU, and you're a pure convert to the church."

Whoa, I thought. *Among my professional colleagues, there will be few who came from outside of Utah, few educated somewhere other than BYU, and few if any converts to the Mormon Church?*

That should have raised a red flag, but it didn't. We were too excited about the possibility of my being hired at the Lord's University, as Mormons call it. Living outside the homeland of Mormonism meant we came from "a Gentile mission field." (Many Mormons refer to all non-Mormons as Gentiles.) Utah, meanwhile, was "Zion," with Salt Lake as the epicenter and BYU as the instructional hub for prospective secular and religious leaders. The LDS "saints" had crossed the plains to Utah by wagon and handcart in the mid-1800s when they were chased out of Nauvoo, Illinois, for various reasons. Polygamy was one. Soon I would learn that they had lived primarily isolated from the rest of the United States for a long, long time, cultivating a rather peculiar culture. It was an incredible blessing that God could even consider us worthy for this opportunity—to live in Zion and be at BYU.

There were other warnings we didn't understand. Our own bishop in Indiana had cautioned us, "You won't like Utah. They don't live the gospel in Utah." How could that be true? Utah was Zion, the base of the one true church. How could people there call themselves Mormons and attend church but just pretend to believe?

I passed the BYU colleagues' scholarship interview, passed the GA's ecclesiastical interview, signed a contract weeks later, and agreed to start fall term. We embraced what we saw as our calling—we were being gathered to Zion.

Alpine, Utah

No one in our extended families seemed to mind our move west, just as no one had seemed to mind our baptism into Mormonism—too much. My parents had moved to Florida. Mom was in a nursing home with Alzheimer's; Dad was well. Mike's mom had died nine months earlier, and his father was in a nursing home in Connecticut, near Mike's sister. Mike's parents and my family were all Christian, but no one talked to us about Mormonism. We constantly tried to talk to them about the advantages of Mormonism. We sensed they weren't entirely pleased, but we didn't know why. There was one exception: Mike had baptized his sister into the Mormon Church years earlier, and she was thrilled to have family in Zion. She talked about retiring near us in Utah.

In early August of 1999, our family trekked across the plains on a route similar to that taken by the Mormon pioneers, but instead of riding in a wagon or pushing a handcart, we were traveling in our well-worn white conversion van. Our oldest son, Josh, would attend college another year at Indiana University before he too made the journey to Utah, where he would continue college. Matt would be a junior in high school in the fall. Micah was a ninth-grader, and Katie was a fifth-grader.

We moved to Alpine, Utah, a beautiful, sleepy bedroom community of about nine thousand. It sits a mile high on the eastern bench of the Wasatch Mountain Range, between Salt Lake on the north and Provo on the south. We were told that no one from the local ward could help us unload what little we had brought with us, because we had arrived on the Saturday of Alpine City Days — the annual weekend of the rodeo, 5K run, quilt show, youth dance, and more. The elders' quorum president, who arranges physical assistance for any ward member in need, was volunteering there. Mormon neighbors did show up later with food, blankets, a kitchen table, and several things we would need to survive until the moving van arrived two weeks later. Mormons typically stand ready to help.

As the local story goes, Alpine was named by the second prophet, Brigham Young, soon after he sent families to settle there in the 1850s, because it reminded him of the Swiss Alps. Some of the oldest gravestones at the top of cemetery hill say, "Killed by Injuns." Alpine is striking, with incredible views of the sheer rock cliffs of Lone Peak to the left, crystal-clear streams, waterfalls, and alpine meadows in the lower Dry Creek area to the right of Lone Peak called "the cove." The cove is nestled between Lone Peak and the adjacent towering mountain, Box Elder. My new kitchen window framed the view of the cove in all its splendor. In the summer, the brilliant red of Indian paintbrush and other buttery and purple wildflowers in the cove are exquisite. It sometimes rains drops of mud on the car in the summer, a dusty desert rain. Only Nevada is drier than Utah.

The kids adjusted to their new schools, to new friends, and to new activities—although each of us had personal challenges in adjusting. The move had been so difficult financially that we did not have the money to pay the kids' school fees that first fall, but finances were about to improve significantly. We had bought a modest stucco-and-brick home on three-quarters of an acre. Our new LDS chapel (ward building) sat literally in our back yard, just over our fence.

Michael settled into self-employment in the financial industry, working from his home office, where his voice could be heard in endless business phone conversations. He worked long hours, feverishly, surrounded by stacks of legal-size files. For a time after we moved, he made family dinners to support me at BYU, when he wasn't back in Indiana visiting clients. He was very proud of my job and insisted that the children respect their mother.

Mike and I loved the magnificent outdoors in "God's country." On Saturdays, we hiked for hours and hours out of cell phone range—usually just the two of us. We always prayed together when we reached the farthest point. "Heavenly Father, guide our family and protect us from harm." Some evenings we drove up

American Fork Canyon and hiked the cave trail. We never tired of the exhilarating views and heights.

On the contrary, Micah was scared of heights. Mike and another leader took his LDS Scout troop to the top of Lone Peak, where a narrow bridge has drop-offs on both sides. Mike took videos, and in the background we heard a barely breathing fifteen-year-old Micah repeat, "We're gonna die. We're gonna die."

Mike got reacquainted with skiing. He and Josh loved to ski. (Matt and Micah were playing sports, and their coaches forbade them to strap on skis—too great a risk for injury.) Although I was in my late forties, Mike dragged me up a mountain and declared it was time I learned to ski. We were loath to spend the money for a lift ticket, but after 3:00 p.m., we could make several blue runs at Alta for free.

An elk herd wintered near us that first winter, and one winter a cougar nestled in the gully near our home to eat a harvest of deer that ran through. We could sit in the hot tub under a gazebo in the middle of our back yard on a snowy winter evening and see the wildlife, eyes alight, all around us.

The Blessed Life

Every LDS ward in Alpine (as in much of Utah) encompassed members living within a few square blocks of each other. Mormons cannot choose their church or their bishop. They must attend the church to which they are assigned in their geographic area, defined by the LDS Church. Ward buildings are used for Sunday meetings and are open several evenings a week for ward activities. Each includes a full basketball court, so Matt and Micah, high school basketball players, like Josh had been, often went over to shoot hoops. Matt also ran cross country, and both of them ran track.

We were aware of only two families in our ward that were what is called in Mormon culture "part-member families" (some LDS Church members, some not). Everyone else was Mormon. My teens would be raised in the "Mormon bubble," and we believed they were less likely to do illegal drugs or have premarital sex if they were active in church. Utah Valley, the heart of the Mormon culture bubble because it has a higher concentration of LDS than even Salt Lake Valley farther north, was dubbed Happy Valley.

LDS ward buildings never have crosses, inside or out. Their tall, bare spires reach up from the churchyard, watching over the social and spiritual lives of the people in that community. Mormonism does not reverence the cross as a religious symbol. (Mormons ask, "If your brother were killed by a gun, would you wear a gun around your neck?" Technically, Joseph Smith *was* killed by a gun.) Two wards in Alpine besides ours, each with its own bishop, met in our building, with staggered Sunday schedules. LDS ward buildings were everywhere.

In addition to the ward buildings, about eight ostentatious Mormon temples are on display up and down the valley, sitting on the benches — shelflike plateaus — of the mountains and in prominent places in the valley, like droning sirens bidding faithful LDS to submit. They are large white edifices, lit up outside at night for all to see, closed inside to anyone but temple recommend–holding Mormons. Temples, surrounded by landscaped grounds, are typically open for the faithful Tuesday through Saturday. Rumor had it that special ceremonies, such as the second anointing, occurred on the other days. This ordinance was only for people so righteous that they could have their "calling and election" (exaltation and future godhood) made sure. Plus, it was whispered that LDS general authorities met in temples to receive revelations from Christ and make decisions critical to the Lord's kingdom on earth.

At the top of each temple, the angel Moroni sits atop a

spire in gold. It represents the ancient Book of Mormon prophet Moroni, who was resurrected as an angel and who visited Joseph Smith and told him where to find the gold plates. Smith translated the gold plates "by the gift and power of God" into the Book of Mormon.

Mike was soon a member of the bishopric. I was called to work with sixteen Laurels (young women ages sixteen and seventeen). Matt was one of two youth representatives to the stake youth committee from our ward. Micah was the teacher's quorum president for his peers, ages fourteen and fifteen. Too young for a calling, Katie found two perfect LDS best friends.

In the year we moved, 1999, the economy was humming, and people were moving into the Wasatch valleys in droves. It seemed that every two months, a new stoplight was added to my commute. New homes were popping up like popcorn, all with the same beige stucco with a touch of stone or wood for the alpine look. The wealthier a person was, the more wood or stone or brick on the house, the larger the house, and the higher up on the mountain it sat.

The citadel of BYU rests opposite Utah Lake on the bench against the tall Wasatch Range at the eastern end of the town of Provo. There is a large Y on the mountain, hence the name Y Mountain. The elliptical Provo Temple, just off campus and higher on the bench, can be seen from most places in the valley, from the air, and from I-15, forever under construction, which winds through the valley. Utah drivers are crazy, by the way, in jacked-up 4 x 4 trucks or gargantuan SUVs needed for their large families.

I made the forty-five-minute drive to BYU daily and set out to learn how to be a contributing and respected BYU professor and still have dinner on the table each evening, attend all of my children's activities, keep the house clean, attend my Relief Society activities for women, and fulfill whatever other church callings I was assigned. Life in Zion was busy and seemed good. We relied on this scripture from the Book of Mormon: "I would desire that ye should consider on the blessed and happy state of those that keep the commandments of God. For behold, they are blessed in all things, both temporal and spiritual" (Mosiah 2:41). We strove to be among the righteous who kept the Mormon Jesus' commandments, expecting blessings both spiritual and temporal. And for a time, we believed that my new job had helped open the door to a perfect life of blessings in Mormon Zion.

Chapter 8

BYU BLUE
IN HAPPY VALLEY

🙶

Men are that they might have joy.

— The Book of Mormon, 2 Nephi 2:25

You're not in Kansas, anymore, Dorothy.

I'd lived my life in the Midwest but traveled extensively inside the U.S. and outside. I'd seen a myriad of captivating cultures — but nothing like the Mormon culture in Utah. Families, church families, and whole communities were so close-knit! Breaking in took knowing the cultural code and a crowbar.

I had two strikes against me from the outset. I was a convert to the Mormon Church, not a generational member. Whoever heard of a Mormon with the surname Wieting (my maiden name) or Wilder? And I was a working woman. At least I was working at the Lord's University. I was BYU blue. Some gave me a bye for that.

When I enrolled the kids in school, I learned that the open house at Katie's elementary was scheduled during the day. I had to be at BYU. I couldn't attend! In Indiana, the schools accommodated working parents. I was angry. This seemed like a message to working mothers that their poor decision to work would not be tolerated. My ward also held weekday Relief Society meetings for the women. In our first month in Utah, I was outcast twice.

In Alpine, everyone I met was a member of the Mormon Church. Folks held status based on their church callings. If one was or had been a bishop, stake president, church patriarch, mission president, BYU professor, or auxiliary president, one had clout. Church position mattered. We were told that if we got stopped for speeding, we could try showing the police officer our temple recommend.

Large families with lots of children were everywhere. Homes had bedrooms galore. Each home had a front room called the home teaching room, where home teachers (a pair of men) or visiting teachers (pair of RS women) from the Mormon Church could sit if they dropped by unannounced. Even if the rest of the house was in disarray, this room was always impeccable. People were polite but not helpful, and everyone spoke Mormonese—at the post office, at the grocery store, in the schools. There was little diversity; almost everyone was blond with the whitest of skin.

We quickly got a taste of Mormon status consciousness. When we'd been in Alpine a short time, our neighbors across the street and up the mountain began building a swimming pool. One day, a man driving by stopped his car in the road near the end of our driveway to watch the construction. Meanwhile Matt got into our car and backed out of the garage and up the steep driveway to the street, where he looked behind him to the left, to the right, and then backed right into the man's car. The man never saw Matt, since he was looking at the pool. Matt couldn't see the man directly behind him.

When Mike and I came out of the house, the man launched into a diatribe. "*I* used to be a member of a stake presidency!"

We were stunned. Who cares? We had expected an admission of partial guilt and perhaps some Mormon Jesus niceness. It seemed to us that a man should not stop his car in the middle of the road, but what did we know about Mormon culture?

Polygamy Shock

Folks in Utah also had status based on family genes. Names like Young, Nielson, Call, Allred, Marriott, Romney, Huntsman, Larsen, Jensen, and Beck exuded importance. Mormon men who practiced polygamy in the early years had produced progeny in no time. Their descendants lived all around us. There were three Youngs in my department of eleven full-time professorial faculty. At the time we moved to Utah, we believed what we had been told when we joined the church—that few Mormons practiced polygamy in the past and that all Mormons had stopped in 1890 when the prophet issued a manifesto, prompted by a revelation from the Lord, that discontinued it. Nevertheless, we were about to stumble on modern truth about "the principle" that Joseph Smith had established in the 1830s and that six subsequent prophets (along with rank-and-file members of the church) had lived by.

After Christmas the year we moved to Utah, Michael and I spent a few days in a cabin in Zion National Park for our twenty-fifth wedding anniversary. We hiked during the day and went out to eat at night. One evening, next to our anniversary table, the restaurant placed several long tables side by side to accommodate a man entering with several wives and his children. Mike and I could not help but gawk. The women were dressed in pastel-colored to-the-ankle and to-the-wrist handmade dresses. They wore a peculiar swooped-up-front, long-braid-in-the-back hairdo.

The waitress saw my reaction and bent down to whisper, "Polygamists." Polygamy was alive and well in Utah.

When we asked our new neighbors about modern polygamy, they explained that the polygamists live in southern Utah, known as Little Dixie, and in northern Arizona. They told us, "There are some in Mount Pleasant too. During the time of the 1890 Manifesto, their descendants split from the Mormon Church to continue practicing polygamy. They couldn't be expected to walk away from their wives and their children, could they?" Many influential people in Utah — the governor, legislators, policemen, judges, and BYU professors — had polygamous ancestors. The pervading attitude seemed to be, let them be. Some were Fundamentalist Latter-Day Saints (FLDS). These fundamentalists actually lived Joseph Smith's D&C 132 scripture, I realized. This section of scripture, hailing polygamy as an eternal principle, is still in LDS scripture.

Modern polygamists were not confined to southern Utah and Mount Pleasant. And they didn't all dress like pioneers. As part of my work at BYU, I was assigned to supervise student teachers in Lehi, Utah. Right there in the heart of Utah were polygamist families in the schools. Then I began to look around and notice polygamists in restaurants and stores. These families did not wear the unusual garb we'd seen in southern Utah. They looked like normal Mormon families, like on the TV shows *Big Love* and *Sister Wives*. Except that there was more than one wife trailing herds of kids. (Utah has the highest birthrate in the United States![14]) Polygamists were scattered throughout typical Utah neighborhoods, in huge homes with separate entrances for the various wives and their children. Or they owned several homes or trailers side by side, like a family compound.

Bowl me over. Polygamists still existed in Utah. Although polygamy was technically against the law, and sometimes involved child rape, spouse abuse, welfare fraud, and deplorable poverty, the state largely ignored it. At the time, polygamists and their families comprised an estimated 2 percent of the state's population of just over two million.

Embracing Mormon Culture

One day after an activity at church, Katie came home with the assignment to bring in a pioneer journal from her ancestors. Pioneer journal—you know, from a pioneer ancestor who had joined the Mormon Church, crossed the plains by wagon or handcart and settled in Zion, and then written about it. Oh, we didn't have one. You don't have one? That seemed unimaginable to her leader.

Mormonism pervaded every part of life in Utah. Micah loved that everyone, absolutely everyone, at his middle school went to seminary. Ninth grade is the first year of the church's four-year seminary program. Seminary is the religion class that my husband and I had taught in the early morning in Indiana. The curriculum rotates every four years: (1) Old Testament (including the Mormon books Moses and Abraham, from the Pearl of Great Price), (2) New Testament, (3) Book of Mormon, and (4) Doctrine and Covenants / Church History.

Matt and Micah kept track of their daily seminary scripture readings and memorized required verses. Matt was the ward rep to the stake youth. Micah was teacher's quorum president, then priest's quorum president, and later one of eight high school students on seminary council. In Utah, several seminary teachers were needed to teach one grade at each school. The ninth-graders at the middle schools and those who were in high school had release time during the school day to walk across the parking lot to the seminary building of the LDS Church to take religion classes. Mormonism was the only doctrine offered.

Our bishop's warning about unfaithful Mormons in Utah proved to be true. For example, our sons told us that some of their peers went drinking on Saturday night and showed up to pass sacrament at church the next day. This was a definite no-no in the

LDS Church. Drinking alcohol would make them unworthy to pass the sacrament or to get a temple recommend. But the social pressure was so great to be Mormon in Utah that some merely pretended to believe. They did not follow the Mormon gospel rules and regs day to day. These were cultural Mormons, or "Jack Mormons." These folks decided it was better to pretend than to endure the consequences of family disappointment, social and job trouble, or even excommunication from the church.

Mormon youth can't date until they're sixteen, and then they are supposed to take their date out in a group. Groups would often go to BYU for "hymn sings" in the tunnel—a street underpass on campus where the acoustics were grand. In addition, the cultural ritual for asking someone to a dance was unusual. One didn't just ask someone face-to-face or over the phone. Instead invitations were issued in creative ways. One girl asked Matt to the Sadie Hawkins Dance by putting a jack-o'-lantern on our front porch with a note asking him to light it if he wanted to go with her. Micah was livid when some girls plastered his car with Oreos to invite him to a dance. Didn't they know what that could do to the paint? His now-wife, Alicia, once got my permission to fill his room with hearts and left a big teddy bear holding a heart that asked him to the Valentine's Dance. That worked better, I guess. Guys also were supposed to use creative techniques to ask girls out. The Wilder boys always felt pressure to think up something more inventive than the last time.

The culture shock in Utah was greatest for Matt, a junior in high school. That spring, he qualified for state finals in track, and the coach substituted a senior who wasn't even on the track team to run his race (because Matt was new in town or the son of converts?). He made the varsity basketball team at school, but the rest of the team had trouble accepting him. We could tell by the melancholy chords Matt composed on the piano that he was hurting, but he didn't complain. Competitive on the sports field, Matt avoided personal conflict.

The best spirits in the pre-existence had been born into established Mormon homes, not to converts. I never realized this made me a second-class citizen until I moved to Utah. This was not the only reason why Matt's adjustment to the new culture was difficult his last two years of high school, but it may have been a part of it.

It didn't help that I naturally thought in convert terms. When the father of a colleague at BYU died, I tried to comfort her by saying, "Well, now you can take his name to the temple and have his ordinances done [so he can be a Mormon and live with Heavenly Father and Jesus in the hereafter]."

My colleague responded, "My father knew enough to do his own temple work."

I learned early on not to tell anyone anything I didn't want repeated or judged or told to my bishop. I lived in fear of neighbors' judgment. I was even careful at Katie's dance lessons, at her musicals, and at the grocery store—anywhere in public. Everyone around us spoke Mormonese, that strange language with terms like "ward," "stake," "FHE" (family home evening), "baptism for the dead," "visiting teaching," "patriarchal blessing," "mission call," "homecoming," and—whispered—"apostate." Mothers gossiped, "Did you hear that So-and-so's son decided not to serve a mission?" Or worse, "Did you know he's gay?" Or, "They are definitely headed for divorce." "I heard she didn't get admitted into the Y." "I think he's really struggling with his testimony. He's going apostate." These were all things to be dreaded.

Nevertheless, most of our experiences in Utah were positive. Mormons tend to be extremely service oriented. Many of the youth did remain morally clean, educated, and obliging. At four o'clock our first Christmas Eve there, our doorbell rang. Neighbor after neighbor came by bringing small gifts for the family — jams, ornaments, candy. I returned the favor with cookies that I'd baked for us. The gifts were quite unexpected and most appreciated. When the last guest left at about seven o'clock, I got on my knees to thank Heavenly Father. I even cried. I really was grateful to be living in Zion.

Eventually, our family developed our own LDS rituals. Out of respect, I turned off the radio and remained silent each time I drove by a temple. Micah began attending the temple every morning before school. As in Indiana, we had family prayers at meals and bedtime. We read our scriptures together in the evening. All three sons chose to serve two-year, full-time missions for the church. I attended the weekly devotional in the Marriott Center at BYU. Michael was diligent in his priesthood callings. Oh my heck (more Mormonese), did we ever embrace Mormon culture!

Spellbound

My time at BYU in the archetypical three-pronged role as teacher, scholar, and humanitarian began more than a week before classes started. BYU students had a solitary sameness, although it took me years to put my finger on it. Like many of our neighbors, they wore a plastered smile of outward niceness but were not very accommodating. In my early weeks there, for example, each time I went to a campus office for assistance and asked, "Can you help me?" a smiling young woman with impeccable teeth and blond hair smiled and said, "I'm sorry." (When Josh transferred to the University of Utah the next fall, he complained to me for not telling him that every college-age woman in Utah was blond. He preferred brunettes.) Next office. "Can you help me?" Next worker. "I'm sorry." Everywhere I went in Utah, people said, "I'm sorry." This didn't solve anything; it was a quirky part of the culture.

The students were brilliant intellectually but lagging socially — rather nerdy and clad alike within the requisite dress code. Maybe part of what I was detecting was a lack of common sense. I worried whether they had the multitasking talents required to be teachers who could adjust to different cultures. We were told that about half of our grads never used their teaching certificate anyway. They married young, had lots of babies, and sometimes worked just long enough to put their husbands through school.

My first week at BYU, new faculty participated in several ice-breaker activities. When the dance faculty put the science faculty in lab coats and made them perform a ballet, I laughed till it hurt. I was surprised to meet science professors that week who taught evolution. I was also surprised to find FARMS (Foundation for Ancient Research and Mormon Studies, now the Neal A. Maxwell Institute) religious scholars hired by the Mormon Church working on campus. Basically, they are apologists who defend the church. I thought they would be housed in the church office building downtown. They joined us for orientation.

Early that semester, campus-wide faculty and staff were honored to hear Elder James E. Faust, second counselor to the prophet of the Church of Jesus Christ of Latter-day Saints, speak to us in the 22,700-seat Marriott Center. The crowd showed a hushed reverence for Faust. It was a treat for me to hear him live. Next we heard from President Merrill J. Bateman. He was the president of BYU, a general authority who was a member of the first quorum of the seventy. The speakers assured us we were part of the move of Heavenly Father in these latter days. These BYU youth had been saved in the pre-existence to come to earth for these very times. We had been chosen to prepare them to serve him as they went out into the world. They would have great influence, righteousness, and bring many to the Lord's church.

Whenever I heard a general authority speak, I was spellbound.

Funny, back in junior high when my friends swooned over the Beatles, I dismissed such behavior as silly. I enjoyed listening to their music, but I never offered them god status, as many in my generation did. Here I was, much older and supposedly much smarter, yet getting weak-kneed over grown men. We rose to our feet when the prophet entered the room, and remained standing until he sat or left. The very experience of being taught by general authorities in small groups of BYU faculty was a sure sign to me that I was special to Heavenly Father.

I was unusually weepy while adjusting to my role at BYU. The Spirit on campus seemed so strong. At times it was overwhelming. I sensed I was treading on sacred ground at BYU, as when I first got pregnant and walked on eggshells. My Mormon spirit-o-meter registered straight up.

The BYU Theocracy

From its immense resources, the Mormon Church finances Brigham Young University. The prophet of the Mormon Church serves as the chairman of the BYU board of trustees. His two counselors are the two vice presidents. Six of the twelve apostles sit as members of the board of trustees. The Mormon culture is rife at BYU.

My dean once reminded me, "Like the LDS Church, BYU is a *theocracy*, not a democracy." The theocracy pours a lot of tithing money into BYU and expects it to run efficiently and effectively. It is critical that the outside world respect the scholars in those mountains, and they do. BYU is one of the top schools in the nation for business, law, social work, and engineering. The long arm of the J. Reuben Clark Law School and their International Center for Law and Religion Studies reaches around the world, into many countries and governments, a deliberate influence. Our David O. McKay School of Education ranked nationally as well, according to *U.S. News and World Report*.[15]

BYU's faculty center provides extensive professional develop-ment activities to improve and support faculty so the world will rec-ognize BYU. The orientation program ran an entire year when I was there. My first semester at the Y, the faculty center provided lunch regularly as we listened to various speakers to learn our job. I even gained weight from the lush attention to materialistic comforts.

The majority of my students at the Y spoke a second language. Many served missions abroad. I had to report my second language (German) to my bosses, and one time when the German chan-cellor was on campus, I was invited to a reception. International corporations, the military, and intelligence agencies snapped up our Y graduates. Today there is a National Middle East Language Resource Center (NMELRC) at BYU that trains anyone aspiring to learn Farsi-Persian, Arabic, Hebrew, or Turkish.

There are quite a few famous BYU grads. Mitt Romney speaks French from his LDS mission to France. Jon Huntsman speaks Mandarin Chinese from his LDS mission to Taiwan. Stephen R. Covey, now deceased, was a world-renowned author of the Seven Habits books and professor at the Jon M. Huntsman School of Business at Utah State University. Stephenie Meyer, author of the *Twilight* series, has a degree in English from BYU. Mormons rise to the top in their fields, having learned to master public speak-ing by giving talks in church, holding leadership callings, serving foreign missions, attending good colleges, working in the arts, and engaging intelligently around the world with cultures and peoples of influence.

By the end of my first year at BYU, I was well aware of what was expected of me. Good student ratings, nationally and interna-tionally recognized research, multiple peer-reviewed publications in top-tier journals, and service to the profession, department, university, and community. This was more than I had anticipated. In addition, I was to be a good moral example to my students and colleagues. I kept a requested vita of my church callings for the university. My bishop completed papers annually to declare my worthiness to teach there.

When I presented my research at professional conferences, it was not unusual for someone to come up to me after a presentation to ask about the Mormon Church, not about the research — although our research was well respected in most areas. I was glad to answer questions about Mormonism. I represented not only BYU but also its employer, the Mormon Church.

I worked long hours, sometimes six days a week, twelve hours a day, but I was oh-so-grateful to have a part at the Lord's University, also called "The School of the Prophets," meaning we trained the future leaders of the Mormon Church. Plus, I had a passion for the subjects I taught, and I loved my students.

My presentations, publications, student evaluations, service, and growing network of professional friends in the United States and abroad earned me advancement from assistant professor to associate professor a year early. One thing I know how to do is work hard.

The next year, I earned tenure. I remember the day my boss, whom I adored, ducked her head into my office yelling softly, "Grab a pencil and come meet someone." I rushed out of my office to a chorus of "Congratulations!" It was my tenure party, cake and all.

My reaction to receiving tenure was the opposite of what I would have expected. I stayed composed until I could withdraw into my office, where I burst into tears. I was suddenly sick to my stomach about all the time I had spent away from my family. *For what?* a little voice in my head screamed. That Dancer again? But quickly I pushed the thought aside. It was my spiritual duty to teach here. I believed that the God of Mormonism had sent me.

My students described me in evaluations as passionate about

my subjects, approachable in my demeanor, tough with my assignments, and spiritual. Looking back, I believe I was confident and arrogant. Since I was keeping the rules and regs and progressing at BYU, I thought I was pretty hot. Life couldn't be better.[16]

A Spiritual Tornado

In church we sang about Zion,

> We'll find the place which God for us prepared,
> Far away in the West,
> Where none shall come to hurt or make afraid;
> Where the saints will be blessed. We'll make the air with music ring,
> Shout praises to our God and King;
> Above the rest these words we'll tell — All is well! All is well![17]

But was it all well, far away in the West? About noon on August 11, when we'd been in Utah two weeks, Matt was eating lunch at basketball camp at the University of Utah on the east bench of Salt Lake. The dining room had a gorgeous glass-window view of the city below. It was growing dark outside at midday. Matt just happened to look up and see — no, it couldn't be — a tornado over the city. Tornados were commonplace in Indiana, but in Utah? Never. But there it was, a harbinger of things to come.

Where was that twirling Dancer giving enticing glimpses of grace? Well, we certainly weren't on the lookout for grace then. We were finding our way to the celestial kingdom by ourselves, and we were doing just fine.

In reality, we were headed in the wrong direction. Soon enough, the Wilder family would face their own spiritual tornado.

Part Two

CRACKS IN
THE FACADE

CHAPTER 9

TEACHING DIVERSITY IN A WHITE-BREAD LAND

✢

*The skins of the Lamanites were dark, according to the
mark which was set upon their fathers, which was a
curse upon them because of their transgression and their
rebellion.*

— BOOK OF MORMON, ALMA 3:6

Utah, as I learned soon after moving there, was nothing if not
white-bread land. The Mormon pioneers had been largely
from the eastern United States, Britain, and Northern Europe, hence
so many Scandinavian blonds! African Americans were 1 percent of
the population in Utah and barely half of 1 percent in Utah County,
land of the Mormon bubble, where BYU resided. There were a few
more Asians, Hawaiian and Pacific Islanders, and Native Americans, but just a few. The 13 percent Hispanic population was growing, but Utah, and especially Utah County, was decidedly white.

Although I'd been raised in largely white Indiana, the preva-
lent minority group there was black. It was the early 1970s, and
the civil rights movement was in full swing. I stopped going to

my parents' country club because my black friends were not welcome to join. They were, however, welcome to bus tables and wash dishes in the club restaurant. An indignant moral conscience pierced me. To say I felt passionate about the cause of equal rights for blacks, and later in college the cause of civil rights for the disabled, was to fail to appreciate my enthusiasm. Eagerly I stood beside black friends to hear black preachers denounce the evils of racism. The air was electric. A hundred years earlier, that very county had been a major stop on the Underground Railroad for slaves fleeing tyranny in Dixie. Now we were facing down tyranny of another kind, less overt but no less evil or insidious.

During my senior year, I walked two miles alone to the downtown community center to hear the latest news about the civil rights cause. I didn't breathe a word of this to anyone in my family. They wouldn't have disagreed with my passion for the cause, but they would have thought I was compromising my safety in that neighborhood. Yet I felt perfectly at home.

Prior to my graduation in 1971, a sit-in closed the high school campus. Before the school reopened, the state sent in psychologists who moderated critical discussions between black students and white students about race. Through it all, I was captivated. Even today I like to tell my civil rights war stories to college students in my diversity course.

Over the years, I taught students from many different cultures: African American, Vietnamese, Native American, Mexican, and immigrants from other Central and South American countries. I loved learning from them about their language, culture, and history. Little did I know that the church I loved would not see all of them the same way.

Racism on the Shelf

Just days before our baptism into Mormonism in 1977—the date set and friends invited—Michael discovered that blacks could not hold the Mormon priesthood. The Mormons did not tell us. Someone mentioned it to Michael at work, and he confronted the Mormons. They tried to appease him with these rationalizations: First, "Christ himself said the Jews would receive the gospel first and then the Gentiles. Someday the blacks will get the priesthood." Next, "It is Heavenly Father's will and his order of things. We can't understand his ways." And, "Don't think of it as condescension. Trust him. He surely has his reasons."

This crazy teaching was nearly a deal breaker for us. I was incensed. Mike didn't like such blatant exclusion either, but he'd had that vivid dream, about defending the Mormon people, that he just couldn't shake.

Why didn't we simply walk away? We did not know what the Bible says about the topic. We never thought to look. If we had looked, we would have found an alternative message that could have ended our foray into Mormonism, or at least set up a choice to make. As Paul declared, "There is neither Jew nor Gentile, neither slave nor free, nor is there male and female, for you are all one in Christ Jesus" (Gal. 3:28). And when the apostle Peter was confronted with his first Gentile believer, he declared, "I now realize how true it is that God does not show favoritism" (Acts 10:34).

But in ten weeks, the Mormons had skillfully proselytized us to look to Mormon sources for answers. Also, we had seen racist attitudes in the Protestant churches in which we were raised, so it was natural to think that racism aligned with religion. The question for us was, did we want Jesus/religion even if we had to hold our noses about the racism? Okay, we would get baptized, and if racism ever reared its ugly head during our years in Mormonism, we would do what we could to change things from within the church, or get the heck out.

So we joined the LDS Church knowing they did not allow blacks to hold the Mormon priesthood. I did not know, back then, the full import of what it meant not to hold the priesthood. Years later, I learned that without the Mormon priesthood, blacks could hope only to be servants in the next life. The priesthood restriction disallowed their access to temples for saving ordinances. Therefore they could not reach the highest degree of the highest heaven or live with both Heavenly Father and Jesus for eternity or have plural wives or become gods.

Skin color alone determined who could receive the blessings of the kingdom? Were we under a kind of spiritual spell that blinded us to this viper in Mormonism? Yes, we loved the Mormon people. But did this love supersede horse sense? Unfortunately, we allowed the Mormons to soothe our concerns. We chose to trust them.

So Michael and I put the racism issue on the shelf and tried not to think about it, although it was a matter of conversation between us at times. Eight months after we joined the church, in June 1978, Mike was watching a ball game on TV and I was folding laundry on the couch. Suddenly a news flash broke into the game, and we paused to listen. The Mormon prophet Spencer W. Kimball had just announced to the world that he received a revelation from the Lord to no longer restrict blacks from holding the Mormon priesthood. I exhaled with relief and gratitude. Thank God I would never have to try to defend that nonsense!

The 1978 revelation that all worthy males could now hold the priesthood is the last one the LDS Church has added to their scriptures. The church prepared an official declaration in the Doctrine and Covenants "extending priesthood and temple blessings to all worthy male members of the church."[18] This included blacks; they were the only group previously excluded.

When we lived in the Indiana house by the river, Mike was the ward mission leader responsible to assist the missionaries in spreading the Mormon gospel. One day, he went with the missionaries to teach a young black man and his family who were seeking God. Mike and I were ecstatic about inviting this family into Mormonism, because at the time, there were no members of color in our ward. The Wilder family took this family in and loved on them, just as the professor's family had done for us.

The whole family was attending church. The gentleman, but not his wife, chose to get baptized. Soon after that, they encountered spiteful resistance from our LDS ward members who did not want black members in the church. Indiana was Ku Klux Klan territory, so Mike and I assumed that this prejudice was because of the resistors' racist upbringing in Indiana. We did not connect the dots to realize that the racism might have stemmed from their membership in the Mormon Church as well. I guess we forgot that a few short years earlier, blacks could not hold the priesthood. The family left the church, and we could not coax them back.

The Curse of Cain

Our initial disgust with racism foreshadowed its reappearance in years to come. Little did I know then that I would spend my years at BYU teaching my students that racism was indefensible.

In the fall of 2000, my second year at BYU, I was assigned to teach a course in multiculturalism. Many higher education accrediting agencies, such as the Northwest Association of Schools and Colleges or the National Council for Accreditation of Teacher Education, were requiring proof of attention to issues of diversity at universities. BYU did not want to jeopardize accreditation. I was the new prof on the block, so the assignment to teach a course in multiculturalism fell to me. My BYU boss at the time apologized for making me teach it.

I, however, felt qualified for the class and loved teaching it. Multiculturalism dovetailed nicely with my special education training, since certain minority groups were overrepresented in certain special education classes. In addition, I probably had the most experience with students from diverse cultures of any faculty in my department. I saw the class as an opportunity to help my students gain understanding of and Christlike love for their future students regardless of skin color, native language, or background.

The conservative Mormon element did not enthusiastically embrace the tenets of multiculturalism, to say the least. We were not to utilize the term "social justice." When BYU finally adopted what most universities call a diversity statement, BYU coined the phrase "enrichment statement" to avoid upsetting church folk, especially the large donors. Instead of viewing multiculturalism as real enrichment to education, many Mormons viewed it as a threat to their cherished values and culture. In addition, multiculturalism was considered an ideology of liberalism, anathema to Mormon country. As Mike has observed, "Utah is so conservative that Ronald Reagan would be considered a liberal there."

A student in my first multicultural course informed me about what she said was a Mormon teaching called "the curse of Cain." Believe it or not, I had never heard of the curse of Cain. The student told me the Bible said that because Cain killed his brother, Abel, God cursed him with a mark of dark skin. I'd never heard of anything so stupid. Since Mormons believe that the Bible is corrupt, I assumed she was right; it must say that and was obviously wrong. But as I learned later, the Bible doesn't say that. The interpretation that Cain's curse was black skin and that white skin denotes righteousness is from distinctly Mormon scripture — from the Book of Mormon and the Book of Abraham in the Pearl of Great Price. I took this shocking new knowledge — that racism *currently* existed in my church among BYU students — as a challenge to right a wrong. Here at last was the reason why God told me to go back to school and then sent me to BYU. I was chosen to help the next generation of Mormon leaders at the Lord's University to denounce racism! I could not comprehend that the God of the only true church was racist. In my mind, it was just not possible. It was my charge to persuade my students that dark skin was not a curse. After all, we believed that God was a changing God, so his church could and did update its ideas. I was a woman on a mission, but I was completely ignoring the fact that racism was at present found in the Mormon Lord's own scriptures. I was blind to the full implication of LDS fixed scripture from the church's founding father, Joseph Smith, and, after Smith's death, multiple sermons from Brigham Young.

While the Bible never claims that dark skin is a curse, in LDS scripture it is quite plain that black is less than white. I honestly had never noticed this before. Now I researched it. I found that in the books of Moses and Abraham in the LDS scriptures, the curse of Cain is referred to as black skin.[19] Second Nephi 5:21 states, "He had caused the cursing to come upon them, yea, even a sore cursing, because of their iniquity ... wherefore, as they were white, and exceedingly fair and delightsome, that they might not be enticing unto my people the Lord God did cause a skin of blackness to come upon them." And Alma 3:15 says, "I will set a mark upon him that mingleth his seed with thy brethren, that they may be cursed also." According to this verse from the Book of Mormon, even someone who has sex with someone with dark skin is cursed.

For students who were convinced that this racism had scriptural support, an open-minded discussion about race seemed pointless. So I didn't use words to convince. I used service. My students were assigned to work with dark-skinned students for the entire semester. Black children were as scarce as good wine in Utah County, so my students worked with Hispanic kids. Some volunteered to play with Hispanic children at the community health center. Some volunteered to teach Hispanic adults who were learning the English language. Then they came to class to share what they learned. My goal for them was to love their diverse students.

BYU students did occasionally realize the impact that their negative, sometimes blatantly racist beliefs and subsequent actions were having on real people. Tender hearts recognized the unfairness of thinking that people were greater or lesser because of skin color. Some students softened or even radically shifted their views. I recall an incident in class when a student burst into tears upon realizing that the Hispanic kids she watched at the health center were somebody's children. She *loved* them.

The odd thing for me was that many of my students had served foreign proselytizing missions for the LDS Church, learned to speak other languages, and adjusted to cultures of other peoples. Yet in their own neighborhoods, they showed bias against certain people groups. As Spanish-speaking immigrants moved into Utah, some school districts went from near zero diversity to one-third learners of the English language in a few short years. Some Mormons, perhaps those who believed that dark skin was a curse, declared, "Not in my neighborhood. Not in the schools where my kids attend." Back in 1985, the now Mormon prophet Thomas S. Monson reflected, "In 1956 we recognized that our neighborhood was deteriorating" since the "minority elements were moving into the area."[20]

In 2002, I was presenting at a national conference on research I'd conducted on the overrepresentation of minorities in special education. A Native American gentleman stood up while I was speaking and began to heckle me, inquiring why a professor from BYU was talking about cultural pluralism. He announced to the audience, "BYU didn't even allow blacks to attend in the 1960s."

This was a bombshell for me. If this was true, I'd never heard it. I quieted him by replying, "Regardless of the past, there are some of us at BYU now who are concerned about these things."

When I returned to BYU, I asked a boss whether blacks could

attend BYU in the 1960s. No. What the Native American had said was true. The boss handed me the book *The Church and the Negro* (1967). In it I read, "Frankly, sincerely, and somewhat abruptly, President Brigham Young has told us that the mark of Cain was a 'black skin.' For the latter-day saint, no further explanation is required."[21] Brigham Young also declared, "Shall I tell you the law of God in regard to the African race? If the white man who belongs to the chosen seed mixes his blood with the seed of Cain, the penalty, under the law of God, is death on the spot. This will always be so."[22]

The tenth LDS prophet, Joseph Fielding Smith, said, "There is a reason why one man is born black with other disadvantages, while another is born white with great advantages ... the Negro, evidently, is receiving the rewards he merits."[23] Church leaders taught that who you were and how you behaved in the pre-existence determined which family you were born into on earth. In *The Church and the Negro*, I learned that Joseph Smith, in his own, supposedly correct translation of the Bible, added considerably to the story of Cain. What I read repulsed me. I was now aware that several Mormon prophets and general authorities in the past had taught their people that the curse of Cain was black skin, resulting in the priesthood restriction. According to those leaders' words, blacks were "justifiably" second-class citizens. Because of this view, the second prophet, Brigham Young, advised the Utah territorial legislature to vote to become a slave territory, and it became the only slave territory (as opposed to state) in the United States.

Did all this cause me to rethink the Mormon Church or go digging into the scriptures to discover what they said about this? No. Instead it was all about me. I thought I had received a personal revelation that went like this: "That's why God sent me here — to teach the future generation of LDS leaders that racism should have no place in the Mormon Church." How arrogant I was to think that God had personally given me a platform because

I knew something others needed to know. I had not yet learned that as a follower of Jesus, he is the master and I the servant.

Hidden Vipers

The next year, our accrediting agency visited the BYU McKay School of Education (MSE). The school was placed on probation and given two years to improve two areas of poor performance. This news was all over the papers and an embarrassment to BYU. One of the areas cited was diversity. The agency required us to (1) attempt to hire diverse faculty, (2) admit and retain diverse students into our program, and (3) send our future teachers into diverse school environments. Two colleagues and I set about to help the McKay School of Education pass accreditation and broaden the views of BYU's future teachers at the same time. We applied for a federal grant.

Out of 160 grant applications, the feds funded fifteen. We were one of them. Funding could have been an indicator of how critically the BYU patient needed diversity intervention. We received about eight hundred thousand dollars for four years to bring ethnically diverse, linguistically diverse, and individuals with disabilities into the School of Education. I was grant co-director and mentor of students.

The adventure began. My cell phone rang constantly. These students, many first-generation college students for whom English was not their native language, came to BYU. Some felt inadequate, some unwanted. I remember one faculty member challenging me in a meeting, "How did *this* student ever get in *our* program?" I was sandwiched between my students' hopes and fears and their professors' expectations and prejudices. I prayed with the students, advocated for them, taught them, worried about them, and mothered them. They were my new passion.

In addition, I served on the MSE diversity committee and continued to research, publish, and speak on the interface between special education and multicultural issues. I wrote about the over-representation of blacks in classes for students with emotional/behavioral disorders. I published professional articles, books, and book chapters related to multiculturalism, homelessness, and special education. I also served as the managing editor of a multicultural journal. I presented research in Russia and later in China. BYU was pleased with my efforts.

Consumed by this work, I felt sanctioned by God. Rather than think there might be vipers lurking in the foundational basement of Mormondom, I had a mission, a cause, a purpose, and I believed my work was critical to the surviving and thriving of the Church of Jesus Christ of Latter-day Saints. I also rationalized that white majority colleagues might listen to a white colleague like me before they would listen to a dark-skinned one. As evidence, a black colleague had just been fired. At the time, I didn't know why, since the Mormon Church is skilled at keeping things hush-hush. Later I learned he had written a controversial book about blacks and the Mormon Church.

The truth was that the viper teeth of racism easily penetrated the vulnerable skin of church members. For 130 years, church members followed the racist policies and scriptures of their leaders. And even though some of the policies toward blacks may have changed, those scriptures have never been removed.

Although I had been LDS for more than a quarter of a century by then, I was still oblivious to the *severity* of the racism in the Mormon Church. It wasn't until 2007 that I fully examined the scriptures quoted earlier and faced the truth about the church's history. Life in the Mormon Church seemed too good to entertain the idea that the church might not be true. I really believed it was true. Although I had encountered some of these facts throughout the years, when I finally honestly scrutinized the Mormon scriptures on black skin plus the words of past latter-day prophets on the subject, what I read shook me to the core. Was I deaf, blind, and dumb to think the church would apologize for the racism or remove the offending scriptures?

The founding father who birthed the Book of Mormon, the Pearl of Great Price, and the Doctrine and Covenants (that would be Joseph Smith) was a vehement racist. Smith was considered less so than Brigham Young, but Smith *was* responsible for bringing forth the words of the racist scriptures. Of course, this was the same Brigham Young my prestigious university was named after.

Young said, "You see some classes of the human family that are black, uncouth, uncomely, disagreeable and low in their habits, wild, and seemingly deprived of nearly all the blessings of the intelligence that is generally bestowed upon mankind."[24] Third Mormon prophet John Taylor taught that blacks are the Devil's representatives on earth.[25] As recently as 1964, the prophet David O. McKay stated to a reporter that blacks would not receive the priesthood in his lifetime.[26] This was the church's stance when Mormon George W. Romney sought the U.S. presidency in 1968.

One event that prompted me to examine these facts more closely was hearing Darius Gray speak on campus in February of 2006. Gray was an African American church member affiliated with the Genesis Group, the LDS Church organization that helps blacks acclimate to the Mormon Church. I took notes and wrote down his words in my journal: "I have the permission of the brethren [general authorities] to tell you the priesthood restriction [for blacks] was not imposed by God but was allowed by God. It tested whether whites would exercise unrighteous dominion. It tested whether blacks would cry, 'Unfair. I deserve privileges.' It tested our character."[27]

This statement was significant to Mike and me, because if God never imposed the priesthood restriction for blacks, why did the curse of dark skin exist in LDS scripture? Precisely who had been talking to the Mormon prophets? God would never tell his prophets to be racist, would he?

Believe it or not, this was the first time I really *saw* the discrepancy between what I believed about God and what the Mormon scriptures said. I wasn't sure how easily I could put this aside again, as I had done for years. And in the meantime, I wasn't at all sure my efforts at BYU would make much difference in the area of Mormon racism. But for now I persisted.

CHAPTER 10

SOMETHING IS ROTTEN IN THE STATE OF DESERET

ψ

Denmark is "an unweeded garden" of "things rank and gross in nature."

— SHAKESPEARE'S *HAMLET*, ACT 1, SCENE 2

Throughout our experience with Mormonism, we saw hints of things not quite right—something rotten in Deseret. (*Deseret* is a Book of Mormon word that purportedly means "honeybee" in a "Jaredite" language and is used in the name of numerous Mormon enterprises.) Then, when we moved to Utah, we faced a culture that was decidedly offbeat, if not noticeably "rank and gross." Yes, racism was definitely a rotten piece of fruit, and so was polygamy. But it was a series of events after we moved that really caused us to wonder about the trustworthiness of the Mormon Church.

The Family in Utah

When we had been in Utah one year, Josh was working in Washington, D.C., to earn money for his upcoming third year at Indiana University. He woke up one morning in late July 2000 with the strong impression that he needed to transfer to a school in Utah. He quit his job, drove to Bloomington, Indiana, subleased his apartment, packed up his belongings, and drove to Utah. There he applied to and was accepted at the University of Utah.

Josh was twenty and had not yet made the choice to serve a Mormon mission. Mike and I had faith that he'd serve when he was ready. His first year in Salt Lake, he met a great LDS friend who encouraged him to seriously consider a mission. During the winter semester, Josh submitted his mission papers, then waited for the prophet to receive revelation as to where he would serve.

In March 2001, to our family's delight, Matt's basketball team at Lone Peak High School won state. The entire family cheered wildly at every game. One article announced, "Knights go 'Wilder' in Win over Provo." Another sports reporter wrote a front-page article about Matt, detailing his skills not only in basketball but also in music. In fact, Matt was headed to BYU in the fall.

Mike's LDS sister came from Connecticut for Matt's high school graduation. She, Mike, and I went to the Timpanogos Temple and baptized Mike's dead parents. They had both died in Connecticut in recent years. Mike and his sister completed their parents' temple endowments by proxy in order to allow them to be freed from spirit prison and sealed their parents together so they could continue in marriage on the other side of the veil.

Meanwhile Micah loved everything about the Mormon Church and Utah. He served as one of eight high school students on the community's church seminary council. He played basketball, ran track, and received a math award given to only three out of six hundred students. He was driving now and would be a junior in high school when Matt left for college and Josh for his mission.

Katie was headed to seventh grade in a middle school where I supervised student teachers. I would get to see her at school hanging with her friends. She was involved in gymnastics, dance, choir, drama, babysitting, and of course the Young Women organization at church.

A Dangerous Fever

Then, in early July of 2001, Matt, Micah, and Katie went on the traditional LDS pioneer trek for the youth in the ward. This was a weeklong reenactment of what it was like for the Mormon pioneers in the 1840s to cross a difficult section of the trail west through Wyoming, pushing handcarts. Micah didn't feel well after he got home, and his fever spiked to 104 degrees. I called a doctor friend who had been on the trek, and he said the symptoms sounded like Rocky Mountain spotted fever, a dangerous tick-borne disease found in the western United States.

I took Micah to the emergency room but couldn't get the doctor to give him the critical antibiotics that were needed as soon as possible for that disease. He said, "No one gets that anymore." He didn't care if Micah had been in sheep country sleeping outside at night with the ticks in the sagebrush. The nurse overheard him and whispered to me, "Yes, people do get it. My own father had it last year." Of course, he was a doctor and we were LDS females. It was expected in the culture not to question males in authority. Micah went home without the drugs.

In parting, the doctor had said to me, "When he has the characteristic rash and you can prove he was bitten by a tick, come back." The next morning, Micah had the rash. Not only that, the Dancer of grace placed a large tick in the bottom of my washing machine, in the load containing Micah's shorts from the trek. We went back to the ER, tick in a Ziploc bag, and he got his antibiotics, but by now Micah was seriously ill. They sent us home.

We couldn't get the fever to stay down. Micah stopped talking, moving, eating, and even sleeping. For the first seven days, he had severe headaches, chills, shakes, muscle aches, and muscle weakness. When his fever relented some and he ate a little, he erupted with fifteen or more canker sores under his tongue, on the inside of his mouth, and down his throat. Eating and drinking were excruciating. I had to beg him to sip through a straw. I stayed with him day and night.

Since Mike was out of town when Micah fell ill, I called Micah's Young Men leaders, begging for someone from church to *please* drop by to visit him, pray for him, see what he was enduring. He was in need of a blessing for the sick, which required two worthy priesthood brethren. One night in desperation, I ran through the neighborhood knocking on doors, looking for two men to give him a proper oil-anointing blessing for the sick. I was able to find one Young Men leader and one neighbor's brother willing to come. We had LDS neighbors all around us, but few came to check on Micah or offered to pray, even though we'd told everyone we knew of the illness.

Then Micah's liver was malfunctioning. In five days the canker sores improved, but his feet began to itch. The only relief he got was when his feet were immersed in a cooler filled with ice and water. In twenty-four hours, the itching and burning drove him wild. His body's immune system was attacking his nervous system, as with shingles. Then the itching and burning spread to every inch of his body, lasting another seven days. Micah screamed in agony and stood in cold showers for some small relief. A couple of trips to the emergency room relieved him with morphine, but as soon as it wore off, his misery was back.

Unable to sleep for more than forty-five minutes at a time, Micah slept sitting up, with his feet in one cooler and his arms in another. The attack on the nervous system resulted in muscle weakness and numbness caused by Guillain-Barre syndrome. He was too weak to walk and could only hobble from the couch to the bathroom using crutches.

The illness started on July 10, and Micah began to improve slightly on August 5. That evening, we all walked with him to the corner of the block and back, celebrating this small victory. By August 10, he got on the riding mower and mowed a couple of perfect golf course stripes. "Mom, I was never so grateful to see a sunset," he told me. In the fall of 2001, Micah was still so weak that he was barely able to go to school. He returned home exhausted each afternoon to sleep the rest of the day and the night.

Micah had contracted this deadly illness on the trek with the youth and the ward leaders, and they all knew about it, but in the month when he was most ill, it seemed none of them called or visited of their own volition. I'd had to make phone calls and knock on doors. At one point, I thought he could die. I was exasperated with my ward friends and neighbors.

Now that I look back, I think God was trying to show me something. People who have truly given their lives to Christ are branches of the vine — him — and have access to his unending love when others need it. It was this love we longed for, and perhaps those who did not know the God of grace could not possibly give it. But I wasn't seeing it yet. I just knew that something about their aloofness at our time of need was callous.

To help me be brutally honest with myself, maybe God allowed me to be hurt. I was helpless and exhausted from Micah's illness and then angry because of others' disinterest. Maybe I needed a few slaps to wake me from my cataleptic allegiance to the Mormon Church. Maybe only experiences like this could break my trance. Through this, I did learn that I was not God and that I could not control all things by my righteous acts.

The day after September 11, 2001, was Katie's thirteenth birthday. Out of respect for people who had died in the Twin Towers, she wanted no party, just a puppy. We negotiated a kitten. She named him Manhattan (Manny).

Two Mormon Missionaries

While Micah continued to battle his illness that fall of 2001, Josh was preparing for his mission, which we had learned would be in Russia. He received the higher Melchizedek priesthood and for the first time attended the endowment session in the temple with Mike and me. In November, we took Josh to the torture room in the Missionary Training Center, the room where the parents and missionaries separate. It was difficult to send our first son to Russia, knowing we would have little contact with him for two years. Mike held Josh and sobbed until I thought his heart would break. Katie later commented dryly, "I thought we were going to have to carry Dad out of there."

We received weekly emails from Josh detailing his missionary adventures. These letters fueled his younger brothers' desires to serve missions too. So nine months after Josh left for Russia, in July of 2002 Matt left to serve a mission in Denmark. That second MTC torture room experience was a little more bearable. Matt hugged each of us quickly and was the first missionary out the door. Katie quipped, "It sure is easier to separate from someone who's eager to go."

Micah was still terribly ill and had been for fourteen months now. Josh emailed us from Russia on September 5 that he had asked the Lord to take Micah's suffering and put it on him, for it would be an honor to suffer like Christ did for his brother. Almost immediately Micah improved. He was able to play on the basketball team and run track his senior year. Jesus—the true, life-giving Jesus—had come through, even for this very confused and lost Mormon family.

A Family Loss

On Sunday, January 12, 2003, during sacrament meeting, I felt a growing unease, so I walked home. In prayer, I asked God what was wrong, then felt impressed to call my father in Florida. He told me Mom had the flu and they were not sure she could recover. She'd had Alzheimer's for about thirteen years. Dad, with some help from his daughters, who were raising their own families in three different states, cared for her most of that time, but she was now in a nursing home. She was seventy-two.

Josh and Matt had taken care to see their grandmother before leaving for their missions, but Micah hadn't seen her for a while. He wanted to see her, so we sent him to Florida. A hospice nurse promised to keep me informed so I could be there for Mom when she got close. I called the nurse every day and left messages, but she did not return my calls. Finally, she did call me to say Mom likely had just a few hours. Mike booked the next flight for Katie and me.

But it was too late. Mom died in the night before we got there. When I heard the news, my body shook uncontrollably for four hours with shock before I could even pray. The nurse told me that in the last few days, she saw Mom smile twice, once when she saw Dad and once when the nurse told her she'd talked with me. Micah was blessed to spend time alone with her the morning after he arrived. He, Dad, and my Christian sister Cindy had been with her until late into that evening, singing "How Great Thou Art." She passed away soon after they left. When Katie and I arrived, we visited her empty room in the nursing home and held each other, grief-stricken.

Josh and Matt were, tragically, not permitted to come home for the memorial services. No missionaries are. That was tough for them. By the grace of God, Josh was in Lithuania renewing his Russian visa when she died. He stopped by the mission home in Moscow on his way back to Voronezh, and his mission president told him to call home. We got to talk three times over several days as he grieved over the phone with the family. If he had been back in Voronezh, this would not have been possible. Matt was allowed one brief phone call home from Denmark the following Sunday. Mike spoke with him and said he was unusually quiet and subdued.

Mission to Russia

Josh was scheduled to return from his mission to Russia and Belarus in November of 2003. Instead of waiting to meet him at home, Mike and I made the long flight to Moscow and disembarked into the dark Sheremetyevo International Airport. Seeing Josh after two long years was balm to our souls. We held him tight a long, long time. He took us to buy Russian coats so we'd be as warm as possible in the frigid Russian November. Then, well equipped with his skills in the Russian language, he took us on a tour of this vast Dr. Zhivago country.

Over those two years, Josh was assigned to different geographic areas and various missionary companions. He served in Lipetsk, Tula, and Voronezh, Russia, and Vitayebsk, Belarus. In Tula, he and his missionary companion chopped wood by hand and performed other arduous services for a children's home. Their main purpose, though, was to increase the ranks of the Mormon Church.

While assigned to Voronezh, Josh was a branch president for a small ward in Borisoglebsk and sent the first Mormon missionary, an elderly woman, out from that congregation. He and his companion traveled by bus from their apartment to the branch, five hours away, every other Sunday to conduct services. Often the bus was so jam-packed that they had to stand the entire trip. We met the people of this ward in Voronezh and immediately loved them, especially for the way they had lavishly cared for our son.

One night Josh and his companion found an elderly woman with dementia wandering at night in a bathrobe. She reminded Josh of his grandmother. She said she had gone to the store and couldn't find her way back to her apartment. She would have frozen to death if out all night, and Josh said it was not unusual to step over a frozen body on the sidewalk.

So first they took her to the fire station to get some help. The men there turned them away. Then they took her to the hospital. No one would help. Finally, they got the idea to go into an apartment building and knock on doors until someone with compassion would take her in for the night. They eventually found someone. Missionary rules did not allow them to take her into their own small apartment.

Next we traveled to St. Petersburg State University, where I presented research to Russian sociologists. The divorce rate in Russia is among the highest, sometimes cited as *the* highest, in the world. I presented U.S. research that connected emotional/behavioral problems in teens with divorce rates. They disputed with me. Divorce was commonplace in Russia, and most of them were divorced. Even as sociologists, they refused to entertain the idea that divorce could be linked to emotional/behavioral issues in their youth.

We took a train from St. Petersburg to Minsk, Belarus. LDS missionaries were not allowed to proselytize door-to-door in Russia, but they could talk to people on the streets and in public. Carrying copies of the Book of Mormon or the Bible in public, however, or mentioning religion might result in deportation. They invited people to free classes to learn English, and there they got to know them and talked with some about religion. In Belarus, the missionaries removed their name tags and were considered volunteers for a nonprofit organization of the Mormon Church. They taught English classes, coached sports, volunteered in children's homes, and met church members' family and friends, all in an effort to proselytize covertly. Most people were curious to meet the foreigners.

When we finally took Josh home, he was a skeleton of the son we had kissed goodbye two years earlier. Life as a missionary in Russia was difficult. He had faced both personal and impersonal threats to his health and person. He had shoveled asbestos in Belarus, and 50 percent of missionaries returning from Russia tested positive for TB, his mission president told us. He had also suffered encounters with the Russian mafia and with skinheads. One time several skinheads surrounded the missionaries and for twenty-five minutes threatened to kill them. I knew about that one. The Dancer of grace had alerted me that Josh was in danger. I prayed fervently, and their lives were spared.

The Missionaries Return

Even after Josh's return, the distress his mission caused did not end. The culture shock was brutal. He still wanted to speak Russian and eat Russian food, so I learned to make a mean borscht. He struggled to adjust from his missionary life of poverty to the plush materialism of the United States. Starved too from the lack of physical touch, he got a black Lab puppy for Christmas to help him heal the scars from what he'd been through.

After Christmas, he returned to school at the University of Utah. The house he lived in wouldn't let him have the puppy, so Katie, Mike, and I loved Kisa for him. He relearned to eat American food and seemed to be adjusting. The judgmental, closed-minded, nondiverse culture in Utah made him crazy, he said later. He didn't want to try to fit into Utah's culture, although he did want to stay in the church. To get away and breathe, he took a summer internship in New York City at Sotheby's, translating for Russian art customers. Josh loved the beat of a big city.

In Denmark, Matt proselytized for the Mormon Church and composed and played church-appropriate music. When it was time for him to come home from his mission, in the summer of 2004, Mike, Katie, and I traveled to Denmark for a few days. Matt was required to maintain his missionary schedule, so we visited with LDS Church members and potential converts and attended the new Copenhagen Temple. The Danish culture was less of a departure from U.S. culture than Russia had been. Back home,

Matt adjusted quickly and went back to BYU. By then, Micah had already left for his mission to Florida.

Repentance Mormon Style

In the fall of 2004, when Josh returned to school in Salt Lake from New York, he decided to repent of some past sins and go back to church. He had been weekend-drinking and sleeping with a girlfriend before he went to New York. She was LDS. He was twenty-three, and in the eyes of the world, legally permitted to drink. But drinking alcohol, tea, and coffee are against the church health code, the Word of Wisdom. And, of course, premarital sex was a problem in the church. In New York he'd decided not to attend church, so he rationalized that he wasn't being a hypocrite. But now that he wanted to go back to church, his former behaviors put him in danger of losing his temple recommend.

His buddy, Ammon, also a returned missionary, had committed the same sins. To repent, Ammon went to see his bishop at the university singles ward (a ward reserved for single members of the church, as opposed to the ordinary family ward). His bishop waved away these sins as common college stuff. He probably saw it a lot. Ammon got a three-month probation. He couldn't pass the sacrament or pray in church. Other than that, it was basically a hand slap. Three months—done.

Josh kept his church membership records in our home ward in Alpine, not in his university ward, so he had to repent to our bishop so the sin janitor could sweep his sins away. He expected disciplinary consequences similar to those his friend had received. The bishop listened kindly for two hours through Josh's tears of genuine repentance. These sins had been over for a while now. The bishop thought he could take care of it himself. But he said he was required to report it to the stake president, President Hansen.

A few days went by, and Josh did not hear from the bishop,

but the stake president's executive secretary called, and he set up an appointment for Josh. The next week, Josh confessed everything all over again to the stake president. The stake president scolded him for the people he had affected. The girl was LDS. President Hansen requested her name so he could contact her priesthood leaders, who would call her in. He discharged Josh with, "We'll get back to you."

The next week, on Friday, the executive secretary called again to tell Josh he was to appear in front of the stake high council Sunday morning. *Okay*, he thought, *they might take away my temple recommend for a year or tell me I can't take the sacrament.* He felt he did the right thing by repenting and was ready to accept the repercussions. It's not as if he'd been drinking and driving—he hadn't—or had had unprotected sex. No DUI. No pregnancy.

Early that Sunday, Josh's problem was last on the high council's agenda. The men seemed anxious to get home to their families. Josh sat in President Hansen's office with the door shut, nervously waiting his turn. The president's office adjoined the high council room. Before Josh was called in, the stake president gave the high council a few details from the one conversation he'd had with Josh. Then Josh was ushered in.

The men sat around a huge, polished, rectangular conference table, as in a corporate boardroom. The stake president sat at the head, with his two counselors on each side and his executive secretary taking notes. The twelve high counselors sat in rank order around the table according to their seniority, which was dependent on when the Mormon Lord had called them. All sixteen men plus Josh wore dark suits, white shirts, and ties. Josh was told to sit in the middle of the table on one side of the men. He was, a third time, instructed to report his sins.

He was emotional and distraught. This was humiliating. He began to speak with his head down, talking to the table. Josh was a communications major, and speaking to people was normally not a problem, but this was different. Soon he was weeping liberally, not bothering to wipe his tears. When he tried to look up, his tears were so thick and his shame so real, he could barely see the men across from him. To his blurred vision, they looked stern and emotionless. He received kindness from one source only, the man to his left, the high councilor from our home ward, who knew him a little; he nodded. Where was the God of love and reconciliation?

Josh was returned to the stake president's office. The priesthood brethren — the stake presidency and members of the high council — deliberated. Before long, the executive secretary called him back. Then he, very formally, read the decision like a courtroom verdict.

"Joshua Michael Wilder, go home and take off your garments. You are no longer a member of the Church of Jesus Christ of Latter-day Saints. You are stripped of all related blessings. You will work closely with the stake president if you hope to be rebaptized ..." Josh could not absorb the rest of what was said. In a state of shock, he was compelled to hug or shake hands with every man in the room. He did so mechanically.

Josh left the stake center and came to our front door as we were getting ready for church. He rang the doorbell, and Mike went to the door. There stood Josh in his suit and tie, his face contorted, his eyes red and puffy, with traces of tears on his cheeks. Mike said, "Josh, why are you here so early? Is there a problem?"

Josh looked at his father and burst out, "Dad, I've been excommunicated!"

Father and son embraced for a long time. Josh was sobbing great gulps of air. His heart was broken, and he was ashamed to the core. In one swift, unexpected drop of the guillotine's blade, he had been separated from his salvation. His baptism was removed.

The two of them came into the bedroom, sat next to me on the bed, and delivered the news. "I might have to borrow a few dollars to buy some underwear," Josh said. I ached for him. Mike went with him, and they broke the Sabbath to buy him underwear. And so began for Josh one of the most dark and painful times in his life.

Discipline in the Mormon Church

We had no idea before that morning that Josh had confessed or had been called before the high council. If Mike had known, he would have prepared him and gone with him. For a decade in Indiana, Michael served two succeeding stake presidents as one of twelve members of the stake high council. He'd worked his way around the table to high councilor number two. In this capacity, and also as counselor to bishops in both Indiana and Utah, he participated in numerous church disciplinary councils. In his experience, Mormons might be called into court for abortion, fornication, adultery, incest, physical abuse, forcible sexual abuse, rape, homosexual relations, abandonment of family responsibilities, robbery, burglary, embezzlement, theft, sale of illegal drugs, fraud, perjury, false witness, attempted murder, or apostasy. An apostate is a church member who speaks publically in clear opposition to the church or its leaders. Criminal charges did not necessarily bring down the strong arm of church discipline, but apostasy would.

Serious transgressions were reported to the bishop, who would report them to the stake president. The bishop and the stake president based their disciplinary action on the sinner's church calling, church activity, gender, and level of sincerity in repentance. Is this person adequately sorry for his or her sin? The stake president always made the final decision, and it was considered spiritually inspired. The four possible disciplinary outcomes were: no action, formal probation, disfellowship, or excommunication from the church.

Excommunication was the most severe discipline, reserved for predators who could create victims, prominent members who could impact the reputation of the church, or disfellowshiped members who remained unrepentant. Offenders were stripped of their church membership and their baptism. Although they could attend church if not openly oppositional, they could not hold a temple recommend or a church position or exercise the priesthood in any way. They were forbidden to give a talk in church, offer a public prayer, partake of the sacrament, or vote in the rote sustaining of church leaders. They were denied blessings of the church, such as wearing temple garments (underwear) for protection and tithing to ensure they would not be burned at Christ's second coming.

Of course, we always knew who had sinned a great sin. Everyone on a pew noticed if someone passed the sacrament without taking it. Although confidentiality was emphasized, stories leaked easily into our closed-culture gossip cesspool.

The Weight of Mormon Sin

Several things bothered me about this church discipline, besides Josh's obvious hurts. First, I had never known the reality of excommunication—that a Mormon Church leader could remove salvation from a person, even someone who had put his life on the line for the Mormon Church. How could a mere man do such a thing? Wasn't it Jesus' job to separate soul from spirit (Heb. 4:12)?

Second, I began to realize the full weight of sin in Mormon doctrine. The Doctrine and Covenants 82:7 said, "Unto that soul who sinneth shall former sins return." In other words, you could never be entirely free of sin; you would likely be tempted back into the same behavior. All that weight returned, the stake president in effect told Josh. How terrible a burden.

Then there was the issue of how disciplinary consequences could differ so greatly from one "inspired" priesthood leader to another. Mormonism taught me that truth comes to earth directly from Christ to the priesthood leaders. I could understand allowing a certain degree of individualization for discipline from one person to another—but opposite consequences for the same sin? One loses his salvation, and one walks away?

This experience got me wondering why someone who sincerely repented should receive man's punishment at all. Didn't God forgive anyone who genuinely repented of anything, even on their deathbed? What would happen if Josh died before he earned his baptism back?

Are there really sins, as Mormonism teaches, that cannot be forgiven? Blasphemy against the Holy Ghost (denying that the Mormon Church is true once you have declared that it is), adultery the second time, and the shedding of innocent blood are all unforgiveable sins. And apparently, there is a problem with any sinning, because sinning returns all sins back on your head, according to the D&C.

"No," Josh's leader told him, "the problem exists when you repeat the *same* sins again." Or at least when you report the same sins again. The church keeps track of certain repented sins on your membership record. That's likely why Josh was excommunicated. He'd repented of the same sins before, and apparently they were on his record.

And the really big concern: "Does that mean I have a Mormon Christ whose atonement of blood on the cross does not cover all sins, and there is no forgiveness in Mormonism for sins committed a second time?" Whoa. That's exactly what it meant.

We Mormons thought we loved our children unconditionally. Now I wonder if Josh's sins were his way of reaching for the unconditional love absent from his life, a love we *all* need so much. But in a judgmental system like Mormonism, there is no such thing as unconditional love, forgiveness, or the Dancer of grace.

Racism was a rotten piece of Mormon fruit, and polygamy stunk, and now this: a weak Jesus whose sacrifice was not enough. Something indeed was rotten in the state of Deseret. Nevertheless, we, like other Mormons confronted with the church's faults, continued to declare, "But the church is still true."

CHAPTER 11

"THINGS WILL NEVER BE NORMAL AGAIN"

⚜

I have been crucified with Christ and I no longer live,
but Christ lives in me.

— GALATIANS 2:20

O hhh, go away."
I wanted to sleep longer, but words were running through my head: "Awake and arise to a sense of your awful situation."

Ugh, must be a scripture we read last night. My family and I had been reading Mosiah 6 and 7 in the Book of Mormon.

I pulled my pillow over my head. "Who are you, anyway? Are you Jesus? What awful situation? Awake and arise, like I'm asleep?" I wished I still were.

I looked them up; those words weren't in Mosiah. My thoughts in Utah Mormon lingo were, *Oh my heck, I thought life was pretty good!*

Yet now I had to figure out what kind of mess I was in.

This happened on April 13, 2004, the same day Micah left the Missionary Training Center in Utah and flew to Orlando to begin his mission. It was several months before Josh's excommunication, but already there was a shift in the atmosphere, a change in the wind.

Strange Ideas

We sensed that something profound happened to Micah early on his mission, because his emails were filled more and more with a faith language we did not understand. But it was difficult to ascertain what was going on. We were forbidden to talk on the phone except on Mother's Day and Christmas, so his one email a week and our answer back was our only thread of contact with him, other than the packages I sent. The LDS Church owned our sons those two years of profound Mormon acculturation. Back home, we were left with a ward-issued wooden plaque with his picture, his mission, and a scripture he had chosen. Micah had selected this obscure— for a Mormon missionary—verse: "I am crucified with Christ: nevertheless I live; yet not I, but Christ liveth in me" (Gal. 2:20 KJV).

On Monday, June 26, 2004, Micah wrote us in his email, "Tuesday we went back and talked to that Baptist minister. He was nice but he basically condemned us to hell and said we were a cult ..." I didn't recall him writing about a Baptist minister.

How un-Christlike! We weren't a cult. Couldn't Christians get that through their heads?

On September 20, he wrote, "Well, I'll be honest with you, this has been the hardest week of my mission. It's like all the success and blessing came crashing down and I am struggling. But I have also found peace and comfort through the Savior, knowing He went through what He did for those that rejected Him. How bad that must have hurt Him!"

Years ago in that hospital room with Jesus, I'd experienced his peace and comfort. "Thank you, Lord, for showing that to my Micah," I prayed. I did love Jesus. But the pain of Jesus' sacrifice and rejection were mostly just words to me. It wasn't something we talked about in Mormonism. Honestly, I'd rather go hiking than give it much thought. Why was Micah contemplating the pain of rejection?

Micah survived three violent hurricanes that season—Charley, Frances, and Jeanne. Wherever his mission president transferred him, the eye of the storm followed and pummeled him. Jeanne came ashore near Stuart, Florida, on September 26, 2004, and crossed into Winter Garden, where Micah was serving. On that foreboding afternoon, missionaries and the elderly hustled to the shelter of a quaint, three-story red-brick hotel in historic downtown Winter Garden, and Micah befriended one of the LDS owners. On the top floor, large plate-glass windows blew out. Glass and debris tornadoed wildly. Micah ducked and covered.

This third storm must have jolted something, because the next day we received this odd email: "September 27, 2004. I know why I came here. I can't really tell you right now but things are happening with me I can't explain. A great thing is coming forth. I am changed forever ... I pray you will always love and support me in the changes I make and the things I do. Things will never be normal again. You have prepared me my whole life for what is happening now. One day you will understand. I pray for your endless love and know that mine will always be here no matter what."

He's nineteen, changed forever, and he'll have to pray to get us to love and support him in these changes? What had he done, robbed a bank? Joined a cult?

That fall, the girl Micah dated his senior year in high school, Alicia, began stopping in to see me at BYU or just leaving sweet notes: "Love you. Have a great day!" Auburn-haired Alicia (Leashy) is an unassuming, delicate ballroom dancer from a strong Mormon family that was recognized and respected in town. A naturally kind and loving young woman, she reminded me of my mom. Leashy was at BYU collecting general education credits, hoping to transfer to another school as an architecture major. She has an artistic eye and a flair for technology.

After Micah had been out on his mission several months, he and Alicia began sending letters back and forth. When he called home at Christmas, she came over and talked to him alongside us. We realized this could be going somewhere, although Micah had not left for his mission with the expectation that Alicia would wait for him. On the phone, he encouraged her to read the New Testament. We didn't know it yet, but soon they were both reading the New Testament and using each other as safe houses to share their insights.

On November 1, his weekly email to his family contained this plea: "I will need your support and love."

On November 8, he wrote, "The [mission] president has complimented me over and over with the success that has happened in this zone. The Lord is the source of it all. To Him I give honor and glory. You have to understand the Lord has a plan and a timing for everything."

To the Lord he gives honor and glory? That struck me as a strange thing to say. Wasn't he proud of *himself* for what he'd accomplished for the Mormon Lord in his leadership positions? After all, Micah had become a district leader after barely four months out and a zone leader in his mission a mere five months out. This early call made him the senior (longest serving) zone leader during his mission. There were approximately one hundred sixty missionaries and eight zones in the mission. Mike commented that Micah didn't sound like Micah; he sounded like the apostle Paul. What was going on?

On November 15, Micah wrote again with mysterious requests for our loyalty. "I need your love and I need your support. If my own family does not sustain me, then who will? I know God does. He always will. But I need you. Take these things to the Lord. Call upon Him. Ask Him to teach you and your eyes will be opened."

Take what things to the Lord? What should I ask him to teach me? My eyes *were* open. I knew the truth, through Mormonism, that few souls knew. I was one of the saints. Of course we would always sustain Micah. We were family.

"Families are forever." Most of my neighbors displayed these words on a wooden plaque in their homes. As Mormons, we believed that in the next life we could have sex with our spouses, live with our current children, and have millions of spirit children. That's what the temple marriage/sealing was all about — forever families. But only if you're Mormon, of course. And since families were forever, we were expected to stick with Micah through thick and thin, unless he committed the colossal unforgiveable sin — apostasy.

On January 31, 2005, Micah wrote, "God is so good and just knowing that He lives is all I need. He is my source of true joy in my life. He does live and love us. He is always there. He is always listening, and He runs to our aid. My greatest joy is raising my cross next to the Savior's, and denying myself to be His true disciple." That is *not* how Mormons speak about faith. First of all, we say "Heavenly Father," not "God." We don't express praises to him. The cross is rarely mentioned. And it would be joy to have a cross next to his? What did *that* mean?

Blinded

Alicia visited us often and became a welcome part of the family. She and I talked, mostly about Micah and his emails. Soon she began to speak to us about what she was learning in the Bible.

In Alicia's words: "Originally, I felt like the only person I could talk to about what Micah was going through was you, Lynn. I needed to have someone who would let me share and confirm the beginnings of my new faith." As Alicia discovered new ideas in the Bible, she came to me for wisdom, because she trusted my objective mind to discern truth. Boy, was she wrong! I was Mormon through and through and could not see outside the citadel. As much as we loved her and she loved us, our LDS faith was an impenetrable wall between us. Nothing was getting through. We weren't reading the Bible, as the two of them were. But as Alicia read, she began to shed Mormonism ideals. The Bible, the living Word, was her new source of confirmation instead of me, or even Micah. She relied on it alone.

One evening Alicia, Katie, Mike, and I had dinner at Fazoli's Italian Restaurant. I used the phrase, "I don't mean to play the Devil's advocate, but ...," and what I spoke as truth was the opposite of what Alicia had read in the Bible. In her mind (now illuminated by the Word and the Spirit), I *was* advocating the Devil's stance. She quit confiding in me once she saw I was fighting against any change related to faith. She realized that the pearls she was throwing before me were coming too early in my journey.

With my strong personality and pride, I trampled on Alicia's fragile new faith. She was forced to stop sharing with me until my eyes could be opened. It saddened Alicia that the deep spiritual connection with me ended. She prayed for our family often, and for her own family as well. She prayed specifically that I would understand and accept the changes in her life and in Micah's.

Micah too was pleading with us to seek the real God, but truthfully, I thought I *knew* the real one. The Mormon Church taught me his words and his will. I did not understand what I was missing, so I didn't understand what Micah wanted me to do.

I heard from Heavenly Father so infrequently that seeking an answer to prayer seemed an exercise in futility. Sincere prayer was left for the brief moments of rumination in the celestial room at the temple, that glorious, thickly carpeted, chandeliered room in which we meditated after the endowment ceremony. A normal prayer went like this: "Dear Heavenly Father, I thank thee [we had to say *thee* because it was respectful] for [fill in the blank]. I ask thee for [fill in the blank]. In the name of Jesus Christ, amen."

If I had told a Mormon leader that I had heard an answer to prayer (like the night I was told to go back to school), or if I had shared my spiritual experiences with him (like the time I was awakened and saved from fire), he might have branded me as crazy. A close LDS friend of mine often had dreams and premonitions she considered communications with Heavenly Father. She told a leader at church about her dreams once when she was a teenager, and he told her it was the Devil. I simply avoided judgment by telling no one but Michael of my spiritual experiences or answers to prayer.

Mormons do believe in a spiritual realm, but as far as making sense of the experiences or receiving answers to prayer, I was taught that those interpretations were to be made by a priesthood holder with stewardship over me, like my husband or my bishop. I was not able to receive revelation for anything outside of my personal stewardship. For me that included my role as a mother, as a spouse, and whatever fell within the boundaries of my church callings. Helping the LDS Church shed racism would not be within my purview. Since I wanted to make my own analyses about answers to prayer and all things spiritual, I kept my mouth shut. Maybe what I longed for was my own personal relationship with God.

In addition, the Mormon life was just too exhausting to allow for much prayer. I prayed quick, rote prayers but seldom if ever spent time in conversational prayer with Heavenly Father (wait, Micah was calling him "God" now). I wasn't aware that he was the conversational type. As Mormons, we embraced the Jesus and Heavenly Father who, as exalted men, had worked their way to godhood. With worlds to rule and multiple wives producing myriads of spirit children, they had a lot to do. They couldn't be more than one place at a time and couldn't be bothered with my prayers unless it was an emergency.

There was no time for serious scripture study either. I went to work and tended to my students' concerns anytime they needed me. There were the functional tasks of meals, laundry, house-cleaning, gardening, and church callings. Then there were the fun tasks of hiking or skiing with Mike, walking with Katie, visiting the eight children she nannied, and attending her activities—voice lessons, dance lessons, plays, and musicals. These are poor excuses, I know, for not doing what Micah and Alicia were asking us to do, even if we didn't really understand what that was.

Well, Micah *had* asked us to read the New Testament, but the prophet said we had to read the Book of Mormon every night as a family. So on a typical evening, Mike would read aloud, "I, Nephi, having been born of goodly parents ..."

I would yawn, waiting for my turn to read. "And now I know that the record which I make is true ..." After I finished, I would get up to start the dishwasher. "Katie, it's your turn." She'd be wrapped in a blanket near the fire, half asleep. But she would rouse to dutifully read her portion.

That was all the scriptures I could handle in one day. After all, I read and studied all day long at work. Where would I find the time and energy to read the New Testament?

Tragedy and Triumph

We were sure it would all be clear when Micah returned to us. The family talked often about how we couldn't wait to see Micah again so he could teach us whatever it was that was altering his life. We mailed him funny videos of us to cheer him, and he passed them around the mission. Everyone soon knew the Wilders. Micah called us collectively "The Beast," a grand honor.

In August of 2005, Micah's best friend from Indiana, Schuyler, and his mom died in an automobile accident. I sent him the news in my weekly email. These tragedies are especially horrid on a mission, because the missionary cannot leave, not even if his or her own mother dies, unless they plan not to return to finish the mission.

Micah got permission to call me. He was scrunched over, grieving for Schuyler. I could hear it. Then I confided to Micah that Josh had been excommunicated from the church. I'm not sure how it came up or why I told him, just that I trusted Micah. Only Mike and I knew, but I remember telling Micah that this excommunication might be good for Josh. Now I can't fathom saying such a Cruella de Vil kind of thing when Micah was mourning, but at the time it fit my worldview. I thought excommunication was a useful tool to rein in sin, as if I had no sin myself.

On Saturday, October 14, Josh called about ten in the evening to say he was headed to our house for the night. President Hansen had called to request that he appear in front of the stake high council at 7:30 the next morning. Josh asked if we would go along and sit on the couch outside the room for support.

We squirmed and fidgeted on that couch. The wait seemed endless as we tried to imagine what Josh was going through on the other side of the door. Finally, the stake executive secretary, loyal scurrying serf to the stake president, asked Mike and me to enter the high council room. Now what? As we entered, every man stood. It was announced that Josh's membership would be reinstated and that he could be rebaptized. Kind of like when I heard the announcement that blacks could hold the priesthood, I was greatly relieved.

Two days later, Josh was rebaptized by his father at the stake center, in the presence of seven people: his parents, the stake president, our high counselor (the kind man from our ward), our bishop, Josh's new LDS girlfriend of several months, who may have been waiting for his temple recommend to be renewed for a temple marriage, and the scurrying serf, for recording purposes. I felt great peace. Only *one more year* until Josh could earn back his temple recommend.

More Disturbing Emails

Toward the end of Micah's two years in Florida, it sounded like he was saying goodbye to us. On November 8, 2005, Micah wrote to his father, "Dad, thanks for your continual love and support that you have never stopped giving me throughout my life. You are a good father and you have taught me how to have faith in Christ and trust my God."

Was he dying? His health *had* continued to be a challenge. He'd been hospitalized more than once on his mission, with recurring complications from the Rocky Mountain spotted fever.

And to me he wrote, "I wish, Mom, I could sit with you and talk with you all night and all day about everything that has transpired in my life these last two years. But I will not have that opportunity until I come home. Don't feel left out or neglected, there is just too much to tell, sometimes it's easier to tell nothing until I can tell everything. You have been a rock in my life and your testimony of Christ has strengthened my faith in the Master. You never gave up on me even when I gave up on myself ... I am nothing more than a simple boy trying to follow my Shepherd ... At times it seems all odds are against me but in those times I have to be strong, for the path that Christ walked was not easy ... But Christ's blood has been spilt ..."

Alicia and Micah decided they would get married after he returned in early 2006. At first they said they would attend BYU and maybe live with us, but by the end of November, he decided that he wanted to play in a band that honored God with music, instead of completing his astrophysics degree at BYU. After his mission, he would come home and stay about two weeks, then return to Florida to manage the hotel he'd stayed in during the hurricane and begin work with the band. That was cool with me. I knew how much he enjoyed music and had loved his band, whose equipment resided in our basement during high school.

But what did any of that have to do with some mighty life transformation? Would he become a prophet and rend his clothes? He did quote a lot of Bible Scripture, which we already thought we understood. "Yes, yes, I know that," I would say, nodding, as I read the verses he quoted. But I perceived them through a Mormon glass darkly.

Three months from the end of his mission, perhaps even Micah did not know that all of his prayer and study would lead him away from the Mormon Church. In early December, I accompanied Alicia to the wedding reception hall in Alpine, where she was employed, to reserve a date. But when Micah talked to us on the phone for the second time that year, on Christmas Day, he dropped the bombshell that he and Alicia were indeed getting married after his mission — but in a Baptist church in Winter Garden, Florida. He didn't tell us yet, but an assistant pastor there had answered some of his questions. I felt the ton of bricks raining down. Could this be the colossal, unforgiveable sin he'd hinted at — apostasy? If so, he'd be doomed to outer darkness, a place of weeping, wailing, and gnashing of teeth reserved for Satan, his angels, and the sons of perdition who have denied the Holy Ghost and left the Mormon Church.

"Maybe in a year," he said, "we'll get sealed in the Mormon temple."

"Okay. What's so bad about that?" Mike and I asked each other. "We were married in a Presbyterian church, and we're doing fine."

I tried to be positive. Though we didn't fully understand it, Mike and I accepted Micah's desire to marry in that church. We loved him, and we wanted to know and understand whatever was happening to him, even as we were still comfortable with our placid, wide-eyed sacred Mormon cow. That cow, however, was about to get slaughtered, so God reached out to prepare me.

On the morning of December 30, my birthday, the Dancer of grace appeared again. I dreamed I saw the face of my sweet mother, who had been dead for three years. She was offering me God's alluring, unconditional love. Did God know what I was about to suffer? When I reached out to touch Mom, the dream dissolved.

This was not a visitation from a dead ancestor; this was only a dream.

Against the mission rules and completely unlike him, on January 1 Micah called my cell phone and left a haunting message.

"Depressed. At the end of my rope," he cried. "I need to talk with my mom."

I have no idea how I missed that call or the message he left, but I did not discover it until January 18. When I finally did, I wept because he had reached out for me and I was not there. I was supposed to always be there. That was my mom job!

Bending the rules, I called him back. He didn't pick up, but I left him a message of genuine repentance, weeping. I kept his message on my phone for the next two years and listened to it over and over. Each time I did, I felt the same wave of sympathy for his pain, and the same shame for my negligence. This message — his voice — was one of the few connections I still had to the Micah I knew for sure loved me.

Although Michael and I knew about the upcoming wedding, Micah and Alicia had not told her parents yet. On January 1, 2006, Alicia left BYU and moved to Florida to work at the Edgewater, the hotel that Micah planned to manage after his mission. When her parents learned about their plan for a Baptist church wedding, it was an even greater shock to them than it had been to us. To them, it was a sure sign of apostasy. Her father reacted like a protective Mormon dad, arguing vehemently against the idea. Micah and Alicia were getting a sense of just how difficult this faith change was going to be.

"Jesus Is All You Need"

One of Micah's last emails from the mission field, dated January 6, 2006, read, "I have learned that God is everything to me and He has reached to me and lifted me greatly. I could do no less than boast of His greatness, His glory, and His perfect and endless love. Christ is the One and only True King, the heir to this earth and our Master forever. In all that this world sees to be important, in all that we worship and praise, one day we will all realize that it means nothing, and only God through Christ can save our souls. I love you all so much. The time is short."

On January 18, we received an official letter from his mission president that announced the details of the close of Micah's mission. It stated, "Elder Wilder will be returning home after serving an honorable mission in the Florida Orlando Mission. A copy of his itinerary is enclosed." He was scheduled to come home on February 15, 2006, at 4:09 p.m. We looked forward to his homecoming with eager anticipation.

What we didn't know was that on this same day, about three weeks before his mission was supposed to end, Micah attended a meeting of approximately sixty missionaries. At the meeting, he was expected to bear testimony of all things Mormon that he had learned the past two years. His mission president was a distinguished, graying gentleman I'll call President Smoot. At the point when Micah spoke, President Smoot had just reminded the missionaries that a proper Mormon testimony included:

1. I know the church is true.
2. I know Joseph Smith was a prophet of God.
3. I know the Book of Mormon is the most correct book on the face of the earth.

4. I know we have a living prophet today.

5. Jesus Christ is the Savior.

Tentatively Micah rose to his feet and took the mic. He knew well what all those ears expected to hear. But the Spirit of the living God appeared when Micah ignored the first four points of a good Mormon testimony and, very simply, professed faith in Christ Jesus alone. This packed a powerful punch.

"Jesus is all you need." He stood a little taller and gazed at the missionaries he'd come to love. "Don't you think that when Jesus was on the cross, that he saw your face? Don't you think that he looked into your eyes and said, 'I love you and I would die for you so that you could live'?" This testimony was so unusual and so tender that many were weeping.

For most of his mission, Micah had been reading the New Testament. There he found a completely different gospel than the gospel of Mormonism — a gospel of grace. He came to know a completely different Jesus than the Jesus of Mormonism.

The colossal miracle occurred when the triad of Micah, a Bible, and the Holy Spirit converged. The other colossal miracle was that it had happened 2,300 miles away to Alicia too. I can only imagine the sensations that surged through Micah as he summoned the courage to tell his fellow missionaries what he had learned. He had been crucified with Christ, and soon he'd feel the full impact.

President Smoot, of course, could not take Micah's testimony as a true Mormon declaration. In addition, unbeknownst to Micah, both Alicia's father and a bishop had phoned President Smoot to let him know about the impending marriage in the Baptist church. President Smoot had no choice but to haul Micah in for an interview. Two days after the suspect testimony, Friday at noon, January 20, 2006, Micah faced the first of his inquisitors, both official and unofficial. Micah, we were soon to realize, had done the unthinkable. He had gone apostate.

CHAPTER 12

HOME SWEET HORROR

*

"Do not fear their threats; do not be frightened." But in your hearts revere Christ as Lord.

—1 PETER 3:14 – 15

Micah's several-hour inquisition occurred early on a Friday afternoon in Florida. It was just after it was finished that he called me on my cell phone: "It's over."

I resigned right then and there to be fine with whatever was happening, even if I did not understand it yet. After all, this was Micah — trustworthy, warm, kind, service-oriented, Heavenly Father – loving Micah. I knew right away that he meant that his mission was over early. But why, exactly?

Micah continued, "I'm being sent home. The mission president here in Florida said I wasn't following Christ. My stake president back home told me I have a demon. I think they're gonna release me dishonorably. I'm going to the hotel to think."

What in the world could Micah have done to get sent home dishonorably? I tried to express love and support for him. I think

I was in a state of shock, trying to absorb it all. Michael was also at home working in his office, so we communicated after the call in stunned whispers.

Since missionaries never call their families except on Mother's Day and Christmas, and since Micah had told us at Christmas that he and Alicia intended to marry in a Baptist church after his mission, and since his weekly emails had given us hints, we knew something big was up, but what was it?

Micah said he felt at peace and told me some passages of Scripture he felt the Spirit had given him for direction and comfort: Luke 21:12 – 19; Matthew 19:29; Psalm 18; and Psalm 23. He prayed a lot that morning before the interview. He said, "The drive was about forty-five minutes, so I had a lot of time to pray in my mind and heart. I really tried to heed the advice 'don't meditate beforehand how to answer ... God will give you a mouth and wisdom.' I was terrified, but tried to have faith."

We hung up at 12:30. I felt some anxiety but did not panic. We were not angry with Micah, nor did we feel he had been deceived by a demon. (What a silly thing to say!) We were just eager to see him again, feel his love for us, wrap him in our love, and hear what was in his heart. We loved and trusted him and wanted to learn what he had learned. In the meantime, we knew that going to a neutral location like the hotel seemed reasonable. Micah was an adult with tough decisions to make. He would need breathing room to make his next one.

Our stake president in Utah called at 5:15 that evening to tell us that Micah had left his apartment and was at the hotel. Of course, we knew that. "The mission president in Florida will try to visit him there to talk him into coming home to family [i.e., back to Mormonism]," he said.

A few minutes later, President Smoot in Florida called as he was driving to the hotel. Out of respect for him, Micah had told him where he was. The president explained to me, "Alicia's parents and a bishop called me last week concerning Micah, so I arranged to interview him this morning. During the interview, Micah said that after his mission, he plans to get married, go to school, and work. But he and Alicia plan to marry in a Baptist church."

"Yes, we are aware of that. He told us when we spoke on the phone at Christmas," I replied.

"Micah also said he believes he has a personal mission to bring together all people in Christ, to unite the seven churches. He said he could not sustain Gordon B. Hinckley as the only prophet of the world, nor Joseph Smith as a prophet. He denied that the Father and the Son appeared to Joseph Smith in the Sacred Grove. He said the Bible was the Word of God.

"Micah is well intentioned but resolute and emotionless," President Smoot continued. "I have felt close to Micah. He is dutiful. He has committed no gross disobedience, but for the last four months he has only testified of Jesus Christ and not the restored gospel." He said he had talked with a member of the quorum of the seventy, in Salt Lake. (My BYU interviewer seven years earlier had been a member of the seventy.) "The brethren in Salt Lake told Micah's leaders to try to keep him in the church."

We learned that they decided to give Micah an *honorable* release and send him home. This seemed like good news. Better than a dishonorable release.

Later that night, Micah told me on the phone that President Smoot verbally attacked him during the Friday interview in the church building. He believed that President Smoot was not led by the Holy Ghost. In contrast, Micah felt that the Holy Spirit had directed his responses. Although this was challenging new territory, Micah was learning to trust this greater God. I felt dizzy. The line between good and evil was wavering.

Micah told us, "I believe I will be excommunicated. That is

their only option after what I have done. Like Paul before King Agrippa in Acts 25 and 26, I pleaded my cause."

No, they would never do that, I thought. He almost sounded paranoid.

He wanted to be officially released as a Mormon missionary, and he would decide soon whether he would come home to Utah for that. Then he added, "People will see the truth if they follow God. I do not want to hurt the Mormon Church."

President Smoot called us again that night to report on their meeting at the hotel. He said, "Micah agreed to think about getting on a plane and coming home to Utah. He needs to come home to counsel with his parents and his stake president. The brethren believe he needs to clarify his thinking." He noted, "Micah is charismatic and has had great influence on other missionaries. Micah needs time to process and to think. The important thing is that we do the right thing. I suspect Micah will come home. He will get to report in his home ward." President Smoot promised that the stake president in Utah would avoid any confrontation. "It is all done in love," he said.

I asked President Smoot if this was a common occurrence with missionaries. He said he had never confronted anything like this before. "Micah is very altruistic and loving. He hugs a lot and tells you how much he loves you. He has great right brain and left brain capacity, but he needs to stay channeled and work through the conflicts.

"Micah feels like he has received a call," President Smoot added, "but he needs to be open and teachable so his feelings about the priesthood can be put in proper perspective. The changes in Micah have been subtle over time. Please feel free to call with any promptings or impressions you have." We didn't.

Micah called us again early the next morning to say he would come home to Utah to be released honorably. He told President

Smoot. Then he called us back an hour and a half later to say he was flying into Salt Lake at eight o'clock that night.

Later that morning, President Smoot called us once again, assuring Mike that no action would be taken against Micah and that Micah would be honorably released. His assurances, we would soon discover, were meaningless.

The Lion's Den

We picked up Micah at the airport, our hearts a cauldron of mixed emotions: joy at seeing him, hope that he would help us understand, and anxiety about how the homecoming testimony in the ward would go. But most of all, we were afraid. Afraid of what would happen at Micah's upcoming meeting with President Hansen — the same priesthood leader who had excommunicated Josh more than a year ago.

We were in two cars, and Micah rode with his siblings home from the airport. On our way, Mike called the stake president.

President Hansen told him, "Come straight to my office, and do not bring any other family members with you to the release."

After the call, Mike turned to me and said, "From President Hansen's tone, this doesn't look good."

Mike was not about to allow the church to excommunicate Micah. After all, the mission president in Florida had promised that Micah would be honorably released, not dismissed from the church and separated from his salvation. Nevertheless, Mike called the kids and informed them of the stake president's wishes. We pulled into our driveway, and Micah got out of the other car and joined Mike and me in our car.

I turned on the roof light so I could see him in the back seat. He was frowning. "Dad, I'm not sure we should go," he said as we sat there in front of our home. "I know President Hansen promised you he would not excommunicate me, but I think he will.

I think it's a trap. Please hear me. He was really angry when we talked on the phone. He said I had a devil in me."

"Son, I can't believe they will excommunicate you," Mike said. Priesthood trusted priesthood. "For what? You've done nothing wrong. [Mike and I were unaware at this time that Micah had borne testimony of Christ alone before a roomful of missionaries. We assumed this was about his marriage in the Baptist church.] We're just going to his office so you can be honorably released. I've talked with him. It'll be fine. Let's just go and get it over with." Mike backed out of the driveway.

It was late on that cold, dark Saturday night when we arrived at President Hansen's office.

Accusations and Insinuations

Up the stairs to the side door, we entered the stake office portion of the church building. President Hansen greeted us with his firm handshake, smiling. He had the classic stake president CEO look — dark suit, trim hair, thin build, early sixties, commanding presence. He was alone. He led us to his office and bid us sit in three stuffed chairs.

I was nervous. *Let's just get him released*. President Hansen called on Mike to pray. Arms folded, head bowed in the typical Mormon-culture prayer posture, I prayed silently that the stake president would reach out to Micah in kindness.

President Hansen asked Micah to share what he'd learned on his mission. Micah bore a brief and heartfelt witness of Jesus Christ. Next, President Hansen took a turn to pontificate, stating his testimony of the Mormon gospel, the true restored gospel. It went something like this: "I know beyond a shadow of a doubt that Joseph Smith, a boy of fourteen, did see the Father and the Son that day in the grove." Et cetera. "He restored the true church, the only one on the face of the earth with which the Lord is well pleased." Et cetera. He was preaching. His voice was forceful, his pitch and volume rising. "He translated the Book of Mormon, the most correct book on the face of the earth, by the gift and power of God." It sounded like scolding. Maybe this wouldn't be so quick.

"We have a living prophet who speaks for God today. He is the *only* one authorized to speak for God!" A moment of silence. Why was he so hostile? I don't think he even mentioned Christ. Where was his sincerity? Where was the kindness I'd prayed for? This sounded accusatory.

Then it was Micah's turn again. "President, I respect that this is what you believe. But I have found the Jesus of the Bible. I will never turn back. I will never be the same again."

"You're confused. The path you are on is the path of the Devil." Head down, President Hansen referred quickly and quietly to Alma 1. That was a passage about one of the antichrists of the Book of Mormon who led the people to hell with priestcrafts. Was he suggesting that Micah was an antichrist with the spirit of the Devil? That was exactly his insinuation.

Indignation rose inside me. To my right, Michael was fuming, ready to blow.

President Hansen tried a new tactic. He disclosed that Alicia's father, a respected man in his ward's bishopric, had called him. President Hansen accused Micah of taking this good man's daughter, Alicia, away from Christ and away from the true church. "You are leading her away from Christ!"

Calmly Micah said, "President, I am leading her *to* Christ."

President Hansen berated Micah in a way that seemed cruel to us and made sure we knew that the Devil was behind Micah's transformation. In thirty years in Mormonism, I'd never seen anything like it. How could he suggest that someone who professed the Christ of the Bible had a devil in him?

President Hansen's attitude so angered Mike that he nearly lunged across the desk for a nose-to-nose contest with him. Just then Micah spoke up and in a calm, firm voice diffused the situation with a courage and maturity that amazed me. "I did not come here to discuss doctrines," Micah said. "If you would like to do that, we can arrange another meeting. I came here to be released as I was promised, and I'm asking you to release me—now."

The room stilled for a few seconds. President Hansen's lower lip quivered. He let out a few puffing breaths, like those of a defeated bull. "I release you, Elder Wilder. You are no longer a full-time missionary."

When we walked out, President Hansen feigned politeness and invited us to bring Micah back in the early morning to appear before the high council. We did not trust him one iota, knowing that Micah would walk into a kangaroo court. He was likely to profess grace through faith in Christ alone and ignore the other four pillars of a Mormon testimony. That wouldn't go down well with the brethren. He'd be excommunicated, regardless of what we'd been promised.

As we left, Mike and I glanced at each other, frowning, and made a pact not to bring him back the next morning. I'd never opposed a church leader before. Never had a reason to—until now. I was starting to feel like a vicious wolf facing down the sacred Mormon cow. Righteous indignation was setting up residence.

Why did Micah even need to come back to Utah to be released? In sending Micah on his mission, President Hansen had entrusted his care to the mission president in Florida, President Smoot. Wherever a church member lives, the priesthood leader there presides over that person—in the name of the Mormon Lord. President Smoot could not have officially released Micah in Florida. Micah had to return to the priesthood leader, President Hansen, who had sent him on his mission, for his official release.

If Micah moved home to live within our stake boundaries, President Hansen would regain authority over him. It's a well-ordered system of male priesthood governance.

Back home and exhausted, we moved to the kitchen, the common gathering place. Micah leaned against the sink, Mike stood by the refrigerator, and I sat in a chair, hunched over the table. I was brain-dead. We had a brief conversation with Micah that he recalls but we do not. We were in terrible shock. It apparently went something like this:

Mike asked, "Micah, do you still accept the Book of Mormon as the word of God?"

Micah replied, "No, Dad."

"Well, Son, please keep reading it."

Silence.

Mike then asked, "How about the temple?"

"No, Dad, I no longer accept the temple either." Micah began to tell us something about the body of Christ being the real church, but none of it made any sense.

Mike interrupted. "Please keep wearing your garments." Although his mouth spoke these words, Mike told me later that he felt sick about not standing up for his son in the meeting with President Hansen. Nevertheless, his Mormon priesthood ruled his actions.

After Matt and Katie's Saturday night guests left, long past midnight, Micah, Matt, Matt's girlfriend Nicole, and Katie huddled in an earnest conversation that we were not privy to. We were glad to see them together, but we were spent.

Whirlwinds

The next morning, we all got up and went to church together in our own ward. To stay home would have been unthinkable. Our neighbors were all members of our ward and would know that

Micah was home from his mission. We speculated on how his homecoming testimony would go over. The bishop announced that Micah was home and called on him during church to bear his testimony. It was fast-and-testimony Sunday. In his dark suit and neatly trimmed hair, Micah strode slowly to the podium. Mike and I held our breath. What would he say?

Micah spoke. "'Nothing,' Paul said, 'can separate us from the love of Christ.' We are saved through faith in Jesus. I am grateful for the path God has set me on. I am doing my best to follow. I love you and thank you for the growth I gained in this ward. I express my deep love for Christ." He sat down. He had borne a sweet witness of Jesus but strategically disregarded the other four pillars of a good LDS testimony.

People noticed that he was home early. After church, several asked, "Hey, is Micah sick or something? Isn't he home early? Is everything okay?" The gossip cesspool was on red alert. We walked home after sacrament meeting, not staying for Sunday school or priesthood.

After church, a steady stream of church, school, and community friends came and went all day long to congratulate Micah, as is the custom in Utah LDS culture. They might also have been trying to find out why he was home early, without asking directly. Mormon culture tends toward polite and indirect communication. That evening, Alicia's family came by. Her father was quite agitated and went downstairs to where Micah was, eager to get some answers about the Baptist church wedding. I was nervous, to say the least, about what conflicts might arise between Micah and him. We wanted answers too, but we would not demand them.

Then came that Dancer again. By the grace of God, our bishop happened by at the same time and accompanied Alicia's parents downstairs to see Micah. I was relieved, since our bishop was a kind man whom I trusted to handle things.

At this point, Micah had been home for twenty-four hours, and there had been no rest, no opportunity to *really* talk with him. I suppose we should have created it, even if it meant isolating ourselves from that insistent Mormon world pressing in. We should have locked the door, turned off the phone, left the house—whatever it took to communicate with and love our son. The adrenaline had been pumping nonstop for all of us since Friday morning.

We were aching to speak with Micah. We wanted to find out what had happened to him. We wanted to express our love for him and have him confirm that he still loved us. But that Sunday night, he approached us with an odd request. "Please get me a plane ticket back to Florida for tomorrow. I would be very grateful. Thank you."

I was crestfallen. Just a few hours of back-and-forth conversation, *please*, when I was fresh, awake, and unencumbered by all the happenings and all the people. But it seemed to us that his life was moving ahead and he might be dismissing us from it. Besides, Alicia was back in Florida, and they had two years of catching up to do.

I guess he never intended to stay home but came home to honor his parents. He always was respectful. And he came to be released from the priesthood authority of Mormonism so he could move on. Of course, priesthood leaders would find him in Florida too. They always do when you are on the church rolls.

Alicia's father called the house again on Monday, looking for serious answers. Alicia was his oldest child and an example to the rest of his children. She was supposed to marry in the Mormon temple. In his eyes, Micah was the reason why she wasn't going to. This young man who evaded his queries had betrayed him. But what could Micah tell him that would satisfy him? "Read the New Testament"? He'd say, "I do!"

Worried and not knowing what to say on Micah's behalf, I

stopped answering the poor man's calls. We decided that Micah going back to Florida until tempers cooled was a good idea, so the next afternoon he flew "home" to Florida. Thankfully, he had already been offered a job and a place to live at the Edgewater Hotel, so we were not concerned about where he would live or how he would support himself.

Whew! What a whirlwind of emotions. What just happened? We had no insight to ease our apprehension. We'd had no long conversations with Micah. No question-and-answer sessions without the duress. The adrenaline wouldn't quit. And what about Micah? Had the verse on his missionary plaque just come to pass?

Gossip and Rumors

When I returned to work the next day, my presence was requested at a privately catered lunch with the president of BYU and a few other faculty members. I'd been at BYU for several years and had never been invited before. Were the priesthood lines of communication buzzing over Micah rather high up the ladder? It never occurred to me that someone even higher up — God — might have arranged this luncheon to show me something I needed to see.

The president of BYU was a general authority of the LDS Church, a leader with great clout. Although I had just survived a nightmare weekend compliments of the stake president, I still had some faith in the Mormon Church leaders and still revered this man's position with Christ. As I mentioned before, general authorities receive rock star status and veneration, and he was one of them. We always rose to our feet as the prophet at the top entered or left a room. We did not need to stand for the president of BYU, but our respect for this general authority was evident in our speech and body language.

At the luncheon, I sat across from the revered man, chatting with him.

"Last Good Friday," I said, "you and I were in the same on-campus meeting." I didn't tell *him* this part, but I had found it strange that at 3:00 p.m. on the day when most Christians remember that Christ died on the cross, he—as Christ's representative—did not even mention Jesus. So at lunch I said, "I missed hearing your testimony on Good Friday. Would you bear testimony of Christ now for us?" I was sincere in my request and leaned forward with anticipation.

Instantly he was angry, as if I had caught him. He snapped, "If you've been here for any length of time, you've heard my testimony!" Then he glanced around, realizing he'd been ill-tempered in front of several faculty members. He did relent to bear a standard LDS testimony, but with gusto: "I know the church is true. I know Joseph Smith was a prophet of God . . ." This time, his testimony struck me as hollow, canned. I was beginning to glimpse the little man behind the Wizard of Oz.

Before long, the gossip cesspool spit foul rumors. I heard them whispered at church, in the neighborhood, in the grocery store, and by students at the university. University friends of Micah approached me on campus to see what they could glean from me, but by the grace of the Dancer, the rumors never surfaced among the colleagues in my department, that I was aware of. Maybe the administrators knew, but my immediate boss, the first female department chair, was a true saint.

Katie heard the rumors at school, from friends, and from Micah's former missionary companions, now home in Utah. Sometimes they stopped by the house, mostly to see her, and to ask why Micah had gone apostate and joined a cult. It was the first time she heard the words *apostate* and *cult*. Christianity was a cult? She chastised one former missionary for believing everything he heard rather than relying on what he *knew* about Micah. Sadly, no one seemed to question whether the rumors were true.

Only one neighbor confronted me directly, may God bless her. I belonged to a group of mothers who all had sons serving missions at about the same time. We shared their emails from the field, got together to mail them necessities or letters of encouragement, and prayed for all of them. I hadn't said a word to anyone in the group, but one of the mothers was in our ward. When this gossip hit the ward, my neighbor came to the house to repeat what was said and to ask me point-blank if it was true. I sorted the truth from the lies for her.

"Yes, Micah was sent home from his mission three weeks early. No, he was released *honorably*, not dishonorably. Yes, he professed belief in the biblical Christ, so is considered an apostate. Yes, they took his temple recommend away. No, he did not join a cult, and no, he is not starting his own church." To a Mormon, the latter would be blasphemous. Joseph Smith founded the only true church. "No, he has not committed any big sins; he did not break the Word of Wisdom or anything like that."

Then my neighbor worried out loud, "My kids have loved Micah so deeply over the years, but I'm not sure I can allow them to talk with him anymore. It's very sad."

Very sad indeed.

Meanwhile, from Florida Micah wrote,

Just wanted to write and let you know how much I love you. I have been suffering in bed for hours with a fever of over 103. I apologize my contact has been so limited since my return to Florida. But I guess it's just hard working so many hours and things going on. It's difficult sometimes, because my life is so filled with emotional and mental stress, along with the health problems that I have been dealing with.

Alicia seems to be the only one that I can have around me. I love her with every part of my soul. It is my weakness in this life that makes me fall so often, and those falls bring hurt and pain that force me to turn to Christ and find peace in His saving grace. Through all of this I feel stronger, and as Christ said to Paul, "My grace is sufficient for you; for my strength is made perfect in weakness."

This has been my time in the wilderness to find myself and to find my God; and the amazing part is that through the pain and heartache I have felt, I have never felt the presence of my Father like I do now. The other evening I found myself alone in my room, as everyone had other responsibilities to attend to. I laid in pain and anguish and cried to my God. I praised Him. I worshipped Him. I called for His mercy to be upon me. I pleaded forgiveness for the sins that keep me from being nearer to Him. No, the pain did not cease. No, the hurt did not go away. But I smiled as I felt His love pour over my soul, and knowing that even through what seemed to be the pains of hell, I still praised my God. I still worshipped His holy name. And He still came to me in His perfect love.

What a refinement this has been and what a fire I have entered to purge me of all my ungodliness. I am weak, yet I am strong. Christ has become everything that I live for, and that will never change. And nothing or no one could change that. So I must come to you with a heart that is being changed, asking for forgiveness and patience from a loving son. I could never forget what you have done for me in my life. I will never stop thanking God for loving parents who taught me where to find true peace and happiness — in Christ. So that is where I am looking, and in no one else am I trying to find Him. I love Him with all my heart and soul. I love you with all my heart and soul. A mother's love cannot be replaced. Thank you for your love and your willingness to see me through difficult times. I will always love you.

Such a burden for Micah, barely twenty-one, to carry on his shoulders. Nevertheless, he was at peace with his God, a peace I had yet to know.

CHAPTER 13

"JUST READ THE NEW TESTAMENT"

✼

God offers to every mind its choice between truth and repose. Take which you please —you can never have both.

— RALPH WALDO EMERSON

Two weeks after Micah's homecoming, Michael and I flew to Florida to see him, hoping in a week's visit to finally have that loving, clarifying talk about his new beliefs. That Sunday, he took us to services in one of the wards he had attended on his mission. To our surprise, he wore jeans, although no one in Mormonism wore jeans to church. After church he asked, "Did you notice how unkindly I was treated by people judging me by my appearance? Jesus himself wouldn't be allowed to pass the sacrament in his own church, you know, with his beard and dusty clothes."

Yeah, I thought, *but you know the Mormon culture rules. You knew exactly what you would get. You set that up.* But I didn't say it. Of course, he set it up to try to open our eyes about something, but we were still blind as bats.

We stayed at the Edgewater Hotel in Winter Garden, where

both Micah and Alicia lived and worked. Since they had both proven themselves to be moral young adults, we knew they would never cross the line with sexual intimacy before marriage. We trusted them. This historic three-story hotel opened in 1927 and is completely refurbished with antiques from that era. One of the owners of the Edgewater, Erik, was a Mormon—or at least had been. Erik was glad to have Micah, with his work ethic and growing managerial skills, and Alicia, who was willing to work any hours.

While serving as ward mission leader in charge of helping local missionaries, Erik had befriended Micah and almost every missionary who came through the Orlando mission. Plus, Erik has a kind heart and young men have gargantuan appetites, so he allowed the missionaries to eat in the hotel restaurants free of charge. When Micah began reading the Bible on his mission, he shared, tentatively at first, what he learned with Erik, who dug into the Bible himself. Erik was a convert to Mormonism who'd had a Christian upbringing. He had earnestly surrendered his life to Jesus during a trip to Moscow in 2001 and joined the Mormon Church soon afterward, when he returned to Florida. His Christian upbringing afforded him some previous knowledge about the Word, and he was a brilliant and quick reader.

In October of 2005, three months before Micah was sent home, Erik had flown to Utah to attend LDS General Conference in Salt Lake with Mike, Katie, and me. Oddly, weeks later he began to call us with questions he was having about the Mormon Church. I was confused about why he came all the way to Utah to General Conference and soon afterward had doubts about whether the church was true. I could listen to his information about church history for only a short period before I passed the phone to Mike; it seemed so negative. Soon Erik came to the same conclusion about Mormonism that Micah did, and he stopped attending the LDS Church.

One day Micah took us to a room on the unfinished third floor of the hotel where he intended to assemble a recording studio. He wanted to play for us a recording of a song that was special to his friend, Elder Joseph Warren, after hearing Micah's testimony that day to the missionaries. Micah was very excited about the song. The recording was a collaborative effort among some musician friends. As we listened, he gauged our reactions carefully. The words went like this:

Whose face did you think that I was looking into
When I was hanging on the cross?
Whose life did you think was passing right before my eyes
As I paid your cost?

And I looked into your eyes, and told you of my love
For you to live I would die for you[28]

I knew the song was supposed to move me, and I tried to muster some spiritual emotion, but it wouldn't come.

On Tuesday, Micah, Alicia, Mike, and I drove from Winter Garden to Fort Myers, in southwest Florida, to spend a night at my dad's. He was very excited to see us. Micah and Alicia told him they were getting married in a Baptist church. Big news for a Christian like Dad, who could not enter the Mormon temple for a wedding because entrance required a temple recommend. His eyes were wide with curiosity. I stood in the background, leaning against the kitchen sink and crying gently. Dad came to me and whispered, "They'll get married right after that in your Mormon temple, right?"

"I don't know, Dad," I said. "That'll be up to them."

Micah had scraped together enough money to fly one of his former missionary companions to the hotel the same week we were there. This young LDS man arrived a few days after we did and then was always around us. His presence precluded us from talking with Micah about his beliefs. We suspected that Micah had arranged this. Did he see his parents as enemies? Nothing could be farther from the truth, as far as we were concerned.

One night in desperation as the week was waning, we tried to talk with Micah and Alicia again. I asked, "What have we done?" They glanced at each other and walked out the door.

I was dumbfounded. Couldn't we just talk about it? Nothing like this had ever divided our family. Did Micah resent us for not standing up to the stake president during that nightmare meeting? Didn't Micah know how much we loved him? Hadn't he always known? What was different now? We still loved him like always. We could never *not* love him.

This supposed rebuff from a son who had reached out to me by phone just weeks ago was a complete mystery. If he were hurt, we needed to talk. Mike and I were sinking fast. Mike was skilled at stuffing. For my part, I kept playing that phone message from January over and over to connect with the place and the time I was sure Micah had loved me.

Intense Pain

Now, it wasn't that I was reluctant to allow my children to grow up. On the contrary. But in this case, the tearing away was so abrupt and confusing and had such dire consequences to our standing as an eternal family that I was beside myself with anxiety and pain.

Alicia and the band were Micah's family now. He repeated to us often over the next couple of years when we asked if he had any needs, "The hotel provides for all our needs." (When he took us back to the airport after that first visit, however, he was driving a 1975 300D Mercedes. It chugged along dangerously slow on the interstate. He didn't shut it off when he dropped us off. (Sometimes it wouldn't shut off, he explained.)

Micah and Alicia had married secretly in a civil ceremony three days after he returned to Florida, on January 26, 2006, his twenty-first birthday. They feared that someone in Mormonism might try to return Alicia to Utah. It wasn't common, but it did sometimes happen in the culture. Later in 2006, the Utah parents of a young Mormon woman named Julianna Redd were charged with second-degree felony kidnapping for taking her out of state and returning her after the scheduled time of her wedding.[29] (They ultimately both pleaded guilty to one Class A misdemeanor of custodial interference.) Whether their fear was rational or irrational, Micah and Alicia had sought legal counsel and found out they had more rights if they married. Weeks after their ceremony, a stake president came to Florida from Utah asking a lot of questions and looking for Alicia. When he found out that she was married, he acted shocked and beat a hasty retreat.

They didn't tell us when we visited in February that they had this fear or that they were married. Maybe *that's* why they had avoided us by putting the former missionary in between. They were compelled to tell Mike and me about their marriage weeks later when Alicia's parents found out.

I remember getting this phone-delivered news back in Utah.

"Hi, Mom."

"Hey, Micah, how's life?"

"Well, I called to tell you Leashy and I got married. Last January, days after I got home from my mission." They wanted to make sure everyone — especially Alicia's family — knew they were committed to each other. They would still have a wedding ceremony in the Baptist church in Winter Garden in April, followed by a reception for family and friends at the Edgewater. I'd need to cancel the reception hall in Alpine.

I took a deep breath and let it out. "Okay ..." This was the same quiet "Okay ..." that I had uttered when he called to tell me he was being sent home from his mission. Still believing in him. Still struggling to understand. What other bombs would drop, bricks fall, wolves attack?

Intense pain began to sear me from head to toe (more penetrating than the physical pain from the auto accidents), although it was a couple of years before I dared to give it a name. The broken-relationship wound was deep and foul-smelling. It became my constant companion and made me ill. I loved and trusted Micah so implicitly, I could not understand any of this. I couldn't sleep at night. I was barely staying sane enough to function in any area of my life. I dreamed I had died and all the family was there except Micah.

I didn't know what was happening. Our kids were wanted and loved. We'd always hung together as an eternal family, supported each other. And now we couldn't lean on our Mormon teachings for comfort or instruction; it was the teachings themselves I couldn't reconcile with the love and trust I had in my son.

I'd seen this pain once before. A teenage girl in our ward became pregnant. She was so ashamed—fornication was a gargantuan sin in Mormon culture—she hung herself in her parents' barn. Pain so consumed the girl's mother that she quit taking care of her diabetes. Depression handed her a signed death warrant. I watched helplessly as she lost her sight, then a leg, and finally her life. She asked me on her deathbed to make sure her son graduated from high school. Like her, some days I wanted to die because of the pain.

"Just Read the New Testament!"

Well, if Micah would not teach us what he had learned on his mission, we would find out ourselves. I had to know the truth.

"Just read the New Testament," he'd said.

My Mormon-wired brain thought, *I trust Christ and Christ alone.*

We rarely used the name Jesus. We were taught in Mormonism that *Jesus* was too precious to say too often out loud, so we used *Christ*. I decided, *I want to read Christ's exact words to discern what is true and what is not.*

So I started in the Book of Mormon, the most correct book of any on earth, to read Christ's direct words. Although I'd been reading the Book of Mormon for a long, long time, I'd never realized before that Christ's exact words were not actually throughout the book. Mostly he spoke through his Book of Mormon prophets.

After he was resurrected, Christ *did* visit the Nephites in the Book of Mormon, in one small section of the book of Third Nephi. He appeared to them and spoke directly to them in the Americas. I read Christ's words in 3 Nephi 12:3–4: "Yea, blessed are the poor in spirit who come unto me, for theirs is the kingdom of heaven. And again, blessed are they that mourn, for they shall be comforted ..." What I was reading was a precise copy of the beatitudes — part of the Sermon on the Mount — from the book of Matthew in the Bible. I saw that. Hmmm. *I'm stuck*, I thought. *I'll have to go to the Bible to read words directly from Christ himself.* So I determined to do just that.

Mormons use only the King James Version and pieces of the Joseph Smith translation of the Bible. One day at BYU, I expressed to a colleague who taught religion that I was curious to know more intimately the words of Christ.

"Why don't you read different versions of the Bible for enlightenment?" he asked.

There are different versions? I thought. I guess I knew that. I'd been to Sunday school at Dad's church one time, and his teacher had a Bible with eight different versions on the same page. I remembered that now.

With my researcher brain, I began to read about these newer versions. There appeared to be a plethora of evidence that they were accurate, having been translated from original Greek, Hebrew, and Aramaic texts. Many texts (such as the Dead Sea Scrolls) had been discovered since the time the King James Version was translated. I began to question why Mormons didn't trust these newer versions of the Bible. Hundreds of linguists and scholars had worked tirelessly to translate them from texts written and preserved by individuals from just after Christ's time.

Relieved to have "Mormon permission" from my colleague to read other versions, I soon became enamored with the New International Version (NIV) student Bible that a new Christian friend had given me.

I started reading in the book of John. John 1:1 said, "In the beginning was the Word, and the Word was with God, and the Word was God." I thought, *The Word is Christ. I get it.* This was what I was looking for, words from Christ himself. *Everything he says is the Word,* I told myself. I read the cross-reference, Revelation 19:13: "He is dressed in a robe dipped in blood, and his name is the Word of God." Christ and the Word of God were the same. I got it.

It's not as if I'd never read these Scriptures before, but this time I was probing for answers. I focused. I read from the beginning of the book of John straight through, so everything I read would be in context. I gave special attention to the exact words of Christ.

I wasn't the only one reading the New Testament. While I sat up in bed at night reading, Mike was reading too. We began to have some very stimulating conversations.

Katie too was reading. Unbeknownst to us, as Micah learned to trust God more than fear his mission leaders, he felt impressed to call Katie one Friday night, just before he was sent home. She was home alone.

In a five-minute phone call, he asked her about her testimony.

When she said she knew that Jesus Christ was the Son of God, he exclaimed, "That's it! That's all! Right there, Katie. Don't make Jesus part of your testimony; make Jesus your testimony." After that one simple phone call from Micah to Katie, she entertained the idea that Jesus Christ was enough. She wanted to know him, so with eyes to see and ears to hear, she began to really read the Bible for the first time.

About this time, Matt called Micah in Florida to ask, "What in the world are you doing to the family?" The direct question was an older brother's prerogative. In answer, Micah challenged Matt to read the New Testament as a child, with fresh eyes.

New Beginnings

Now, Matt had a girlfriend, Nicole, whom he'd met the semester before Micah was sent home. They'd had a memorable first date bowling. Nicole told Matt to bowl a strike; he bowled a strike. When it was his turn again, he asked Nicole to grace him so he could bowl another strike. Instead she chuckled and demanded he bowl a seven-ten split. Matt is fiercely competitive, but as a former high school volleyball player, so is Nicole. He slammed the ball hard, hoping for another strike. As it released, he heard his jeans split right down the crotch, exposing his Mormon garments. Seconds later, the ball yielded a seven-ten split, precisely as Nicole had requested.

Matt shuffled backward to the closest seat. Nicole and the others were hee-hawing because he had bowled the split. When they discovered he'd split his jeans too, they doubled over. Luckily for Matt, he had a pair of wrinkled up, oversized dress pants in the back of his car. So he ran to the car to change and spent the rest of the evening wearing large church pants with a hoodie.

Earlier that evening, they had discussed how horrible it must be for one to have ants in one's pants. Well, after bowling they were sitting in the grass near Nicole's college dorm, talking. All of a sudden she stood up, flipped out, and sprinted to her dorm. She had been sitting on a huge anthill, and ants were crawling all over the place. Apparently, a good number of them had made their way into her pants.

Matt explained, "I could not remember exactly which dorm she lived in. So when she took off running, I realized I needed to follow her. I was so embarrassed because I noticed while I was chasing her that it appeared to other people watching that she was running away from me."

The two tall, thin, blue-eyed blonds were a striking couple. When Micah challenged Matt to read the New Testament, Nicole took the challenge too. On weekends, they came to Alpine so we could all discuss what we had learned through our reading that week. It wasn't as if they could have conversations like that with their roommates at BYU.

Nicole is a great logical thinker. She was really good at chasing a biblical topic from Scripture to Scripture—Scripture chaining, we called it. I looked forward to this weekend stimulation, when we shared excitedly what we were discovering. Katie was busy with theater on the weekends and read on her own.

We all were making progress, slowly but surely, toward absorbing concepts from the New Testament, with Matt and Nicole a step ahead. We discussed John 7:24: "Stop judging by mere appearances, but instead judge correctly." That explained why Micah had worn jeans to church—to demonstrate the difference between judging by appearance and judging by what is in the heart.

We also read John 8:47: "Whoever belongs to God hears what God says." To be honest, I wasn't sure I wanted to belong to God one hundred percent of the time. I was comfortable with my compartmentalized faith, which allowed me to think about Heavenly Father only when I was engaged in church work.

In March, I went to Reno to present research at a conference and came home with pneumonia, spitting up phlegm and blood. Either the Bible reading was cleansing my body of filth or my estrangement from Micah was bringing me death. Perhaps both were true. The day I returned to Utah, Matt had his sophomore piano recital at BYU. Not even pneumonia could keep me away. Rachmaninov, Schubert, Liszt—his piano playing gave me brief moments of relief. Nicole, her grandparents, and a couple hundred others were at the recital.

That night at his recital, Matt called Nicole up on stage, got on his knees, and proposed to her in front of the crowd. We were thrilled. Matt was never more calm and happy than with Nicole's steady love and support. But I was ill. A week later, I tried to be healthy enough to meet and socialize with her LDS family from Seattle. While playing cards with her parents and grandparents, though, I could no longer sit up. I apologized, and Katie drove me home and put me to bed.

For two weeks I was terribly ill. I was given steroids, which caused an electrical problem in my heart—racing and skipping that kept me up nights. I was constantly aware of the emotional pain manifested in physical pain and of how I was barely thriving, barely living. Unable to concentrate for long on anything but the Word of God, I developed an increasing appetite for the Bible. I told God I wouldn't read anything else for a whole year unless I was forced to read something for work.

At the end of April, Micah and Alicia got married in First Baptist Church in Winter Garden, Florida. Alicia's family and our family traveled from Utah. The wedding was glorious and simple and focused on Christ. Micah dropped to his knees and, to Chris Tomlin's song "We Fall Down," mimed throwing his crowns at Christ's feet, a knight with Christian valor. Such a sincere and bold gesture of respect for Jesus deeply moved me. I also loved the chapel of the Baptist church as the sun sent beams through stained-glass windows. The tension was sometimes thick but stayed below the surface.

After the wedding and reception in Florida, the couple flew to Utah, where Alicia's parents held a bridal shower and, three days later, a reception for them in their ward in Alpine. Her mom invited Katie and me to attend the beautifully arranged shower in her home with thirty of Alicia's aunts, cousins, and friends. At the very end, the groom made the requested cameo appearance. The guests had placed the bows and ribbons from the presents in Alicia's hair. Micah tilted his head the way he often did. His look said, "Must be a female thing."

At the reception, some of the guests seemed surprised at Alicia's gown, which was modest and lovely but sleeveless, a bold sign that the couple was not wearing temple garments. The dress was a cultural signal that they were not strong Mormons. I thought she looked gorgeous in it, but I felt somewhat awkward about it too.

Mike and I drove the couple to the airport, where they would leave for their honeymoon. On the way, I asked Micah some questions that my Bible reading was stirring up. He was more than happy to answer with what the Bible said, but the trip was too short for me to absorb the many ideas he poured out so eloquently. Alicia and Micah had a glimmer of hope for us when they realized we were reading the New Testament.

Falling Short

I felt trapped by my own discomfort, others' opinions, my Bible reading, and Micah and Alicia's brave new faith. What I perceived to be an increasingly broken relationship with the married kids paralyzed me more and more. I avoided communication with them except occasionally by text or email. I didn't understand how to relate to them now. When I had to communicate, I was too loud, too friendly, too cheerful, and not genuine. Communication any more intimate than that might find me weeping silently, uncontrollably, stupidly. I was feeling loony, and aging by the minute. In the throes of menopause too. My emotions were out of control. What in the world was happening to me? I had always been calm, confident, and in control — a woman in a business suit who walked in a professional world.

My Mormon brain said, *I must be doing something wrong in order for this terrible thing to happen to my family — to lose Micah and his bride and their future children from our eternal family in heaven.* Salvation depended on righteousness. I needed to find out how I'd fallen short, so I could fix it. I knew Mike wasn't the problem. In this works-based faith, I was responsible to fix whatever I had done that was causing this family rift. I asked the Lord to show me a weakness (Mormons don't use the word *sin* much) that I needed to work on, or at least to show me what the "awful situation" was that needed fixing.

Soon I dreamed I was at a conference center on the beach. To my left, a few seats away in the row in front of me, was a young man of fourteen. I stood up and walked to another part of the conference center. All at once, I heard a loud roaring sound and knew something big had happened. People came to me shouting, "You have to see! You have to know!" A tsunami had torn away the left half of the room, and the fourteen-year-old boy had been washed away. Was this Joseph Smith? We always referred to him as a boy of fourteen, because that was how old he was when he had the purported First Vision of the Father and the Son.

Troubled but not knowing what else I could do, I plowed ahead with my reading of the Bible, liberally applying the balm of reason to the pain of what seemed like rejection.

CHAPTER 14

THE POINT
OF NO RETURN

Truth only reveals itself when one gives up all precon-
ceived ideas.

— SHOSEKI

U p to this point, the Dancer had come and gone, granting me
alluring glimpses of grace. There was the time when I was
twelve that the drugstore burned down but the portrait of Jesus
was untouched. In that moment, the tender God of the universe
removed my fear of dying in a fire. Then there was the time eighteen years later that I was stung by a bee and felt his presence
in my hospital room. His great love saved both Matt's life in the
womb and my own. He came again to awaken me the night of the
flue fire in Farmland and personally protected me and my family.
About eight years after that, he awakened me fourteen nights in
a row, telling me to go back to school. He knew me intimately.
Only Jesus could be doing these things. At the time, I did not
know that experiences in the spiritual realm could come from
two sources, good or bad. But once I saw how they played out, I

CRACKS IN THE FACADE

decided it was Jesus. The experiences were out of the ordinary, yes, but I trusted that they were real.

Not the Same God

As a Mormon, when I had a big problem, a member of the god-head might bother to attend to me. The handful of times when I had sensed the presence of one of them or received answers to prayer corroborated my Mormon belief system, which maintained that Heavenly Father, Christ, and the Holy Ghost were basically unavailable and unconcerned with me personally. It was my job to earn my way to righteousness by following the laws and ordinances of the Mormon gospel. The gods were too busy to address my needs.

In Mormonism, the three members of the godhead are separate gods. The Christ I knew was an exalted man who worked his way to become a god. Some even believed he had once been a sinner. He had a body of flesh and bones and could be in only one place at one time. His blood alone did not wash away all sins. I related to this Christ because he was like me, and I thought of him as a kindly brother. Michael and I, as a temple-attending couple, were on the same path to godhood that this Christ had taken (well, I would be a queen or a priestess to my husband in his role as god); this Mormon Christ was just farther ahead.

The Heavenly Father of Mormonism also had a body of flesh and bones. He could not be in more than one place at a time either. He lived near the star Kolob. I thought of him as a merciless judge.

The Holy Ghost of Mormonism could be in only one place at one time as well. I received the gift of the Holy Ghost after Mormon baptism by the laying on of hands, and the Holy Ghost's influence remained with me (shining down like the sun), but only until I sinned. If I did anything wrong, his influence left me, and I would experience trials until I repented. We took the sacrament every Sunday to have the sin janitor—the Mormon priesthood, who represented Jesus—sweep away these sins so the Holy Ghost's influence could again shine down and we could be delivered from our sin-induced suffering.

In the pages of the Bible, however, I found a different God. This was a much bigger God whose words challenged my Mormon godhead. "Biggie-size your God!" a Pastor Shaw later told us. And that's just what happened.

As I learned, this new, big, Christian God discerns one's heart, honors meekness, creates universes out of nothing, performs miracles for individuals, loves me like a spouse, and remains God from eternity to eternity. He doesn't change. He hasn't worked his way to godhood. He knows everything. He has power over everything. He is everywhere at once. He is always working on our behalf. He answers prayer all day, every day, and every night, and he never sleeps. Therefore he has the love, the desire, the time, the knowledge, and the capacity to be *personal*. His love is wide and long and high and deep. As I began to get to know this God, I couldn't get enough.

This bigger God has a message that conflicts with Mormonism. As I read the New International Version (and checked with the King James Version used by Mormons), I came upon blatant contradictions between teachings in the Bible and Mormon Church doctrine. Even though I'd taught the Bible in Mormon seminary, I had never paid attention to these contradictions.

Each night after Mike and I sat in bed reading the Bible and discussing what we had read, I drifted to sleep thinking about the words. Then I woke up the next day with fresh insights. We were testing the forbidden waters of biblical Christianity. In Mormonism, this was heresy. We had been taught that we could read the Bible, but since the Bible was corrupt, we could not interpret it in any way that opposed Mormon doctrine.

One obvious contradiction between the words of the biblical God and those of the Mormon Lord had to do with the subject of trials, a topic of interest to me at the time. In James 1:2–4, I read, "Consider it pure joy, my brothers and sisters, whenever you face trials of many kinds, because you know that the testing of your faith produces perseverance. Let perseverance finish its work so that you may be mature and complete, not lacking anything." In 2 Corinthians 12:10, I read, "For Christ's sake, I delight in weaknesses, in insults, in hardships, in persecutions, in difficulties. For when I am weak, then I am strong." Consider it joy when you face trials. Delight in hardships. The message was crystal clear. Trials were not necessarily a punishment. They had a purpose.

But as a Mormon, I worked hard to make myself righteous so I could *avoid* trials. Trials were fodder for the weak and sin-ridden, which may be why our Mormon neighbors seemed so callous during Micah's terrible illness. They, like I, believed that the best were blessed. The Bible, however, was saying the opposite. Believers in the biblical Jesus can expect to experience trials, hardship, persecutions, and difficulties. And they are to be *grateful* for them. Trials test faith, produce perseverance, refine, teach, and mature. One trial, our distance from Micah, was beating me to a pulp. Something good could come from that?

This gospel was not the one I had learned in thirty years of Mormonism; this God was not the same God, and this message was not the same message. Mormonism would have me declare Micah lost to outer darkness for denying the Holy Ghost and turning from the Mormon gospel. Did I dare think, *March on and forget he exists. Your eternal family has one less child. Root out the cancer before it infects anyone else?* This was how President Hansen expected us to think about Micah. But the biblical Jesus says to love God above everything and everyone and love others as you love yourself. He doesn't say, "Make your family an idol before me, and if one member turns from God, cast him out." Besides, what if all this studying led us to the place where Micah was?

Stepping Out

That summer of 2006, we mustered the courage to drive two hours away to attend a Protestant church on a Saturday night. That way, no Mormon friends could possibly see us. We were paranoid, worrying that if someone from BYU saw me at church, I would lose my ecclesiastical clearance and my job. And I would have. Only at BYU would someone lose their academic position for even considering disagreement with church doctrine. Micah had faced the same danger as a missionary. He risked every-thing—faith, family, friends, college scholarship, home, respect, Mormon salvation—by stepping out of Mormon belief. He had been willing to do it. I didn't understand how or why.

My professional colleagues in secular universities would never have believed I could lose my job over religion. I could imagine the talk.

"You got fired at BYU?"

"Yes."

"Why?"

"Because I decided to follow a different faith."

"No one would ever fire you just for that! You must have done something wrong."

Mike just knew that if we bucked the Mormon Church, I'd never work again. My sin of apostasy would be splashed across the pages of the Mormon-owned newspaper and the Mormon-owned TV station out of Salt Lake. Who knows what else they would dredge up to report? Then all those years, all that money, all those skills would go down the drain, and we still had three kids to put through college. But Mike and I were in agreement, our relationship was strong, and as we had vowed long ago, whatever we decided spiritually, we would do together.

When we parked at the church that first night, I realized that one of my BYU colleagues lived close enough to recognize my car. Every time we drove the two hours there, we sweated bullets for fear of being discovered.

The first night we were there, the pastor preached right out of God's Word on Jesus' cross and blood. Whew, powerful! These were foreign concepts to me. Mormons don't reverence the cross, and instead of a representation of Jesus' blood (grape juice or wine), they use water for the sacrament.

That night, I dreamed of a square, three-story, concrete building that was dark and dingy with filth, dust, and cobwebs. It had stairways, hallways, and elevators that went nowhere—there was no way out. The next night, I dreamed of the same building again. I barely recognized it. This time, all four walls were glass. They sparkled. Light streamed everywhere. It was orderly, with stairways, hallways, and elevators going somewhere.

Soon after that, I read, "You are God's field, God's *building*" (1 Cor. 3:9, emphasis added), and Christ loved his church, his believers, and died for her, "cleansing her [his church, his building] by the washing with water through the word" (Eph. 5:25–26). Reading the Bible was washing me with living water through the Word.

In the midst of this sorting-truth-from-fiction process—reading the Bible, thinking through the doctrinal conflicts, and dealing with broken relationships—God sent a week of grace. In June of 2006, Katie and I went to New York City to take in Broadway shows with her drama teacher and students. Being with Katie and receiving her love was an oasis for me. Maybe everything would be okay. But truthfully, I still had no idea how it could ever be okay, with Micah and Alicia not with us in the eternal family circle.

Joseph Smith's Egyptian Papyri

In New York, Katie and I visited the Metropolitan Museum of Art. Besides reading the Bible, I had begun to research Mormon Church history. Boy, is that a closet full of skeletons!

Here's the history I'd learned: On July 4, 1835, Smith and his latter-day saints were living in Kirtland, Ohio. A traveling Irishman set up a paid exhibit of four Egyptian mummies and some Egyptian papyri. Eager to prove that Smith did indeed have the power to translate all ancient texts — the gift described in the Book of Mormon as that of a *seer* — the brethren purchased the entire exhibit for $2,400 and presented it to Smith.

Some people in Kirtland had been claiming that the Book of Mormon was a fraud. Smith could not prove otherwise, because the angel Moroni had returned the original gold plates, from which he'd translated it, to heaven. So, to prove he was a seer, Smith "translated" these ancient Egyptian texts. No linguist in the United States could read ancient Egyptian at the time, so Smith had no fear of scholarly reprisal. Smith called his translation of these Egyptian papyri the Book of Abraham and included it in the Pearl of Great Price, *current* Mormon scripture. In other words, Mormons still revere Smith's translation of the papyri as scripture. His translation was first published in 1842 in Nauvoo, Illinois, the town to which the saints had moved.

Joseph Smith's Egyptian papyri resurfaced at the museum in the 1960s. The world had assumed that these famous papyri had been destroyed in the great Chicago fire of 1871, but they had survived.

In 1967, the Metropolitan Museum of Art presented the rediscovered papyri to the Mormon Church. Huge. This was exciting. Now modern Mormons could prove that their founding prophet Joseph Smith was a true prophet of God, a seer. Then the world would accept their modern Mormon prophet, his counselors, and the twelve apostles, also seers.

Since the discovery of the Rosetta Stone, however, linguists could decipher ancient Egyptian. Egyptologists translated Smith's papyri. The Mormons held their breath; they were sure the translations would match.

They did not, not even close. The papyri were common Egyptian funeral texts that said nothing about Abraham.[30]

Still today, Mormons cling to this scripture translated from the papyri as accurate. Most are unaware of the story of the resurfaced papyri, and the original documents haven't been seen for years. They are probably buried in a church vault somewhere.

In July, Josh, Katie, Michael, and I went to China with some colleagues from BYU for eleven days, at the invitation of the Ministry of Education. While I spoke to a crowd of more than four hundred, a government official yelled at me in Chinese. He objected to my citing a study that showed the rise in emotional/behavioral problems in Chinese male youth. This censorship reminded me of the LDS Church when it came to church history. As their response to the Egyptian papyri revealed, only *their* telling of history was valid, regardless of the truth.

A New Bride

In late August, Matt and Nicole got married in the Seattle Temple. They took me with them to Nicole's home in Seattle for nine days before the wedding/sealing. This was a sweet experience, getting to pray together with them each night while Matt and I stayed in Nicole's brother's room. I loved Nicole already — her energy, intelligence, organizational skills, work ethic, and ability to live frugally. Matt and Nicole were eagerly anticipating their wedding, but they lived through some anxious times as her family hoped she would reconnect with a certain returned LDS missionary who would keep her in Seattle, instead of marrying the quiet but strong, square-jawed musician she'd met at BYU, with whom she would eventually go to Florida.

As I watched her parents' concerns, it occurred to me that it is not unusual for well-meaning adults in Mormon culture to be pretty involved in their adult children's lives, trying to sway their decisions and behavior. I saw several instances of this in Utah. In psychology, we call it being enmeshed. Most Mormon families are enmeshed, with adult children sometimes overly dependent upon parental direction or still talking with their parents daily or coming home each Sunday for dinner. This helps to keep them Mormon. I explored whether Mike's and my closeness to our kids might be in any way unhealthy. I was beginning to entertain the idea that it could be.

Although Matt and Nicole were coming to know the Jesus of the Bible, they had opted to get married in a Mormon temple. This was partly because Nicole wanted to experience the temple before she made her final decision about Mormonism and professed faith in the biblical Jesus, and partly to appease the family she loved so much. Nicole had spent her entire life trying to please her parents, who'd sacrificed a lot for their children, and she couldn't bear the thought of disappointing them. She knew they would suffer greatly if they — like us — had to endure the pain of believing they were losing their eternal family.

Even though he'd been rebaptized, Josh was in his second year of church discipline, earning his way back to a temple recommend, so he could not yet go into the temple for the wedding. To his credit, he endured the embarrassment of standing outside the temple during the ceremony, to support Matt and Nicole. Standing outside was a sure sign that a returned missionary was unworthy to enter. Every LDS person associated with the wedding and the family would know. But for the couple's sake, he put his own discomfort aside and danced at the reception in Nicole's parents' ward building after the wedding. Like many temple weddings, there would be a second reception sponsored by the groom's parents as well. Matt and Nicole honeymooned and later attended a reception in their honor in our back yard in Utah. Micah and Alicia did not come to Seattle or to Utah for either the wedding or the receptions; the business kept them occupied. Matt seemed disappointed, but as is characteristic of his ability to assume positive intent, he didn't complain.

By the time of the wedding, Matt no longer believed in Mormonism, but if he acknowledged belief in the biblical Jesus, he would be forced to walk away from his academic and music scholarships, and he would not be allowed to graduate from BYU as per the Honor Code Statement in the BYU undergraduate catalog.[31] He was entering his senior year, and he wasn't sure he was ready to sacrifice everything he'd worked so hard for. But after the honeymoon and the reception in our back yard, Nicole suggested they move to Florida. Matt agreed. He stood solidly with the Jesus of the Bible and could not live a lie for another year by pretending to be Mormon at BYU. Nicole had accepted the biblical Jesus too. Knowing how difficult this profession of Christian faith would be for her parents, she was not yet ready to tell them.

The Word had pulled all of us into a bizarre state of transition in which normal affairs swirled around us as we were led somewhere else. But where? Matt and Nicole would figure it out together. No longer trusting my LDS instructions on how to parent, I struggled with how close to get and what role to play with my new daughters-in-law, whom I loved dearly.

Matt and Nicole's sealing was the last time I entered a Mormon temple. Mike attended the temple another nine months as ward redeem-the-dead committee co-chair. I was called and set apart to be the other co-chair, but my Bible reading was transporting me farther and farther from Mormonism. So Mike bore the weight of the callings for both of us. In this role, we were responsible for encouraging others to attend the temple.

My two-year temple recommend was still good for another year and a half. I'd just renewed it the Sunday before Micah was sent home. Good thing. If I had been asked those questions six months later ... Well, it's not that I had any great sins to report, but I might have had trouble with temple recommend question number three—confessing a testimony of the restored gospel of Mormonism. And I had to have the temple recommend in order to keep that coveted job at BYU. What was it Micah had said in that missionary email? "The Lord has a plan and a timing." Maybe he was right. Did I dare hope that God knew me and loved me that much, even timing the events of my conversion?

When I read what Jesus said in John 6:44, "No one can come to me unless the Father who sent me draws them," I knew I was being drawn—sucked, pulled, conveyed, transported. In physics, an event horizon is a boundary beyond which the gravitational pull is so powerful that there is no escape. The object is sucked right in when it reaches this point of no return. As I read the Bible, my appetite for God was growing exponentially. I felt myself drawn to him at an ever-increasing speed. I quit fighting, began to relax, and trusted that this new, bigger God indeed had a plan.

Leashy's Letter

Micah and Alicia were still in Florida managing the Edgewater Hotel. They maintained the building, managed the lessees on the first floor, cleaned the twenty hotel rooms on the second floor, and cooked breakfast for the guests. Meanwhile Matt and Nicole were working in the restaurants on the first floor.

In September, in answer to her father's continuing concerns, Alicia wrote him a frank, sixteen-page letter describing her new-found biblical faith. She sent us a copy. I read Alicia's letter eagerly, hungrily. Never once that I could recall since he returned from his mission, except during the car ride to the airport, had Alicia and

Micah had a conversation with us about what they had learned from reading the Bible. Finally she'd laid it all out in a letter. And as I read her letter, I realized with growing astonishment that after reading the Bible for myself over the last eight months, I knew the same things she did. The Bible's message is undeniably clear. It's simply a matter of choosing whether one believes it or not.

I had so much empathy for Alicia's parents, just as I'd had with Nicole's. Not long ago, Michael and I would have been as shocked and dismayed as they likely were upon receiving this letter.

Gently and lovingly, Alicia had addressed their major concerns.

The first concern was that she and Micah were headed to outer darkness, the Mormon equivalent of the Christian hell. Alicia wrote, "My faith in Christ has brought me to the understanding that He has died for me, and through my faith in Him He has a place prepared for me ... I have taken a serious look at this path, and thanks to the Words of Christ, 'he that believeth in me, though he were dead, yet shall he live: and whosoever liveth and believeth in me shall never die' (John 11:25–26), I have eternal peace knowing my place in Heaven is secure through my faith in the grace of God."

The second concern was that born-again Christians merely want to believe in Christ and feel his love. To a Mormon, this is getting off scot-free. In the Mormon faith, one must obey the laws and ordinances of the gospel, in addition to faith, and that means hard work.

My whole life, I thought I had to work for salvation. Tithe to the church, be faithful and active in the one true church, get married in the temple, receive special saving ordinances, obey the leaders of the church. But I was beginning to realize that because of Christ, we no longer need to work for our salvation, because Christ has secured that for us by his blood. Salvation is so much simpler, yet so much deeper, than what I ever believed. We simply must believe that such an act of mercy and grace is real in our lives, and our lives will reflect our faith. As Alicia wrote, "We are saved by faith alone, not by our works; nothing we can do besides believe will save us. After we recognize that we are saved, then we will do works because we love God and desire to build His Kingdom; but not for our own salvation." I was beginning to understand that I was saved through grace. Period.

The third concern was that Mormons need living prophets to lead them in these latter days. Alicia's reply was that the Bible is enough. "The Bible is the only account of Christ's mortal ministry to the world, and of His teachings of salvation. Don't you think that if God wanted us to know what was most important, He would have told us through the mouth of His own Son, the only Perfect Man to ever walk the earth? Of course He would, and He did. That is why billions of believers love and cherish the words of the New Testament. They are the words of Christ Himself, and are heralded as the most important teachings in the history of humankind. That cannot be changed, nor can the words of Jesus be taken for less than what they are ... So tell me, what could be more important than the words of God through the mouth of His own Son? The words of a 'prophet?' I think not. The word of God through Christ will always stand supreme over all other things that prophets have said, or ever will say."

Finally, Alicia shared how wide and long and high and deep the biblical God's love is for us, and how much she loved him. "I have a love for Christ that is greater now, since I have let Him lead me and show me the truth by words spoken from His own mouth. I have found the truth. Christ is a loving Savior who has made it possible for a personal relationship with Him. He gave us salvation with the gift of the atonement. Christ is all we need; He can be in us. He knows our hearts; He calms our fears and He guides our lives ... Remember that it's not about what we do, but about what He's done; and it's not about who we are, it's about who He is."

"I Am Yours"

Alicia's words sank in, confirming what I was beginning to believe was true. It's not about what I do, my good works, but about what Jesus did for me on the cross. It's not about who I am; it's about who God is. His sovereign will be done. Amen.

I thanked this bigger God for the perceived rejection from Micah and Alicia that tore me apart emotionally and physically that year. Nothing less than the loss of a dearly loved child could have taken me to the place of profound, prolonged suffering where I was ready to meet Jesus. Their rejection hit so hard that I became frantic to know the truth. Desperate, I had devoured Jesus' own words in the Bible. I don't know how else God could have commanded my attention to teach me what I needed to know to be saved. The loss of my child left me hungry, out of my mind, and craving truth.

These things I knew for sure: This new God was big. His love was personal. His words in the Bible were truth. He could save me. I would offer the remainder of my life to him.

In John 5:24, I read, "Very truly I tell you, whoever hears my word and believes him who sent me has eternal life and will not be judged but has crossed over from death to life." Just as I knew I was being drawn, I *knew* I would cross over from death to life. He indeed had a plan and a timing.

One night in October of 2006, Katie, Mike, and I watched the movie *Luther*. As I followed the tale of Martin Luther, the Holy Spirit, the one who leads us into all truth, showed me the parallels between the strength Luther's faith in God gave him and the changes I needed to submit to. The legalism that Luther opposed in the Catholic Church in the sixteenth century had the same root I now needed to oppose in Mormonism. The Scriptures that Luther loved were the Scriptures I believed. The God Luther knew personally was the God I had met. Like Micah in front of his mission president and fellow missionaries, Luther stood before the church leaders and declared, "Unless my errors be proven by Scripture, I cannot and I will not recant. Here I stand. I can do no other. God help me."

I made my decision. I knew from my reading that only a good killing could reap a bountiful harvest. My contented sacred Mormon cow had to be slaughtered. I had to die before new life could begin and bear fruit (John 12:24). I was finally ready. Gathering speed toward the point of no return, I lay facedown on the carpet, arms extended, and cried out to God as Martin Luther had. "I am yours. Save me." Instantly I was sucked over the event horizon.

Part Three

———

STARTING OVER

Chapter 15

THE
EXTRICATION

✒

Ye shall know the truth, and the truth shall make you mad.

— Aldous Huxley

Describing this moment as a sudden sweep across the event horizon may sound a bit dramatic. Honestly, I'm not sure what happened—I'm no theologian—but looking back, it seems that the point of surrender was the beginning of a shift in perspective. I finally understood enough truth to discern I could never go back. But I wasn't sure precisely where I was headed.

In the weeks following my choice to follow the Jesus of the Bible—what most Christians call conversion—not a lot changed in my life outwardly.

I continued to teach and research at BYU, on target to becoming full professor. I was now a managing editor for a professional journal. Mike lived life as usual. Katie settled into her senior year in high school. After graduating from the University of Utah in 2006, Josh got a great job in Salt Lake, bought a townhouse, and took Kisa to live with him. Because the family was questioning its faith, he now felt free to question his, and he put on hold his plan to be reunited with his temple ordinances. His LDS girlfriend moved on to find someone else to marry in a temple. And our newly married sons continued to work at the Edgewater Hotel in Florida.

Though my outer circumstances hadn't changed much, my inner life changed every day. Michael and I were studying the Bible and attending both LDS and evangelical services. Katie eagerly joined us. We settled into the Sunday routine of attending the three-hour block of LDS services and then sprinting by car to an evangelical church by 11:00 a.m. for another hour plus. There were no Christian churches in Alpine, our town of about nine thousand people. Not one. So we got brave enough to attend one we found closer than the church we'd attended sporatically last summer two hours away, a congregation of about thirty on-fire believers fifteen minutes away. There we were introduced to people worshiping God with guitars, vocals, keyboard, and drums—in church! Mormonism allows only the piano and organ with an occasional vocal, and perhaps, with permission, a stringed instrument. Brass and percussion are verboten.

The strangest thing began to occur in that evangelical church. Whatever questions my Bible readings had stirred up that week, Pastor Jim answered in his teaching. I kept thinking it was just coincidence, but it happened week after week. Personal attention from God was awesome!

Christians told me I needed a "birthday," a date when I knew I was saved. Honestly, I didn't know what day in October I crossed over. I didn't know if I fit the mold of mainstream Christianity. All I knew was, I wanted Jesus and I met him in the Bible, so whatever those two things brought into my life, I would accept—no more and no less.

The month of my conversion, October, Matt's wife, Nicole,

developed serious blood clots in her legs, lungs, and pelvis. She was hospitalized in Florida. I flew there and prayed a lot for her. I prayed for her health and also that God would show her his love. Her parents came too, and we stood helplessly around her bed. Matt wouldn't leave her side, and I had to make him eat. When completely exhausted, he folded his six-foot-four-inch frame on a small two-cushion sofa near the elevator close to her room and tried to sleep. Would this bigger new God take Nicole away from us?

After a couple of surgeries, Nicole was released with a swollen leg. It had been a terrifying experience. I didn't know or understand this bigger God. But I was watching him, thinking about him, praying like never before, and beginning to know myself better. And I saw things I never had before.

The Hard Truth

Christians said that the way to become "saved" or "born again" in Jesus is to pray a sinner's prayer. It goes something like this: "I know I am a sinner. I know that as a sinner, I cannot hope to live with God for eternity; I am headed to hell. I need Jesus to save me. Jesus, I surrender my life to you. You are the way, the truth, and the life."

Now, I might have done this instead of saying, "I'm yours. Save me." Except that at the time, I did not know I was a sinner. Sounds unbelievable, I know, but as a Mormon, I was sure that the sin janitor (the Mormon Jesus) kept sweeping my sins away, and I was basically clean.

God knew I was in need of some major humbling. I was about to get the truth I'd asked for. It was brutal, not the "I'm sorry," Mormon-Jesus-niceness I was used to but cold, hard, real truth. In John 9:39, Jesus said, "For judgment I have come into this world, so that the blind will see ..."

It's a good thing we have a loving God, because what he was

about to let me grasp about myself was oh, so hard. I was uglier than I ever imagined. I was a sinner—big-time. After I surrendered to him, the first thing he did was open my eyes to my sins, one by one. I could never have stood them all at once. I'd have begged to die, for sure. This process took more than a year. I'd had my head in the sand, as it were, for a very long time.

Finding Freedom

The first sin God showed me was my pride. It was repulsive. I saw the haughtiness, the confidence, the blindness. I thought I was intelligent, hardworking, righteous, and deserving of reward. I thought I was something when, on my own, I was nothing.

The Mormon idea that I could work my way to goodness blasphemed the God of the Bible. Mormonism gave me a way to measure my righteousness using the LDS measuring stick of laws and ordinances. I thought I was doing fine because I had a temple recommend to show.

The truth is that one sin, one breach of God's Word, made me a loser, a sinner, blemished, and unworthy to stand in the presence of God. Nothing I could *do* would make it right. Only what Jesus did on the cross because of his immense love for me made it right. I was just beginning to absorb this gift.

Soon after my surrender, I was headed to the restroom from my prestigious view-of-Y-Mountain office at BYU (I'd earned my way up from the dark corner office). One of my students with a multicultural scholarship came running up to me and hugged me. "Dr. Wilder, I can't thank you enough for what you have done for me. Because of your letter, my visa has been extended and I can stay in the country! It's all because of you. I'll never be able to thank you enough."

I grinned from ear to ear and hugged her back. "No problem. I was glad to do it." Afterward I stepped into the empty restroom and smiled at myself in the mirror. Thinking I was being generous by including God, I said to him, "Look what *we* did!"

A voice within promptly said back to me, *"We?"*

Oops, I was convicted straightaway. I got it. The student would not have received the visa if God hadn't willed it. He was sovereign over everything. My actions had nothing to do with it. It was my pride that wanted to believe I was powerful and good.

Scripture warned me about this. Philippians 2:3 says, "Do nothing out of selfish ambition or vain conceit." Matthew 23:12 states, "Those who exalt themselves will be humbled." It was something I needed to learn. Again and again, God's word in the Bible was intimately personal. In this fresh new world, he was constantly teaching me.

Soon I got brave enough to tell a group of Christian friends that I was prideful. In the past, I rarely recognized my sin, and if I did, I would *never* confess it to others. Something about doing this was so freeing! I felt a burden lifted. So what if I was prideful? Jesus could help me change. I could name it and not be afraid of it. The ugliness of sin and its guilt and shame could have no hold on me. I was beginning to understand how the truth literally freed me. *Authenticity* became my new favorite word.

Getting Over Myself

God also showed me my selfishness. First Corinthians 13:5 says, "[Love] is not self-seeking." Katie was drama club president her senior year. Her drama teacher told me he chose Katie because actors were selfish and she had the chutzpah to say to her peers, "Get over yourself!" I needed to do just that—get over myself. As Matt got closer to Jesus, he once told me, "Mom, it's not all about you."

But the old nature kept rising up. *What was so wrong with me?* I wondered. Most everyone had always liked me because I worked hard to "choose the right," as Mormons say. This is what I'd been taught to do to please Heavenly Father. At least, I *thought* people liked me. My student evaluations were good. My bosses were usually pleased. My church leaders were pleased; one told me in a blessing, when Mike and I were set apart as redeem-the-dead committee co-chairs, "You are one of the great spirits of the ward." My husband and kids didn't complain — much.

The truth was, as a Mormon, I'd been decidedly self-centered. All day long, I worried, perhaps not consciously but unconsciously, if what *I* was doing was the right thing. I worried whether each decision *I* was making throughout the day was moving *me* closer to being good enough to be accepted by Heavenly Father.

A scripture from the prophet Nephi in the Book of Mormon informs Mormons, "We know that it is by grace that we are saved, after all we can do" (2 Nephi 25:23). Mormonism taught that we are saved only if we have done all we can do first. The purpose of my so-called good works (doing genealogy, attending the temple, fulfilling my callings, tithing, performing acts of service, etc.) was to be recognized by Heavenly Father, to earn brownie points that mount up. I was continuously thinking about *myself*, about how I was being watched by a Father who was testing me to see how I would do. This was not the same God I was watching now, who declared most decidedly, "It is by grace you have been saved, through faith — and this is not from yourselves, it is the gift of God — not by works, so that no one can boast" (Eph. 2:8–9).

Back then, I had the hope that perhaps I could earn the celestial kingdom in the end, if I did absolutely everything I could possibly do for Heavenly Father. How did I know what that was? I listened to and obeyed the Mormon leaders. Then his grace could kick in. The Mormon Church set the rules, and I was responsible for playing a righteous game. My husband, my bishop, my stake president, and my BYU bosses were the refs. If I didn't play according to their terms, I got a whistle and a penalty.

All day long, my thoughts stirred. *Am I doing the right thing? Choose the right, choose the right.* I planned my next move and then the next. My success was up to me. This tension was continually humming, like electric lines, in my ear. I liken this to being my own helicopter parent, forever watching, guiding, directing, corralling, correcting, and keeping sin at bay.

So each Sunday, I took the sacrament to chase away any sin I had failed to prevent, so Heavenly Father would not have to punish me. In the Mormon Church, we used leavened bread and water as the sacrament, the food fed to prisoners throughout all human history. Christ as Rabbi would have used unleavened bread and the fruit of the vine—grape juice or wine—to *free* the prisoners. These parallels were evident to me now that I was in the Word daily. My understanding was heightened.

I read that all my works were filthy rags (Isa. 64:6). All my efforts were like boxing empty air. I did not realize that constantly evaluating my own righteousness was self-centered. I thought I was honoring Christ and Heavenly Father according to the Mormon gospel. But this worldview *is* self-centered, and this is why: I had to constantly think about myself and my behavior to determine where I stood. I was thinking about *me* all the time. Plus, I gave myself credit for being able to stave off sin. This groundless belief was toxic to my soul, blinding me to the many sins I *did* have. With heightened senses, I felt I'd been duped, deceived, and lied to, and it made me mad.

Twistiology

The problem with twisting the truth is, it's no longer the truth. In order to get fully extricated from Mormon boundaries and authority, I needed two things. First, I had to know what *was* true, and second, I had to recognize lies so I could untangle the two. Believe it or not, this took years!

For example, Mormonism took the biblical idea "people sin and need a Savior" and twisted it into "people sin and can be their own savior." Isn't that the same lie Satan told Adam and Eve in the garden when he promised them that if they ate the forbidden fruit, they would "be like God" (Gen. 3:5)?

A part of the temple ritual involves putting on a green apron, which supposedly represents the fig leaves worn by Adam and Eve. In the ceremony, a person portraying Satan gives the order to put on this apron. With my new insight, I wondered, *Why should we obey Satan? And didn't the Bible say that Adam and Eve realized they were naked and made the coverings for themselves* (Gen. 3:7)? *So why is Satan involved in the whole fig leaf thing?*

In the temple endowment ceremony, Eve is esteemed for recognizing that she needed to eat the fruit so human beings could know all things and begin the great progression to godhood. I was taught in the Mormon Church that the fall was a fall upward. But in the Bible, God cursed Adam and Eve for the *sin* of eating the fruit and banished them from the Garden of Eden (Gen. 3:14–24). The esteem of *felix culpa* (happy fall) resides not in Eve but in the greatness of the one who rescues us from the fall, Jesus.

In Mormonism, every good Mormon has the potential to become a god. Josh's patriarchal blessing said, "Those who receive you and the message you bring will one day recognize you as a Savior on Mt. Zion." Mormonism declared that my own son would be recognized as a savior! How many Saviors are there, really? The Bible points to just one: Jesus.

In Mormonism, Jesus' atonement allows you to be resurrected, but if you want to live with Jesus and Heavenly Father in the hereafter, you must work your way there. The Bible says that only God's grace can save us (Eph. 2:8–9).

Mormonism takes elements of truth and twists them into something very confusing. As the old saying goes, "Round and round and round we go, where we stop, nobody knows." Because Book of Mormon doctrine often conflicts with Doctrine and Covenants doctrine, Mormon scriptures exist to argue both sides of some theological issues. But the Bible was my standard of truth now. I wanted to be disentangled. Never again would I allow myself to follow this twistiology of man: the Book of Mormon, the Pearl of Great Price, and the Doctrine and the Covenants. How did I ever believe this stuff?

Drinking Poison

During high school, Katie attended Mormon seminary as one of her classes. On the weekends, she was busy reciting Shakespeare, dating, and delighting audiences in her role as the elderly Martha in *Arsenic and Old Lace.* Her model-thin frame, bent-in-half walk, trembling hands, large expressive eyes, and squeaky voice had audiences roaring.

Abby: "The man died because he drank some wine with poison in it."

Martha: "Elderberry wine."

Mortimer: "How did the poison get in the wine?"

Martha: "Oh, we put it in the wine 'cause it's less noticeable. When it's in tea, it has a distinct odor."

Now as I look back, I have to roar at the humor of God. There in front of me night after night onstage were two little old sisters, Abby and Martha, sweet elderly women in shawls whom anyone would trust. Routinely, carefully, they selected a lonely old gentleman with no family and invited him to their home for a glass of wine—elderberry wine—laced with arsenic. Friendly conversation ensued until the unsuspecting gentleman keeled over dead. The old ladies dragged his heavy body into hiding until their deranged nephew, Teddy, hauled the body downstairs for a burial. The ladies, thinking they were putting lonely old men out of their misery, conducted a nice funeral as they trifled politely over whether this gentleman was number eleven or number twelve.

The deaths resulted from the gentlemen's innocence, their *lack of knowledge*. They drank something they thought was good for them, but it was laced with poison. The people who offered it were *so nice*.

How many times and in how many ways did God show me, right in front of my face, the answer to my question about my "awful situation"? The truth was in Micah's emails, in the Word of God, in Scripture-chaining with Matt and Nicole, in Alicia's letter, in dreams, in *Arsenic and Old Lace*, and in the Mormon culture all around me. Although I'd suspected it earlier, once I crossed over, I saw clearly that the spiritual waters I drank from in the Mormon Church were not just a little murky; they were poison. Not only did they not satisfy; they were death. Mormonism was not just twisted; it deceived.

Matt Untangles the Truth

In order to work out my salvation after accepting Jesus (Phil. 2:12), I had to untangle the lies of Mormonism from the truths of the Bible. Matt too was going through this process of disentanglement. After he and Nicole got married and moved to Florida, they went to the Mormon Church once or twice but then started attending the church where Micah and Alicia had married. As he reflects back on that process now, Matt says, "I prefer to dwell on the positive aspects that brought me closer to Christ rather than the negative things that drew me away from Mormonism. But for me to fully come to Christ, I first had to realize and accept that I had been deceived. As I became open to the possibility that the LDS Church wasn't right about everything, I started seeing things in the church organization that I was blinded to before. I was reading in the Gospels about the pharisaical 'woes' (Matt. 23), and then my eyes were opened to how the woes applied to the Mormon Church."

The Pharisees were teachers of the law, just as the Mormon priesthood emphasized law. These are a few of the accusations Jesus made to the Pharisees: "You shut the door of the kingdom of heaven in people's faces. You yourselves do not enter, nor will you let those enter who are trying to." And, "You travel over land and sea to win a single convert, and when you have succeeded, you make them twice as much a child of hell as you are." Also, "On the outside you appear to people as righteous but on the inside you are full of hypocrisy and wickedness" (Matt. 23:13–15, 28).

Matt noticed in LDS Church meetings that Jesus wasn't the central focus. A year earlier (November 2005), Micah had tried to tell us in an email from the mission field that there was more Joseph Smith than Jesus Christ in Mormon meetings. "No," I wrote back. "It just seems that way because this is the two hundredth anniversary of Smith's birth and we are focusing on him this year." The very next week, on the cover of our church magazine, the *Ensign*, was a picture of Joseph Smith instead of Jesus Christ at Christmas. No baby Jesus in a manger?

Matt read in the Bible that you can recognize a false prophet by his fruit. With that in mind, he took time to examine the teachings and actions of past LDS prophets, in order to see their fruit. He discovered many strange and diverse doctrines previously hidden from him, as well as historical accounts that were very disturbing. Matt used to rationalize away anything negative about past LDS teachings and history, because his mindset was to defend the LDS Church. When he started to seek truth, he took a more neutral approach, and he began to see how unbiblical the teachings of past Mormon prophets were.

Without going into too much detail, there are a few doctrines that concerned him in light of the biblical warning "Do not
be carried away by all kinds of strange teachings" (Heb. 13:9).
Matt discovered the second prophet Brigham Young's teachings
on "blood atonement"—the teaching that a person who committed an unforgiveable sin might have to allow his own blood to be
spilled in order to be saved. Christ's blood was not enough.

Brother Brigham also taught the Adam-god theory—Adam is
our god, while other planets have other gods. Matt realized that
the concept that God was once a man and that God has a God
who has a God was another strange doctrine. Even the Word of
Wisdom health code seemed unbiblical as a commandment when
he read Bible verses such as, "The kingdom of God is not a matter
of eating and drinking, but of righteousness, peace and joy in the
Holy Spirit" (Rom. 14:17). And Jesus said that it is not what goes
into a person but what comes out of a person that defiles him or
her (Mark 7:14–16).

One day Matt was reading in the history of the LDS Church
and stumbled across a quote that outright terrified him—especially since it came from the LDS Church's own accounts. This
quote itself was enough for him to know that Joseph Smith was
a false prophet: "I have more to boast of than any man had. I am
the only man who has ever been able to keep a whole church
together since the days of Adam. A large majority of the whole
have stood by me. Neither Paul, John, Peter, nor Jesus ever did it.
I boast that no man ever did such a work as I."[32]

Joseph Smith was boasting that he was able to do something—by himself—beyond what Jesus Christ had been able
to do. Mormonism gave glory to Joseph Smith, a man, instead of
to God.[33]

Every work of a Christian comes through the power of God.
Jesus himself always gave glory to the Father. The even greater

works that Jesus promised in the Word that believers would do come from God (John 14:12), never oneself. When Joseph Smith proclaimed his own work as his and not that of Jesus, he was acknowledging that he was not in Christ and the biblical Christ was not in him. Matt could see that this line of thinking had fed the pride monster (just as the doctrine of polygamy had fed the lust monster) in many subsequent Mormon leaders.

Other strange doctrines that started to creep under Matt's skin were the doctrines of the temple and of "work for the dead." Genealogy work put one's focus on the dead instead of on the living. Matt remembered hearing accounts in Sunday school of LDS prophets seeing dead spirits (like the founding fathers of America that supposedly appeared to Prophet Wilford Woodruff) in the temple. In church he heard a family history expert share an experience in which her deceased great-great-grandfather led her with his voice to his own grave so that she could retrieve the necessary information about his life that would make it possible to save him in the temple.

Matt knew people who sought out spirits of the dead to see, hear, or feel so they could give an account of them. With that in mind, he was remembering things Jesus had said, such as, "Let the dead bury their own dead" (Luke 9:60). And he stumbled across biblical passages such as Paul's instruction to Timothy: "As I urged you when I went into Macedonia, stay there in Ephesus so that you may command certain people not to teach false doctrines any longer or to devote themselves to myths and endless genealogies. Such things promote controversial speculations rather than advancing God's work—which is by faith" (1 Tim. 1:3–4).

Matt was also beginning to realize how deceit played a role in the LDS Church. We were, for example, taught that the Book of Mormon contained the fullness of the gospel. Yet many of the temple recommend questions sprang from teachings from other sources—like the D&C. When Matt was a missionary, he and his co-missionaries did not give prospective members a D&C to study and accept. They gave them only a Book of Mormon. He understood that the less people knew about the "deep doctrines" (strange and diverse teachings) of the LDS Church, the better chance the missionaries had of baptizing them. So Matt recognized deceit even in the way the LDS gospel was presented to others. The Mormon gospel was masked to appear as Christian as possible.

One day in church, the ward was singing "Praise to the Man." This is the song revering the name of Joseph Smith. Matt realized that he really should be singing praises to Jesus. He started to see that the LDS Church liked to honor men, and he wondered why. It made sense when he discovered that its leaders have been honoring the leaders of their organization from the beginning. Brigham Young said, "I honor and revere the name of Joseph Smith. I delight to hear it; I love it. I love his doctrine."[34] Smith once told Young and "the twelve" that "the good love me, weak and humble as I am, and the wicked hate me."[35]

After this research and months of reading the Bible, Matt no longer believed that the LDS Church was what it claimed to be. He believed that salvation came through Jesus, and not through any organization. In other words, that salvation exists outside of human-made organizations but not outside of Christ. Focusing just on what Jesus taught in the Gospels filled him spiritually. And the gospel began to make so much more sense to him. It seemed so simple.

"You believe in Jesus, he baptizes you in the Holy Spirit, and then you live for him," he told me.

Jesus' Gospel of Grace

Matt was right. The true gospel *is* simple. Salvation exists outside of human-made organizations, but not outside of Jesus. And, as Matt was discovering, the biblical Jesus imparts his gospel of grace to the poor. "Listen, my dear brothers and sisters: Has not God chosen those who are poor in the eyes of the world to be rich in faith and to inherit the kingdom he promised those who love him?" (James 2:5).

During Matt's mission to Denmark, he gained a special sensitivity for the poor. Near their missionary apartment lived a fragile old man, who was often on the street. He was weak, disabled, and could barely get around. Without help, it could take this man nearly an hour to walk the 150 meters from his second-story apartment to the shopping center, and then another hour to return with the bags. He forced his debilitated body forward at the pace of a snail, resting after a few feet—all the while trying to keep a grip on his shopping bags. Although hundreds of people passed him, no one stopped to help, and he didn't ask for or expect it.

With permission from the frail gentleman, Matt and his fellow missionary took his bags. Standing on either side of the man, they helped him walk. In order to make progress, they practically had to bear the weight of his entire body. They reached the apartment building and helped him struggle up the steps, enduring his body odor and bad breath as he gasped for air. Matt remembers opening the door to his apartment. "Inside was the most putrid and rank odor I had ever smelled. He directed us toward a chair near a window in his room on the far end of the apartment. When we entered his room, the smell got worse, and I began gagging and decided to hold my breath in order to prevent myself from throwing up. We hurried to set him in the chair and tried not to appear sickened by the environment. We asked if we could do anything else for him, and he said no. It seemed that he wanted to be left alone. So we left. Then I stood outside his apartment contemplating the horrible plight of that poor old man."

After that first time, Matt and his friend visited the old man routinely. One day, exhausted and with a lot to get done, Matt and his companion spotted the man struggling up the street. He saw them and looked pleadingly at them, wanting help. Matt and his companion hurried into the shopping center to avoid being inconvenienced, because it was their missionary preparation day. Matt's brain rationalized that he had worked so hard the other six days of the week, he deserved one day to relax and do what *he* wanted to do.

Even now, Matt carries with him the image of that old, incapacitated man looking to him with hope, only to be rejected. Matt says, "It still breaks my heart when I think about how I neglected to help a needy old man in the street one day." This awakened in him a desire to offer the gospel to the poor who need Jesus, a desire that flourished as he broke away from Mormonism and embraced the God of grace.

Beginning to Hear

One night during this time of change, I had a dream. I was standing in the swift current of a shallow river. As I looked up, the sun blinded me and I heard someone say, "You're beginning to hear, but you still don't see very well yet."

Outside of the real Christ, I had been deaf and blind. "The god of this age has blinded the minds of unbelievers, so that they cannot see the light of the gospel that displays the glory of Christ, who is the image of God" (2 Cor. 4:4). But my ears were being opened, and soon my eyes would be as well. Thanks to Jesus, "the blind receive sight, the lame walk, those who have leprosy are cleansed, the deaf hear, the dead are raised, and the good news is proclaimed to the poor" (Matt. 11:5).

Maybe God heals some new believers of blindness and deafness all at once. For me, having been so entangled with false teachings for so long — exactly thirty years — it was taking a long time.

Even as I faced my pride and selfishness, I was reluctant to commit to God one hundred percent. Sometimes I would rather be my own god, as in Mormonism, than trust him. I struggled with a judgmental spirit and anger — especially anger that I'd been deceived and had wasted my life teaching our kids untruths. I still had a knack for sensationalizing, exaggerating things to stir up peoples' excitement. (That went with the professor territory.) My mind needed to be renewed, so that truth replaced the lies and incorrect thinking.

As I read the Word, I sensed some progress. Every day was new at this juncture. After my surrender to Jesus in the midst of extrication just before Thanksgiving 2006, Micah and Alicia announced that they were expecting our first grandchild, a tremendous gift of grace. In December, Alicia traveled to Utah for a baby shower her mother gave their son-to-be. Alicia was encouraged to see some further growth the Word had stirred in Mike and me. Still, Mike was fulfilling his temple calling, wearing his garments, and attending both LDS and the evangelical church. But we were both *devouring* the Bible. Even as I wrestled with my own weaknesses, I was hopeful. I couldn't wait to wake up each morning and see what Jesus would do next.

CHAPTER 16

BIGGIE-SIZE YOUR GOD

⚜

They were all amazed at the greatness of God.

— LUKE 9:43

When Micah was on his mission in Florida, he tried to convert anyone he met to Mormonism, including Christian pastors. One day when the missionaries were out on bikes, Micah's companion needed a restroom, and they tooled into what they thought was an old warehouse to find one. The warehouse turned out to be a church, the Faith and Power Worship Center, with an imposing black pastor, Matthew Shaw, a former football player. This was the first of two pastors that Micah tried to convert to the Mormon gospel.

Pastor Shaw listened patiently to the LDS spiel. Then he opened a Bible and showed Micah and his fellow missionary where Mormonism conflicted with the gospel Jesus taught. He said, "Elder Wilder, you are like Saul, trying to destroy the church of God. One day you will be like Paul, a great minister of the Word of God."[36] Pastor Shaw held Micah in a great bear hug when they parted, and prayed aloud that the spirit of blindness be broken over this young man.

Fast-forward four years. Micah and four companions have formed a Christian band, Adam's Road, and together they are ministering God's Word—just as Pastor Shaw declared. One day, the young men in the Adam's Road ministry helped a friend set up electronics for a Christian band event, Worship under the Stars. Jonathan, a pastor's son and one of the logistics coordinators, was in the sound booth enjoying the event with Micah toward the end of the evening. When a pastor took the stage and began appealing to anyone in the audience of thousands to accept Jesus as Savior, Micah, looking astonished, tapped Jonathan on the shoulder and asked, "Do you know the man onstage?" Jonathan answered, "Sure, that's my dad. His church is sponsoring this event." Grinning, Micah told Jonathan he'd met his father before. Micah told him the story, and Jonathan realized that, amazingly, the Mormon missionary his father had said he'd prayed over years ago was now the Christian right in front of him.

Jonathan urged Micah to go with him down to the stage. Compliant, he went. There ensued a mighty reunion—black and white, older and younger, broader and thinner, pastor and baby Christian—right there in plain view of thousands, reminiscent of what it must be like to meet our Christian brothers and sisters in heaven. Overcome, arm around Micah, Pastor Shaw shared the powerful testimony of what the seed of God's Word had accomplished, and many accepted Jesus that night!

This instance of grace belonged to Micah Wilder and to Matthew Shaw, but it blessed many others in its wake, including me. When we met the Shaws, Matthew and his wife, Pam, told us their own conversion stories. To my surprise, I started crying. It hit me that if they had not accepted Jesus, Matthew would not have been in the position to challenge and pray for Micah. Then the second pastor who challenged Micah to read the Bible as a child might not have been able to water the seed Pastor Shaw had planted, and then Micah would not have been able to challenge us. What an intricate plan!

As I began to know this bigger God, such incidents increased exponentially. The biblical God began painting a landscape so beautiful, it would one day take my breath away. At the start, though, all I could see was disconnected splashes on a canvas. I struggled between reservation ("Can he really do that?") and exhilaration ("I know that was you!").

I think what is hard for so many of us is not just to believe *in* Jesus but also to believe *Jesus*. Everything he says is true. Believing his Word in the Bible opens a whole new world.

"You did not choose me, but I chose you and appointed you so that you might go and bear fruit—fruit that will last—and so that whatever you ask in my name the Father will give you" (John 15:16). I couldn't imagine a love so great from a Father so gifted. I had to keep shutting my gaping mouth.

Adam's Road

At the end of October 2006, just after I gave my life to Jesus, I was back in Florida to visit the two couples living and working at the hotel. In the ten months since Micah ended his mission, the band that he seemed to know would come together *had* come together. The band for Jesus now consisted of Micah and Matt Wilder, Joseph Warren, Steve Kay, and Jay Graham, all former Mormons. All but Jay had served LDS missions—Micah, Joseph, and Steve in Orlando and Matt in Denmark.

These five young men had dedicated their lives—until the grave, they said—to teaching others about the biblical Jesus through music directly from the Word. They christened the band Adam's Road, to symbolize the road of every man and woman to

God. God had walked beside each member of the band, taking them out of Mormonism and down the road to the biblical Jesus. And each band member had a train-stopping testimony to tell.

Jay Graham

I knew Jay from when we first visited Micah and Alicia at the Edgewater. Dark-haired Jay was the only band member under six feet two inches. He was a little older than the others, serious, and his road to Jesus was dramatic.

In 2001, at his twenty-third birthday dinner, Jay announced to his Christian parents, who'd been fervently praying for him, that he'd given up on God. He conceded defeat to the drug and alcohol addiction he'd wrestled with for seven years. He would never be free from his dungeon.

Yet this was when God began drawing Jay to him. Three days after Jay renounced his faith, a Christian friend shared the love of God with him. This opened his eyes to the fact that God had a plan for him and that only by submitting his will to the will of God could he be freed from his bondage. Later, alone on his bed, contemplating a life without hope, he cried out to God one more time. He could not, in his own strength, conquer his demons. He was at the end of himself. He *did* need God.

At that moment, Jay dedicated his life to serving God. His torment disappeared. Through his bedroom window, Jay saw an ugly black cloud recede from him, gathering speed. He remembered that his friend had shared a Scripture with him from the book of Matthew (12:43–45), and he scrambled to read it again: "When an impure spirit comes out of a person, it goes through arid places seeking rest and does not find it. Then it says, 'I will return to the house I left.' When it arrives, it finds the house unoccupied, swept clean and put in order. Then it goes and takes with it seven other spirits more wicked than itself, and they go in and live there. And the final condition of that person is worse than the first."

Recognizing that this was his story, Jay knew his house had just been swept clean, and he didn't want the ugliness to return—ever. But he did not know how to serve Jesus. While he was searching for a church to attend, Mormon missionaries came into his life. He joined the Mormon Church, thinking it was a Christian organization. Three years after his conversion to Mormonism, Jay was working at the hotel when he met Elder Micah Wilder, who was frequenting the hotel restaurants for the free meals. Micah was devouring the Bible as well as the hotel food, and with Jay's Christian friend, he urged Jay to read the New Testament. When Jay did, his eyes were opened to the errors in Mormonism, and he chose to stay with the Bible and Jesus. Jay just happened to play the guitar, to write songs, and to sing.

Steve Kay

Originally from Seattle, Steve served a mission in Orlando. Early in his mission, he became good friends with Jay, who had recently joined the Mormon Church. At the time, missionaries serving in the Orlando mission could visit the local theme parks for one day during their last week as missionaries. Steve was serving several hours south of Orlando, so after a full day at the parks, he spent the night at Micah's apartment close by, so he wouldn't be out too late. He'd received special permission from the mission president to stay out to watch the fireworks. Reaching Micah's apartment after the usual curfew, he had a brief encounter with a self-righteous, grumpy Micah, who was ready for bed and wondering why Steve was out late.

Micah had recommended to the hotel owner and to his brother Matt that Matt work at the Edgewater in Florida the same summer Steve was working there (2005). Steve had completed his two-year mission in 2004. Hotel employees with musical talents occasionally jammed a Mormon-style music. That fall, Matt and Steve became roommates back at BYU. Mike and I knew Steve from the times he, with a different girl each time (on the hunt for his future wife), showed up for Sunday dinner at our house in Utah.

Steve started as a pre-med major at BYU, then switched to a music media major. He sang in concert choir. He was an intelligent, agreeable young man with dimpled smile and chin who believed sincerely in the Mormon faith. His LDS father had died of colon cancer when he was in high school. That event generated a crisis of faith for him in 1999, and he chose to cling to Mormonism, wanting to live with his father again in their eternal, temple-sealed family in heaven. Steve took a New Testament course at BYU and fancied himself knowledgeable about the Bible.

The summer of 2006, after his and Matt's junior year in college and after Micah's mission, Steve noticed that Micah, Matt, and Jay weren't attending the Mormon Church anymore. He asked about it, and the others challenged him to read the New Testament as a child would.

Steve was hesitant to believe he could learn anything new, but eventually he took the challenge, asking Heavenly Father to show him the truth. Lo and behold, when he read the Bible like a child open to truth, he found it (a repeated theme among the band members). It seemed to be a whole new book with a brand-new message. He was reading the same verses he'd read before, but suddenly — with his blindness lifted — his eyes saw the truth that had been hiding in those verses all along. Steve, who played bass, was excited to talk about his faith. He, like Matt, chose not to return to BYU that fall. They worked at the hotel, devoured the Word, composed music, practiced together, and played gigs. Incredible. Changes were happening at breakneck speed!

Joseph Warren

Joseph, named after Joseph Smith, grew up in quaint Kaysville, Utah, in a very strong LDS family. Life was saturated with the Mormon gospel. Joseph served his mission in the Orlando area with Micah and was drawn to the nonjudgmental love he felt in him. They quickly became close friends. Micah offered Joseph the challenge he had received from the second pastor he tried to convert: "Read the Bible as a child." Because of the love Joseph had for Micah, he picked up the gauntlet. In the New Testament, Joseph recognized the gospel of grace for the first time.

As missionaries in suits and badges, Joseph and Micah spent hours reading and discussing the Bible. Joseph was hungry for the Word, and he asked God to show him the truth. When the young men knocked on doors or instructed their potential LDS converts, they increasingly taught more about the love of the Jesus they had met in the Bible and less about the Mormon Church being the only true church. They both sensed a positive change, but they did not yet know they were headed out of Mormonism.

The book of Hebrews was key for Joseph. It dawned on him that the Mormon Church was built on a foundation of one modern-day prophet who spoke for God and on priesthood, temples, and high priests. But each of these was fulfilled in Jesus and no longer had a function in faith.

Then came the day when he heard Micah, unashamed of the biblical Jesus, boldly bear a Christian testimony to about sixty Mormon missionaries. One of the band's first songs, "I Would Die for You," stemmed from Joseph's surefire personal touch from God that day. Soon God planted in him a desire to use his musical talents to help others know Jesus. With bright eyes, light hair, and a friendly demeanor, Joseph Warren is now passionate about Jesus and the Word. Joey plays the guitar and the mandolin and sings.

-≍-

As I pondered the formation of the band, yet another miracle, I remembered the sincere prayer I had prayed as a little girl—that I would make music that honored God. Was I watching the answer to that prayer through my sons? It didn't really matter, because it was less and less about me these days and more and more about the work of Jesus, except that I felt God was showing me many intricate, personal connections, as if his hand were in our lives and had been all along. I watched the guys perform at the Winter Garden Music Fest on a warm Florida night and was awestruck, seeing what this bigger God was capable of as he added paint to the canvas.

Joyous Baptisms

During my visit to the Edgewater late that October, Joey talked about his faith relentlessly as he cleaned hotel rooms and I put fresh sheets on the beds. I listened intently. I knew some of what he knew, but I was also absorbing truth.

Listening to Joey and Steve was easier than asking Micah my endless questions. Micah always answered my queries from the Word with rich wisdom and pointed me to Scriptures to read, but he usually didn't offer new information.

I eventually figured out that Micah understood that a person's relationship with God will be more solid the more that person turns to God and to his Word rather than relying on the testimony of others. I sometimes asked Alicia or Matt or Nicole about the biblical gospel. Matt didn't talk much—he never has, although he has a hilarious sense of humor and perceptive insights when he does—but he sometimes let me read his journal. And of course I asked questions of the Christians back in Utah, but many of them in Pastor Jim's church had never been Mormon, and that made it hard to communicate. So talking to Steve and Joseph was a breath of fresh air, with both of them so eager to share the Word.

I was thrilled, therefore, when God blessed me on that visit by allowing me to experience the rebaptisms of both Steve and Joseph. The baptisms took place at Kelly Park in the most beautiful, clear spring of living water I had ever seen. Florida foliage in brilliant colors was all around us, even reflected in the water with the fish and turtles. Plants in shades of deep greens with red, yellow, and purple flowers hung nearby, above a carpet of green grass and sand. I couldn't believe that God just happened to arrange the baptisms when I was there. The Dancer of grace seemed to be always with me now since the surrender. My senses were heightened, and this Christian thing was rising like a river, becoming a flood.

Morning by Morning

When I took the employment aptitude and interest test at the end of high school, it said my number one ability was visual-spatial, that I could see geometrically and fit patterns together. The number one career choice for me, the test concluded, was auto mechanics.

I thought the test was inaccurate, because I'm very auditory. I can close my eyes during a lecture and listen, organize my audio notes, replay, and remember what was said. I even talk to myself for auditory input or replay. It helps me remember. I think in words, not pictures. (Soon after Mike and I were married, it was obvious that he *did* think in visuals. This was something we had to contend with when we attempted to communicate.)

Well, now that I had given my life to Jesus and all things were being made new, an extraordinary thing happened: God seemed to be communicating with me in visuals, especially dreams, in addition to the voice inside me. It was as if my life had greater dimension, IMAX 3D and Dolby Digital surround sound. I developed an interest in photography because I *saw* things I hadn't before. It scared me at first. I wasn't sure it was biblical. Using the Bible as my standard, I was feverishly sorting truth from error, pitching Mormon lies and deceit as quickly as I spotted them. Was this a lie or the truth? From God or not? Then I read Acts 2:17–18, in which Peter quoted the prophet Joel, saying, "In the last days, God says, I will pour out my Spirit on all people. Your sons and daughters will prophesy, your young men will see visions, your old men will dream dreams. Even on my servants, both men and women, I will pour out my Spirit in those days, and they will prophesy."

So the dreams, the heightened senses—I could be experiencing an outpouring of God's Spirit. I stumbled on Isaiah 50:4, which says, "He wakens me morning by morning, wakens my ear to listen like one being instructed." Maybe I wasn't going crazy. Perhaps the Holy Spirit was teaching me in the early morning through an impression or a voice in my mind. I trusted no feelings anymore, because we relied on them exclusively in Mormonism, and they had led us astray. If I believed the Bible, then dreams, visions, an inner voice, and prophecy from fellow believers were all worthy of consideration, as long as the message did not contradict the Word. I had such a hunger to know Jesus.

After the baptisms, at home in Utah, I had one of those IMAX 3D dreams. It was so real. I felt the breeze, smelled the sea, the sand, the plants, saw in Technicolor, and knew the air temperature.

I was staying in a home with a tiled floor and first-floor pillars, open to the air on all sides. It was in a warm climate, maybe near the ocean, and surrounded by gardens. Others were there too.

We were ushered upstairs one at a time to see someone—Jesus. When it was my turn, I went up the narrow stairs and sat down opposite him, a rough wooden table in between. I could not look up, I was so overwhelmed to be in his presence. There was silence for a long time. When I finally got the courage to glance up, I saw smiling eyes and a Jewish nose on a face so kind, exuding love for me. Words were not necessary. It was a powerful connection, a palpable love. Someone could love me like this? His tenderness washed over me. I stayed in this home for some time and got to walk through the gardens and visit him in the upper room. I rested and experienced a peace I'd never known before.

Some Christians tell me they have never experienced God's communication in the realms of dreams and inner voices. God also talks to me through other members of the body of Christ, through my circumstances, and most important, through Scriptures that jump out to me in his Word. Mike and I learned from Henry Blackaby's Bible study *Experiencing God*[37] that all these ways of communicating with God have scriptural support. Going through that study with other Christians helped me know what to trust—and to believe I wasn't crazy.

It is quite possible to be saved without having such supernatural experiences. I know others who accepted the biblical Jesus more readily than I did. I believe God had to make my experiences with him so dramatic because I was inherently stubborn and needed the supernatural in order to get it. This is a big God, and he works with each person according to the way he can best reach us.

Here I Stand: Nicole

Two days before Matt and Nicole got married in the Seattle Temple, several temple-endowed relatives, Matt, and I accompanied her to the temple to receive her endowments. Although pretty sure then that Mormonism was a false faith, she wanted to experience the temple endowment before making her final decision for the biblical Christ. During that endowment ceremony, she had her answer. The endowment solidified in her mind that the Mormon Church simply was not true. The only reason why she went ahead with a temple marriage was that she was afraid of disappointing her parents. Nicole was on her way to becoming a biblical Christian, but she did not consider herself a Christian at the time, because she didn't fully understand what it meant to take up her cross and follow Jesus.

When her only brother married in the temple in December of 2006, four months after her own temple wedding, the decision about whether to attend was heavy on her heart. Nicole debated whether to tell her parents the truth about her beliefs before the wedding. Katie, Mike, and I saw her just before the big day, and she was miserable. Should she upset her parents and extended family right before her brother's wedding? Should she choose not to go, but not tell them why? Or should she put on the happy Mormon face and go, be there for her family, but step into a place they considered holy and sacred, which—if they knew what she now believed—she would be unworthy in their eyes to enter? She chose the latter. She still had more fear of what her parents thought than trust in this new God she was coming to know.

Shortly after her brother's wedding, Nicole finally decided to tell her parents the truth. She told Matt she could not consider herself a true Christian if she was unable to put God above her parents, live for him, and believe that he is enough. She decided to trust Jesus and to declare that she was not ashamed of his gospel. She and Matt carefully composed a letter explaining their beliefs and read it to her mother and father over the phone. Her parents were in complete shock. I had great sympathy for what they would suffer.

Wearing the Cross

Katie was a senior in high school and not socializing much anymore. Most often, she could be found in her room spending time with Jesus and consuming the Word. Katie was passionate for Jesus. She used to leave her light on next to the bed all night long to remind her of the Light of the World (and to help her drive her night fears away). Katie had had nightmares ever since she could remember.

Before Christmas, Michael and I shopped for crosses for Katie and me. Hers would be a surprise. With my new understanding of what Jesus' love for me had done on the cross, I wanted one too. The jewelry stores in the mall near Provo did not display them publicly, so as not to offend Mormons, but we were allowed to go into the back room and see them. I was drawn to one with red in the middle, like a single drop of blood. We bought Katie a small silver one that resembled the old rugged cross.

When I put on the cross that crisp Christmas morning in 2006, I removed my temple garments and never put them on again. I was fully committed to this new Jesus. I stopped going to the Mormon Church, stopped paying my tithe to the Mormon Church, and hid my cross beneath my clothes at work. If I had showed the cross openly, I'd have lost my temple recommend and my job. I wasn't quite ready to go public yet.

Katie wasn't either. She was stuck in a high school where almost everyone was Mormon. She knew well the LDS Church's stance on the symbol of the cross. It was *not* accepted. If she decided to wear her cross in public, she could be in trouble with the Mormon Church. She said, "As a child, I'd been programmed to think that if I went against the rules and did something wrong, there had to be a punishment. I had no idea what could happen to me if someone important in my church saw me wearing a cross."

As the Spirit taught her more and more from the Word,

though, she became more confident in her relationship with Jesus and began to wear the cross openly. In Mormon country, that was a huge statement, an offense.

The first time Katie saw someone else in Utah wear a cross was at a drama competition. Once a year, thousands of high school students from across the West converge in Cedar City, Utah, for a Shakespearean competition on the campus of Southern Utah University. Katie had just performed a monologue. She and her friends stepped outside into a sea of students moving across campus. Suddenly her eye caught something. A boy about her age was wearing a cross! He caught a glimpse of her cross too and grinned as if they were the only two people in the world who knew Jesus. It was one of those moments in life that happens in slow motion, crowd rushing by. She later told me, "I'll never forget the power of the Spirit that two complete strangers shared simply because we wore the cross of our Lord Christ Jesus."

At school, everybody went to seminary class and carried quads (all four LDS scriptures—the Holy Bible, the Book of Mormon, the Doctrine and Covenants, and the Pearl of Great Price—bound together in one tall book). Katie wore the cross unapologetically to class. One day, she walked into the seminary building across the parking lot from her high school. Her favorite seminary teacher was in the hallway. Now, Katie was the good Mormon girl who sat in the front row and answered all of his questions, so he liked her a lot. When he saw Katie enter the doors, he smiled and waved a greeting.

As she got closer, his demeanor changed. He was staring at her cross with wide, almost frightened eyes, as if he'd seen a ghost. But many Mormons sweep what they are uncertain of or uncomfortable with under the rug. No questions, just a moment of discomfort, then back to Happy Valley, where no one has concerns and no one wears a cross. This was how most of Katie's encounters with Mormon leaders and even close friends went—a flash of realization and horror, then the pretense that everything was fine.

The ironic thing to her was that nobody addressed her cross or her changes. Even her best friend never batted an eye. Didn't anyone care enough to say something if they thought she was slipping away? This is the same question I have asked many times about the Christians who watched me embrace Mormonism and never said a word.

Only once did someone say something to Katie about her cross. A drama friend knew she was Mormon, but at one point she looked at Katie's cross, perplexed, and asked, "Are you Catholic?"

Mike kept wearing his temple garments, not yet ready for a cross. In fulfilling our joint calling at church without me, he continued to accompany ward members to the temple and to teach the temple prep class. He was paranoid that I'd get in trouble for not paying my tithe at the end of the year and lose my job, so he went into the usual tithing settlement with the bishop for me and paid my tithe. No one at church appeared to notice that anything was amiss. For the next seven months, none of our leaders said anything to Mike or to me about my absence. Perhaps the Dancer of grace had shut their eyes, or the culture that doesn't offend was working overtime.

Michael and I kept reading the Bible in bed at night and discussing what we read. Mike was making the steady progress commensurate with his step-by-step, logical brain. He was trained as a mathematician, accountant, and technologist. I didn't worry about him. I knew he'd get there, and when the full import dawned on him, it would be not an emotional decision but a rational one.

Lost and Found at BYU

I had been moved to tears the first time I heard a preacher explain the cross. That's why I covenanted with Christ to wear it instead of the Mormon garments. I had gained a strong witness of the power of the blood of Christ and had read about the saving blood in the New Testament.

During this time of rapid learning, I kept having vivid dreams. One night, in a dream, I saw my daughter being spattered with blood. Soon after, I read the section in Exodus 24:8 where Moses sprinkled blood on the people to signify the covenant God had made with them. Notice I read the verse *after* the dream, not before, and I did not go looking for verses to corroborate the dream. I didn't remember ever reading that passage before, and if I had, it had been years ago. Strange and supernatural things were happening to me as I began to not just believe in Jesus but also believe his words.

I used to wear the cross on a necklace under my clothes at BYU, but I didn't have enough high-necked clothes to wear it every day. On the days my cross might show, I put it in my pocket and reached for it often. One day when I reached for it, it was gone! I assumed it fell out of my pocket when I went to the rest-room. I dashed across the hall to find it—but no cross. This was a covenant with God that I couldn't ignore. I strode across campus to the lost and found, gave the nice female student working there my faculty ID, and asked her to look for a cross on a necklace. I described it in great detail.

Shocked, she looked at me and said, "We wouldn't have any crosses here."

"Would you please just look? Thank you."

She disappeared in the back and returned with about four crosses. I had to smile. I guess I wasn't the only one on campus with a cross. She seemed stunned, but none of these were mine.

As I was leaving, she appeared genuinely concerned—I suppose she saw the anguish on my face—and called out, "I'm sorry we didn't find your family heirloom." Assuming that the cross was

an heirloom was the only way she could imagine that a Mormon —
a BYU faculty member especially — would care about a cross. As I
was walking through the cold to the parking lot quite far from the
lost and found office, I was deep in thought and prayer.

Suddenly I heard the sound of running feet. The young
woman from the lost and found was hurrying toward me, yelling,
"You won't believe this. As soon as you left, someone came in with
your cross. I wanted to make sure you got it. I'm glad you got your
heirloom back."

BYU has thirty-four thousand students, with many parking
lots in different directions, yet this young woman found me. "You
won't believe this"? Of course I believed it. God and I had a thing
going on. I was beginning to expect supernatural happenings and
recognize that my God could do *anything*. I thanked God for his
goodness and mercy, as my relationship with him became more
and more and more personal.

Oh, how we had sold him short in Mormonism, saying he
had a body of flesh and bone! I had always thought of him more
as a man, but now I was beginning to know the God of the Bible,
a God who was so much grander than I had been taught. Upon
receiving my cross back, I sat a long time in the car, astounded
by what this bigger God could do and was doing. Or as Luke, the
physician and missionary companion of the apostle Paul, would
say, I was "amazed at the greatness of God."

CHAPTER 17

GOD PROVIDES

✦

Command those who are rich in this present world not
to be arrogant nor to put their hope in wealth, which is
so uncertain, but to put their hope in God, who richly
provides.

— 1 TIMOTHY 6:17

Katie and Micah had always been close. In addition to the long days growing up in Indiana, when they fished at the river, jumped on the trampoline, rollerbladed, and played parts in *The Wizard of Oz* side by side, something happened that formed an indelible bond between them. Seven months before we moved from Indiana to Utah, joyful, wide-eyed Katie experienced something horrific for a ten-year-old.

At the time, Katie and Micah attended Burris Laboratory School, on the campus of Ball State University. She was in fourth grade and he in eighth—elementary downstairs, secondary upstairs. Since I was teaching part-time at the university and working on my doctorate, I wanted them nearby, and the school was just a block away from my university office. Besides, I was all about making sure our kids got the best education available, and in the area, Burris was it.

Katie was new at Burris that school year, but she quickly made a friend in Megan Stedman. They sat together at lunch every day, read together in the school library, and wore BFF (best friends forever) necklaces. Megan contracted a virus at four months that damaged and severely weakened the heart muscle. Her condition necessitated a heart transplant when she was ten months old—the youngest recipient in Indiana at the time, her mother told me. Her health when she was ten years old appeared good, except Katie said one week that Megan was winded after PE class lately and slow walking back to class. Katie held back with her. That week, her teacher walked with them too, concerned.

On Friday night, Katie was invited to spend the night at Megan's. She was so excited. At 6:00 p.m., Megan called her. "Mom says we have to wait until tomorrow night to have a slumber party. She says I'm not feeling well, but I'm fine. Call you tomorrow!" As Saturday wore on and no one called, Katie was worried. Then the phone rang and I answered. It was Katie's teacher, crying, barely able to speak. "How I hate to have to tell you this—especially Katie." She delivered the news in the kindest way something like that can be delivered. Megan was gone. Now it was my turn to cry.

Katie said, "I remember I was in my bedroom when you came in frowning. You stood in the doorway and immediately told me, 'Katie, Megan died.' I just ran to your arms and cried ... hot tears."

On Saturday morning, Megan had climbed into bed with her mother and died in her arms. No one foresaw the cardiac arrest of a precious little ten-year-old girl. For Mike and me, this was the fourth death of someone close to us in five months. Katie's grandmother, Grandma Gertrude, who had lived with us for the first seven years of Katie's life, had just died two months earlier in Connecticut. Saturday night after the news about Megan, Katie dreamed of burning alive. She said her heart hurt so badly, it felt as if she were on fire. She also said her tears were hot — burning — and she'd never felt that before. It was strange to her.

On Sunday afternoon, the school requested that all the children in Megan's class and their parents come to the fourth-grade classroom. It was a solemn occasion. The school brought in three psychologists, who suggested that Megan's classmates make her desk a shrine of teddy bears and flowers. Katie's desk sat right across from Megan's, facing hers. Katie was distraught. One of the psychologists took us upstairs to the library and told us to encourage Katie to talk. She didn't sleep well Sunday night either.

On Monday, she spent seven hours at school in front of the desk made into a shrine. Students from all the classes filed by with bears and flowers to place on the shrine. Katie burst into tears three times that day. Her teacher offered to call me, but she said, "No, I'm afraid if I leave this class, I'll never be able to come back." So the teacher decided to get Micah.

God Provides a Brother's Comfort

At fourteen, Micah was already five foot eleven, so he had to squat to talk with her. "Kater," he said gently. He held her hand. They tried to get her to eat, but the basement cafeteria where the friends had sat side by side was too much to endure. I picked her up from school and took her out to lunch. All she would eat at Wendy's was a few bites of baked potato and french fries, definitely comfort foods.

We went to the viewing, and Megan's mom gave Katie the other half of the BFF necklace her daughter had worn. It was agonizing for all of us to watch Katie grieve. She was inconsolable; she couldn't eat or sleep. She had nightmares. In memory of her friend, Katie wanted to *do something*. She conceived the idea of singing at the funeral. I called Megan's mom. She was pleased, but the pastor told me that no ten-year-old girl could possibly sing at a funeral in front of so many people. However, when Megan's mom personally requested it, he did allow Katie to sing, but ten minutes before the service began. Three hundred people gathered. Katie was surprisingly calm, her courageous voice clear and sweet as her final gift to Megan. She never shed a tear through the whole service. Her gesture seemed to have relieved the suffering some.

The next morning, she said to me, "I hope we don't even talk about it today." As time went on, she still cried herself to sleep a lot and had bad dreams. This was the beginning of years of terrifying nightmares. I tried to use our Mormon religion as comfort—to tell her that someday we could take Megan's name to the temple and complete the temple ordinances for her so she could become a Mormon and go to the celestial kingdom. (Technically, this would release Megan from spirit prison if she accepted the LDS gospel, but I didn't tell Katie that.) Then Katie could see her again. Megan was undoubtedly a Christian. She talked with Katie about angels and even about Jesus. Katie wrote in her LDS Book of Remembrance (in LDS culture, a scrapbook for personal history) that she knew Megan was with God. One night, she dreamed that Megan came to play with her, and this eased her suffering too, but Katie's once-innocent cheerfulness was undeniably subdued.

The desk shrine of teddy bears and flowers, a painful reminder facing her own desk, loomed large in Katie's classroom. Regardless, it remained until the end of the school year. So did Micah's tender loving care. Now and then in class, grief swept over Katie, and she would sob uncontrollably. Her teacher encircled her in her lap and tried to comfort her as classmates stared.

At such times, rather than calling me, the school sent for Micah. Anytime Katie needed him, her teacher made sure he was summoned, and he came eagerly. Just the sight of him eased

Katie's pain. The touch of his large hands, the feel of his strong arms around her, and his empathetic smile were therapeutic. Sometimes the two of them walked around the outside of the school and talked. At the age of fourteen, he became her rock. He had such a way with her, and I was so grateful he was there. The deep and resolute relationship forged between Micah and Katie during those dark days at Burris endured.

Five-Minute Phone Call

So when Micah made that five-minute phone call to Katie in January of 2006, just before he was sent home from his mission, she was beyond excited to hear from him. They'd been apart too long. In that brief conversation, he encouraged her to read the Bible and to listen to Christian music, and because of her trust in and love for Micah, she did.

She started at the beginning of the Bible, in the Old Testament. She read of the prophet Moses, called by God up to a cloud on Mt. Sinai. The Lord talked to Moses for days, gave him instruction for the people below, and just spent time with him. This all made sense to her because, as a Mormon, she was at the mercy of a prophet. She was one small person waiting at the bottom of the mountain for the prophet to come down and proclaim the revelations he had received from the Lord for all people. As she read about Moses, Abraham, and Joseph, the Spirit of Truth brought New Testament verses to her mind, opening her eyes. The scales blinding her began to fall. She recognized that the Old Testament law and the ways of the Old Testament prophets were accomplished in Jesus Christ. He had come to fulfill all things, so she could approach the very presence of God himself.

Katie had been standing at the bottom of a mountain, waiting to hear from a prophet, when all this time God himself, through Jesus, was calling her. She could now run up the mountain to be with God and talk with him on a personal level, no longer communicating through others. She found that the religion she had followed had fooled her into believing that she needed church leaders, a bishop, a stake president, apostles, priesthood, and a prophet between her Lord and herself. It was all a lie. But Jesus sought her out to free her.

Once her eyes were opened to see that Jesus alone was enough, then Jesus alone became all she wanted—and he was better than anything she thought she already had. Katie even worshiped God by singing out loud and dancing. She prayed to Jesus as though he were her best friend, the only high priest. She began to feel whole, as if she had finally reached out and touched the Lord's robe and been healed. If anyone could have looked into her heart and seen her greatest desire, they would have seen, "Jesus, may I just have you?" The Father drew her to Christ, and he was enough.

God's Salvation Provides Comfort

The week after Christmas 2006, Michael, Katie, and I went again to Winter Garden to have Christmas with the other half of the family. During this trip, Katie met Joseph Warren—Micah's missionary friend, whom I had seen rebaptized at the end of October—for the first time. After returning, on January 21, 2007, one year to the day after Micah was sent home from his mission, Katie became born again in Jesus Christ. The Bible says, "Greater love has no one than this: to lay down one's life for one's friends" (John 15:13). She felt that she could have no greater love for God than to give him her life—to lay down whatever plans she had for herself, whatever ambitions, whatever dreams, and pick up her cross and follow him. Micah's unconditional love at that critical time in her life when Megan died gave her a glimpse of God's immense love for her. Another one I loved dearly had crossed over.

Remarkably, after Katie gave her life to the Jesus of the Bible, her dreams switched from night terrors to dreams of God's love. She had suffered terrifying dreams for as long as she could remember, relying on Manny, her cat, and a nightlight as essentials for refuge. They began when Megan died and involved death, blood, and pain to herself or to others she knew. Often people from the LDS Church were in her dreams. Once, she dreamed she witnessed the shooting death of our bishop. She stepped in the pool of his blood. Katie dreamed of people she knew getting divorces and families being torn apart, children separated from their moms or dads. As a bystander, Katie witnessed horrendous things that had nothing to do with her, but somehow she ended up hurt or discovered. Usually she ran from the situation and got shot in the back or caught or tortured.

When she woke up, it was always the same feeling—a ghastly fear that paralyzed her. Sometimes she felt sharp pains in her back, chest, or legs, and yet she could not move. Her cell phone lay on the white desk in her room, just inches away from her bed, but she couldn't reach it, couldn't scream for us, because her voice was paralyzed too. In her room, she sometimes sensed an evil presence. Katie saw faceless, shapeless figures of darkness, like dark phantoms hanging near. Physically they looked like a dark cloud or an eerie shadow. They didn't speak to us; they didn't hurt us; they didn't move; they were just there to haunt her dreams. A demonic presence that appeared in a dream would be there when she woke, only to leave at dawn when light finally streamed into her bedroom through the window. Only then did she feel like she could move. Only then did she feel relatively safe.

Katie remembers that while we were still entrenched in the LDS religion and living in Alpine, one night before bedtime I knelt beside her bed trying to comfort her. I read a consoling verse out of the Bible to help her sleep. "God hath not given us

the spirit of fear; but of power, and of love, and of a sound mind"
(2 Tim. 1:7 KJV). To this day she remembers how calm she felt
after I read the Bible to her before the night came. Every once in
a while, between dreams of murders and war, she was graced with
vivid and powerful dreams not of fear and death but of love and
forgiveness. Intermingled with those terrifying dreams of worldly
troubles came enlightening dreams of hope and peace. However,
these night terrors never disappeared permanently until she gave
her life to Jesus.

About a month after her conversion, she dreamed of a stone
courtyard in the shape of a circle. On the ground was dark gray
stone mixed with red dirt. There was only one entrance to the
courtyard, like the sheep pens of old, where the shepherd himself is the gate. She saw a small girl, about four or five years old,
led by the hand by a man through that entrance into the courtyard, near the center of the circle. It dawned on her that she was
the small girl. There were small pools of blood on the ground.
Although the sight of blood would seemingly frighten a child, she
felt no fear. She was told that this courtyard was where the Son of
God, Jesus, had been beaten and whipped until near death, and
the fresh blood was his blood—the Lord's blood, since "with his
stripes we are healed."

Katie looked right at the man, who was wearing a cream-
colored robe and a shawl over his head, and trusted him. He knelt
in the dirt to gaze at her, directly at eye level. Taking the shawl
off his head, he dipped it into the bloodstained ground around
them. Then, using the shawl, he gently began to cover her with
the blood, starting with her forehead. She was reminded of the
Scripture in Revelation about his name being written on people's
foreheads (Rev. 22:4). She held out her arms like a cross, so he
could cover them with blood too. He smiled at her while he performed this service, as if she were the *joy* set before him.

I didn't know about Katie's dream until later, but this was about the time I dreamed of her being spattered with blood. Jesus was healing the deep wounds Mike and I, as her parents, could not heal.

And more was happening in her life. In Winter Garden after Christmas, Katie, passionate for Jesus, had met Joseph, passionate for Jesus. Since then, the two of them had texted each other occasionally. In March, one of them called the other, and soon they were talking for hours on end, late, late into the night, about nothing else but God. They had no thoughts of a romantic relationship, she explained, but because she lived in an all-Mormon community, she needed somebody to share her joy, to share God's grace, and to share what was happening to her. Joey was more than happy to oblige. He understood her passion for Jesus the way she understood his. Finally, a God-breathed place for all that pent-up passion for Christ.

God Provides an Answer

Mike and I prayed about what God would have us do next. We felt that God was directing us to Florida. Well, you can't just switch states without a job, and we had no idea that God could arrange one, so Mike got the license he needed to conduct business in Florida and I applied for five professorial positions at various universities there.

I was invited to interview as one of two finalists at three of the schools. As it turned out, my transcript did not include the graduate-level courses required for the first two jobs. The first door closed in February, the second in March. I interviewed for the third job and didn't hear back for weeks. I finally called and was told that the university had pulled the job because the economy took a Florida red-shouldered hawk dive-bomb. I had done all I knew to do in my own strength to leave BYU. In Mormonism, we'd been told, "Pray like the outcome is up to God, then get off your knees and work like the outcome is up to you." That's exactly what I had done, and it didn't work.

It would soon be the end of the year, and we had no job to move us to Florida in the fall. "Now what?" I asked in prayer. "Do I need to stay at BYU and help students know the Jesus of the Bible?" Students often came to see me with concerns. I did pray with them and point them to Jesus, technically not a problem at BYU.

During Michael's and my usual in-bed at-night Scripture reading, I was in the book of 1 Corinthians. When I got to the eighth chapter, the Spirit hit me over the head with a two-by-four. Here was the answer to my prayer about whether I needed to stay at BYU: "Be careful, however, that the exercise of your rights does not become a stumbling block to the weak. For if someone with a weak conscience sees you, with all your knowledge, eating in an idol's temple, won't that person be emboldened to eat what is sacrificed to idols? So this weak brother or sister, for whom Christ died, is destroyed by your knowledge. When you sin against them in this way and wound their weak conscience, you sin against Christ. Therefore, if what I eat causes my brother or sister to fall into sin, I will never eat meat again, so that I will not cause them to fall" (1 Cor. 8:9–13).

What in the world did this section about eating meat sacrificed to idols have to do with teaching Jesus to students at BYU? When I got to the tenth verse, it struck me. I had the knowledge—the truth—but I was not sharing it. Instead, as students had positive experiences in prayer and conversation about Jesus with me, they were associating those experiences with the LDS Church. Because I represented Mormonism to them, I was inadvertently leading them through the sheep gate to the Mormon Church, not to Christ.

I told my husband that night that this would be my last year at BYU. I had already removed my LDS garments and was wearing a cross. The only place to go was out.

God Provides a Grandson

On April 9, 2007, our first grandchild, Micah and Alicia's first little angel, Jacob Andrew Wilder, was born. I flew to Florida for a week to hold that precious baby. That week, I was needed to help with Alicia's hotel work, making beds and doing laundry. As I moved from room to room making beds, I listened intently to Joseph and Steve, who were cleaning the rooms, talk about their love for Jesus and the developing ministry of the Adam's Road band. On Sunday, I went to church with Matt and Nicole at the Baptist church where Micah and Leashy had married. The others stayed back to work.

Once that week, I got to hold Jacob alone in a quiet third-floor room, the same room where Micah had avoided the flying glass during Hurricane Jeanne, now refurbished. They were beginning to renovate the third floor for living and music recording space. This child was an inordinate blessing to me, embodying a way that I could reach out, hold, and love a piece of my Micah. In spite of my conversion, there seemed something not yet healed between us. As I held Jacob, his tiny body was wracked with hiccups. I prayed that Jesus would remove them, and just like that, they stopped. "You do that too?" I asked God. "Very cool."

As the sun set, I softly sang baby Jacob the words I'd memorized from my new favorite song, "Amazing Grace."

Amazing grace, how sweet the sound,
That saved a wretch like me.
I once was lost but now am found,
Was blind, but now, I see.

'Twas grace that taught my heart to fear.
And grace, my fears relieved.
How precious did that Grace appear
The hour I first believed.

Through many dangers, toils, and snares
I have already come.
'Twas grace that brought me safe thus far
And grace will lead me home.

Amazing grace, how sweet the sound,
That saved a wretch like me.
I once was lost but now am found,
Was blind, but now, I see.

I love you, Jacob. I love you, Micah and Alicia.

"Are You LDS?"

When I returned to Utah, one of Micah's old friends, Mormon of course, stopped by my office at BYU to tell me she was deferring her entrance to law school for two years so she could serve a Mormon mission. I had been there to introduce her to BYU, and she expected I would enthusiastically endorse her decision. In LDS culture, for male or female, a mission is wonderful news. But by this time, I could not bring myself to pretend it was. Like Nicole with her parents, I was struggling with not being completely truthful with my colleagues and students.

I forced myself to look up at her, and I tried to smile. I couldn't shake my questions: *Are you glad for her? What are you going to say to her? Are you LDS?* I thought of a patronizing answer, just echoing her excitement with, "You are really excited," without outright lying to her by saying *I* was excited. As soon as she left, I fished for my car keys and headed home, pondering these irksome questions during the drive.

Half an hour later, I pulled into the Super Walmart to buy some things for Easter dinner, still musing over the questions. Especially the question, *Are you LDS?*

As I went through the checkout line, the clerk chattered relentlessly, telling me his son was going to be baptized on Saturday, the day before Easter. Trying to avoid a second bad experience within the space of an hour, I asked what I thought would be a neutral question: "Do you have family coming?"

He answered, "No, my parents are Lutheran, and they are not happy he is being baptized LDS. First they were Jewish, then Catholic, and now Lutheran. At least when I converted, I stayed in the same church." Then he looked right at me and asked, as if in slow motion, the dreaded question looping through my head: "Are *you* LDS?"

Alarmed, I thought, *This is freaking me out. He's a God-plant. God planted this guy to ask me this question.* He waited, his eyes searching mine. I was so shook up by having to face, head-on, the answer to this question, I quickly nodded yes and thought, *Well, I'm on the rolls, but that's about it,* and got myself out of there! Honestly, I was so astonished by his question—it couldn't be a coincidence—that I returned to the store the next day to see if he really worked there. Every register was manned, it was two days before Easter, but he was nowhere to be found. *You can do that too, God—confront me through a store clerk? You are an amazing God.*

Slight Detour

Because we were *so* hungry for truth and what God had to teach us from the Bible, Sunday services at Pastor Jim's church were not enough for Katie, Mike, and me. Pastor Jim had come to Utah to convert Mormons, but to date he'd had little success. He'd been there four years and had not seen anyone fully exit and *openly* accept biblical Christianity except, he said, someone who also believed in little green spacemen. He was a humble, solid Bible teacher, but he had to work another job to keep the church alive and was not available full-time to answer all our questions.

We wanted to fellowship with other Christians and talk about Jesus and the Word more often. So we joined some of the people attending Pastor Jim's church who also met another evening during the week in a home church. They gathered for praise and worship and to hear an ordained Methodist pastor from out of state. Pastor Jim attended now and then to make sure the teaching was biblically sound. The home preacher did not have his own church, and we typically met in a home, but Pastor Jim allowed this man to use the church building from time to time, hoping that the home group of ragtag, seeking Mormons would land converts in his congregation so he could shepherd them and teach them truth.

The out-of-state home preacher was dynamic — friendly, charismatic, personable, a jolly sort — and entertained us with his preaching from the Word. Of course, since it was all new to us, we could not listen closely enough or hear it often enough. We all had our Bibles open and soaked up what he taught. This small group increased to include people from all walks of life, from as far as two or more hours away. There were hordes of people hungry for the truth in Utah, we saw. Many were still members of the Mormon Church who were searching "underground," some without their families' knowledge, so they were not yet ready to show up at a Christian church on a Sunday morning.

One man who met with us owned an empty store at one of the Salt Lake malls, so as our numbers grew, he opened this store to accommodate the crowd. We began to hold potluck dinners there, sing praise and worship songs, and then hear preaching, Bibles open. We were all craving Christian fellowship. We were like family, praying for each other and seemingly operating like the early church had.

In this home church, however, God intended to provide for us something more than we expected. Yes, Jesus provided comfort, salvation, answers to prayer, and material needs, but most important, in this instance, he provided *knowledge*. By May of 2007, we sensed something was wrong. I began to notice that some of the women looked at the preacher as if they were jealous. Then Mike and I knew. Their looks said it all: at least three, maybe four, women appeared to have an intimate relationship with the dynamo preacher. A few inquiries, and we were told he had been defrocked in his home state. So he came to Utah, land of polygamy, perhaps to prey on people hungry for Jesus, using his amazing gift of preaching and the bling of the Bible to attract unsuspecting souls. Right in front of us stood a modern Joseph Smith. What a lesson!

Mike and I stopped attending and spoke with Pastor Jim about our suspicions. He seemed to have figured it out too. This is precisely how Joseph Smith worked to deceive so many about polygamy and polyandry—with enough truth from the Bible to hook the innocent, then a dynamic presentation of deadly twistiology to a select few. We walked away having learned we could trust no man, only the Word of God and a personal relationship with Jesus that was tested and corroborated in the Word.

God Provides a Job

One morning, I was awakened by that early morning voice in my head, the one whose message and delivery I now always check with the Bible. This time the voice said, "The job you should take will come looking for you." That was crazy. Who in Florida knew me or would know I was looking for a job? I did not know God could find me a job or raise one ex nihilo, out of nothing.

Then in the middle of June 2007, I was standing in my kitchen, with the breathtaking view of the mountains behind me, when the phone rang. I answered, "Hello."

"Dr. Lynn Wilder?"

"Yes, this is she."

"I'm the dean of the College of Education at Florida Gulf Coast University. I have your curriculum vitae in front of me, and I'd like to offer you a position."

I held my hand over the receiver and mouthed with incredulity to no one in particular (I was home alone), "I did not even apply there. How would she get my vitae?"

"It's a one-year visiting position. That's why I don't need to post it and can simply hire you. One of our professors has taken a leave of absence to work in Hawaii next year."

"Thank you very much, Dean. I will talk with my husband and get back to you by Monday."

I hung up the phone, astounded, and fell to my knees. *You can even do that? Wow. Amazing grace!*

The job just happened to be in the town in Florida where my eighty something father lives. Dad knew I was looking, asked me to email my resume (I thought he just wanted to see it), figured out how to open the file, and printed it out. He took it to a board meeting of a nonprofit organization where he was a member, and a university provost just happened to be a member too. He gave it to her. She gave it to the dean, and the rest is history.

I took a one-year leave of absence from BYU, retaining my position there since this was only a temporary job, buying another year to see exactly what God had in store. In my mind, I decided, *If, between now and the time I resign at BYU for good, God chooses to make the conversion of a baby Christian a public encounter, as I've seen happen with other professors who disagreed with the church, then — trembling — I will accept his will.*

To give you a sense of how uncommon this job opening was, in my eight years at BYU, no full-time professorial job had opened in my field. In the several years I've now been at this university in Florida, no job has opened in my field. As Micah wrote in that mission email, "God has a plan and a timing."

God Even Provides Money

By now, I realized that I liked the comfort of material goods and the control of money. I'd been brought up to hoard money in piles and count them, much like Scrooge. Over the years, we had paid our bills, had the basics of home, food, and clothing, and paid our tithe to the Mormon Church. Beyond those basics, the kids needed various lessons and mission and college funds. After several years at BYU, we had managed to save some money. We'd spent part of this on the two weddings the year before.

One day, Mike and I were hiking in beautiful, wavy sandstone slot canyons in southern Utah. I was beginning to have God on my mind almost constantly, especially during our wilderness hiking and skiing. I was getting to know him because of the Scriptures I was reading, and I often heard from him as I grew to trust him. He spoke clearly to me that day and told me to write a check to Micah for most of what we had saved over the past eight years in Utah. I had no idea why. Before encountering Jesus, I would never have done such a thing. It would take us a long time to recoup that money. I told Mike. He was hesitant but agreed. Taking this step of faith was huge for us.

Around this time, Katie was getting ready to graduate from high school. When a young LDS woman graduates, she moves from the Young Women organization into Relief Society for adult women. It was a tradition in our ward for the mother to make the daughter a quilt for graduation. Our Relief Society president had a quilting machine in her garage, so I went there to work on Katie's white-patterned quilt. I'm not highly skilled, but I suddenly had an idea. I bought a red ribbon with gold ribbing that looked Jewish to me. Although I hadn't been to Relief Society for months, right there in the Relief Society president's garage, I stitched the accent to the quilt in the shape of a cross.

Katie displayed her quilt with the others in the ward's Relief Society room. It was folded, so it was difficult to detect what the red-and-gold ribbon represented. The women crooked their necks, trying to figure it out, murmuring, "No, it can't be."

Then Katie was asked to address the women. Using her natural drama skills and passion for Jesus, she wove into their souls the story of the woman with the issue of blood who touched Jesus' robe and was never the same again. It was her testimony. They were deeply moved.

For her graduation present, Katie wanted a plane ticket to go see Micah (and maybe Joseph) in Florida. So by the grace of God, she happened to be with Micah when he casually opened the envelope from us and saw the check. She watched him fully comprehend what God had done. He stood with shoulders bowed in humility and shed silent tears of gratitude.

To this day, I don't know what the money was needed for, but I suspect it was the answer to something Micah had talked with God about. Meanwhile God was teaching Michael and me to rest in his love. He provides.

CHAPTER 18

BREAKING THE PHARISEE

Unthinking respect for authority is the greatest enemy of truth.

— ALBERT EINSTEIN

Where was Mike with all this spiritual upheaval? I love and respect both my Jesus and my Michael. I was beginning to know this God and what amazing conversion miracles he wrought, and I also knew Michael's mind and heart. My husband is like a thoughtful turtle, methodical and plodding, with a soft and tender underbelly. He had always wanted Jesus. It was just a matter of connecting with the right Jesus. I had seen firsthand the power of prayer, so I prayed for him.

Mike's church calling when Micah was sent home was to tame a large class of ten-year-olds, mostly boys, in a two-hour Sunday morning Primary class. These boys had driven their last teacher, well, let's say, far away from them. No pushover at six foot two, two hundred and ten pounds, Mike had worked in the Scouting program and raised three sons of his own, so the antics of energetic boys were nothing new to him. Also, as former bishopric coun- selor (assistant pastor) responsible for Primary, Mike had attended Primary class often, so he knew these hooligans—and he abso- lutely loved them.

We'd been reading the Bible since Micah was sent home, and we had traveled two hours to hear a preacher teach about the cross and the blood. Mike felt safe enjoying his boys in Primary as he sorted through his growing questions about the Mormon Church. For Mormon men rotating through leadership roles as Mike did, however, Primary was a resting place, not a permanent stop.

Called to Redeem the Dead

Unfortunately, Mike's Primary calling lasted only a few months. In July of 2006, eight months after Josh was rebaptized into the Mormon Church and six months after Micah was sent home, Michael received a phone call from his high priest (HP) group leader. Mike had been a high priest since 1988. His HP group leader presided over all of the men in the ward who held the rank/office of high priest, which signified the higher Melchizedek priesthood (the lower is the Aaronic priesthood). A high priest was required to serve as a member of a ward bishopric, as a ward high priest group leader or one of his two assistants, as one of the three members of the stake presidency, or as one of the twelve members of the stake high council.

Mike was a little apprehensive to hear that his HP group leader wanted to come to our house to meet with him, because no one in leadership had ever talked with Mike about what had happened with Micah. At this point, Mike didn't really want to have that con- versation, because he could not in good faith say that he supported the actions of the stake president. Admitting that to a church leader would likely place his temple recommend, and perhaps his church membership, in jeopardy. Temple recommend question number four probes whether one sustains the local authorities of the church. Disagreeing with a decision made by a local leader who purportedly hears from God on such matters could label Michael an apostate. Mike would not lie if asked directly, but he had not yet solidified where he stood with the Mormon Church. He was in limbo.

As I mentioned earlier, Mike and I were called to be co-chairs of the redeem-the-dead committee. This is how that happened: Michael's fears of meeting with the HP group leader turned out to be groundless as far as Micah's experience was concerned. The man never ventured into the personal realm. He simply extended the call to Mike for the two of us to serve as co-chairs of the committee.

The ward was experimenting with a new leadership structure — ward councils — and called three couples to lead, one couple for each part of the threefold mission of the church: (1) perfect the saints, (2) preach the gospel, and (3) redeem the dead. In other words, the major work of the members of the church is to (1) help the saints shed sins and stretch toward godhood, (2) spread the Mormon gospel to all the world, and (3) do genealogy, taking the names of deceased relatives and ancestors to the temple so they can be redeemed to the Mormon heaven through the temple ordinances. In short, the fruit of Mormonism is to create gods (polytheism), spawn converts to a false gospel (even drawing people away from biblical Christianity), and save those who are already dead. As Matt had realized, this last one is creepy. And none of these is doctrinally Christian or supported in the Bible, but they mimic Christianity's evangelistic fervor.

As redeem-the-dead co-chairs, it would be our job to motivate members in our ward to get a temple recommend, to keep it long-term, and to attend the temple regularly. Each temple "patron," or attendee, must pass the fourteen temple recommend questions, which assess their personal righteous works according to the laws of the Mormon gospel.

The purpose of temple attendance was, first, to redeem one-self to the celestial kingdom of Heavenly Father through the temple ordinances, and second, to routinely perform the same ordinances by proxy for the dead in order to save *them* to the celestial kingdom. The aim of every temple ordinance, then, was either to exalt oneself to the celestial kingdom or to exalt the dead.

Mike and I would be expected to plan monthly temple excursions, perhaps ending with dessert at someone's home. In addition, we would teach the temple prep class to prepare ward members who had never been to the temple. I recalled our own temple prep course, woefully inadequate to prepare us for the bizarre temple rituals.

Mike was not thrilled about the redeem-the-dead calling. He preferred to hide in Primary for a while, away from the adults. But he rationalized that attending the temple was supposed to be spiritual; maybe all this spirituality—participating in the temple ordinances, listening to the covenants being made, and praying in the celestial room of the temple—would help him sort out Mormonism and its doctrinal conflicts with the Bible. Meanwhile he convinced the reluctant me, "Babes, please, you can't reject the redeem-the-dead co-chair calling. Someone might detect that we've got some questions about the church." He promised to perform the calling for both of us. I attended the first two meetings, then never again. He worked himself silly doing his calling and mine, paying his tithe and mine, and attending the LDS Church with Katie but without me. During the year that Mike carried the redeem-the-dead co-chair football, no one from leadership questioned us. I'm grateful for the Dancer of grace who blinded eyes as he worked with Mike and me in his perfect timing.

Which Jesus to Believe?

One day after a ward council meeting, the bishop told Mike that he was sorry about what had happened with Micah. He thought

Micah should have been allowed to finish the last three weeks of his mission and come home to naturally reassimilate. Whew, someone finally addressed the issue of Micah, and Mike survived the experience. In addition, last year this bishop had told Mike that he would gladly have handled Josh's issue, but the stake president usurped his authority, as he had every right to do according to the church rules.

Neither Josh's excommunication nor Micah's harsh treatment caused our discontentment with Mormonism. But thank God we'd had those experiences, because God used them to send us all searching for truth. What we found during our search is what caused our discontentment.

In Josh's case, we uncovered what Jesus himself said about what should happen to someone who sincerely confesses his sin. People are commanded to forgive. In Micah's case, we uncovered what Jesus himself said about being saved by grace through faith in Jesus alone. In both cases, the biblical Jesus instituted the principles that our sons had followed, yet the Mormon Church staunchly opposed those teachings. Mike began to wonder if the Mormon Church had hijacked the real Jesus and portrayed him as someone he was not. Was this a deliberate effort to take people who truly wanted to follow Jesus and deceive them into following a false Christ? I watched Mike struggle with which Jesus to believe—the Mormon Jesus or the biblical one.

About the time I surrendered my life to the biblical Jesus, in October of 2006, Mike took a ward group on an excursion to the Mount Timpanogos Temple. Fall was in the air, slowly moving down the mountains. A dusting of snow lay on the peaks, with the scrub oak and quaking aspen bright red and deep yellow just below. Like the rugged Utah mountains, Mike was facing a season of change.

The night Michael returned from the Mount Timpanogos Temple, he started to read the Bible instead of the Book of Mormon.

That reading caused an unexpected shift, like the jolt of the earth's tectonic plates before an earthquake.

His Bible opened to Luke 16. As he glanced at this passage, he thought, *I have read this multiple times. Why read it again?* But something nudged him. He read the parable of the shrewd manager, in which Christ says, "You cannot serve both God and money" (Luke 16:13). When the Pharisees hear this, they are upset, because they love money. Christ says to them, "You are the ones who justify yourselves in the eyes of others, but God knows your hearts. What people value highly is detestable in God's sight" (Luke 16:15).[38]

Mike thought, *I attend the temple regularly. To get into the temple, I had to pass the temple recommend question, 'Are you a full-tithe payer?' Yes, I pay my tithing to the Mormon Church. To do God's work in the temple, I was required to pay money to the Mormon Church. Oooh!* This was a new association, one he hadn't considered before — he was paying money to earn temple privileges, privileges necessary to live with Heavenly Father and Jesus in the afterlife. Mormons call tithing "fire insurance." Was that paying your way to heaven?

Mike continued with Christ's words in Luke: "The Law and the Prophets were proclaimed until John. Since that time, the good news of the kingdom of God is being preached" (Luke 16:16).

The law and the prophets ended with John the Baptist? Wait, Mike sustained the president of the Mormon Church as a prophet, seer, and revelator and as the only person on the earth who possessed and was authorized to exercise all priesthood keys. The temple recommend certified that Mike kept his life in harmony with the laws and commandments of the Mormon gospel and that he kept the covenants he made in the temple. Strange, Mike never noticed that verse before. *The law was until John, but no more? Maybe that verse is not translated correctly,* he thought. His Mormon-trained, knee-jerk reaction was to call a foul on the Bible when it conflicted with Mormon doctrine.

Next Mike read the parable of the rich man and Lazarus. *Surely, this story won't also conflict with Mormon doctrine,* he thought. The contradictions were wearing on his last nerve. When the rich man dies and goes to hell, he asks Abraham to send Lazarus to cool his tongue with a drop of water, but Abraham says, "Between us and you a great chasm has been set in place, so that those who want to go from here to you cannot, nor can anyone cross over from there to us" (Luke 16:26).

Now, wait a second, Mike thought, an earthquake beginning to rumble in his spirit. *The whole purpose of going to the temple and performing endowments for the dead is to save them from a lower kingdom to the highest kingdom of heaven, so they can cross that chasm. My calling is to co-chair a committee whose purpose is to redeem the dead. Redeeming the dead is what I do and lead others to do. If there is a great chasm that no one can cross, how do temple ordinances allow the dead to pass from one side to the other? Maybe I don't understand this story as well as I thought I did.*

Michael read on. "If your brother or sister sins against you, rebuke them; and if they repent, forgive them. Even if they sin against you seven times in a day and seven times come back to you saying 'I repent,' you must forgive them" (Luke 17:3–4). Mike was alarmed. During all those years he was on the stake high council and in two bishoprics, he sat in judgment for the Mormon Church on disciplinary matters. He judged people who had already repented, and he bestowed judgment upon them in the name of God by imposing probation, disfellowship, or—worst-case scenario—a removal of their salvation through excommunication. If Christ himself said to forgive each time a person sinned, why did the LDS Church punish people *after* they repented?

Mike's memories came roaring back. His son had gone to see the bishop to repent of his sins. He had not been caught in the act of sin; he volunteered the information. Josh was like the brother in Luke 17:3 who repented. But genuine repentance is not always recognized in the Mormon Church, for Josh was found guilty of violating the law and was sentenced by a high council court under the direction of a stake president to be excommunicated.

Micah was chastened at being released from his missionary service. His sin was believing he was saved by faith alone, through grace alone, in Christ alone. *Oh, what a wretched man I am for not supporting my sons in their time of need!* Mike thought. *I now realize I'm currently under the law of the Mormon priesthood, not under the grace of Christ.*

This reading of the Bible was not going well. *Maybe this is why the prophet tells us to read the Book of Mormon,* Mike thought. Over and over again, the Word of God in the Bible clashed with Mormon doctrine.

Mike wanted to stop, since all the contradictions were making him furious, but he was curious. It couldn't get worse, could it? Again directly from Jesus: "Two men went up to the temple to pray, one a Pharisee and the other a tax collector. The Pharisee stood by himself and prayed: 'God, I thank you that I am not like other people—robbers, evildoers, adulterers—or even like this tax collector. I fast twice a week and give a tenth of all I get'" (Luke 18:10–12). *Wow, this Pharisee sure was righteous. God must have been pleased with him.*

During Mike's life in the Mormon Church, he was taught that he was not like other men either. Since he held the Melchizedek priesthood, he was more spiritual and holy before God. He had worn the garments of the holy priesthood for nearly thirty years. Since he had been washed, anointed, and pronounced clean, he had earned, by his righteous acts, the privilege to stand not only before the temple but also *in* the temple of God. The non-Mormon man (once called a "Gentile" by Mormons) could not go to the temple to do the Lord's work. He was not worthy. He had no temple recommend. Mike did. Mike also fasted at least once a month and paid his tithe and his fast offerings to the Mormon

Church. This Pharisee in the story and Mr. Mike (as his adult children and children-in-law now called him) were really righteous men. God had to be pleased with them, right?

Jesus continued the story: "But the tax collector stood at a distance. He would not even look up to heaven, but beat his breast and said, 'God, have mercy on me, a sinner.' I tell you that this man, rather than the other, went home justified before God. For all those who exalt themselves will be humbled, and those who humble themselves will be exalted" (Luke 18:13–14).

Mike was stunned. He quietly closed his Bible. A feeling of shame washed over him. Was he the Pharisee or the tax collector? He needed to ponder these stinging words from Jesus.

The rumbling got louder.

Growing Discomfort

In January of 2007, the Wasatch Mountains were covered with "the greatest snow on earth," as Utah ski resorts advertised. Michael walked to our ward building around the corner from our home for Sunday services. In his high priest group, the men were starting a new lesson book for the year, called *Teachings of the Presidents of the Church: Spencer W. Kimball*.[39] Each year, the men and women of the church studied the words of past presidents of the Mormon Church, including Joseph Smith and Brigham Young. This year they would study the words of former prophet Spencer W. Kimball, who had been the prophet when we joined the Mormon Church in 1977. *This should be interesting*, Mike thought.

Oh, it was. The lesson that bright, snowy day was called "To Live with Him Someday." In this lesson, Prophet Kimball was quoted as saying, "Celestial life [highest heaven] may be had by every soul who will fulfill the requirements. To *know* is not enough. One must *do*. Righteousness is vital and [temple] ordinances are necessary."[40]

What Mike had read about the Pharisee and the tax collector was racing through his mind.

The teacher continued on page five: "The Lord Jesus Christ, our Redeemer and Savior, has given us our map—a code of laws and commandments whereby we might attain perfection and, eventually, godhood. This set of laws and ordinances is known as the gospel of Jesus Christ, and it is the *only* plan which will exalt mankind. The Church of Jesus Christ of Latter-day Saints is the sole repository of this priceless program in its fullness ..."[41]

Is this what the Bible teaches? Mike asked himself. The men in class were actively agreeing with the lesson. But Mike just sat there, detached and observing.

Next, the teacher read from the manual, "The Lord restored his kingdom [Mormon Church] in these days, with all its gifts and powers and blessing. Any church that you know of may possibly be able to take you for a long ride, and bring you some degree of peace and happiness and blessings, and they can carry you to the veil [death] and there they drop you. The Church of Jesus Christ [Mormon Church] picks you up on this side of the veil and, if you live its commandments, carries you right through the veil as though it weren't there and on through the eternities to exaltation."[42]

For the past thirty years, Michael would have approved, but at that moment he wasn't sure. The words *veil, exaltation,* and *godhood* were ringing in his ears.

The lesson continued: "One must live a life of righteousness, cleanliness, purity, and service" and "be endowed and sealed" in the Mormon temple to reach the goal of eternal life, exaltation, and godhood.[43] The instructor listed on the blackboard all the things a man needed to do in order to reach exaltation.

Most high priests concurred that they, as priesthood holders, were different from other men. Many of the men in Mike's group held or had held major Mormon Church callings, such as patriarch, stake high councilor, stake president or presidency member, and bishop or bishopric member. This was an extraordinarily experienced high priest group. Like all high priests, they knew they had to attend the temple to gain exaltation.

Michael sat still and did not say a word. He was the co-chair of redeem-the-dead committee and was not chiming in to encourage the priesthood to attend the temple. What was up with him? Why was he so uncomfortable with this lesson? As they left the room at the end of the lesson, he said to a friend, "I guess even Mother Teresa would need her temple endowment to gain eternal life." His friend smiled.

Then the story of the Pharisee and the tax collector came to Mike's mind again. This biblical story was in direct conflict with the words he had just heard. Those words, promising exaltation and godhood (D&C 132:20) from Mike's own righteous acts, came crashing down when compared with the words of Christ: "I tell you that this man, rather than the other, went home justified before God. For all those who exalt themselves will be humbled, and those who humble themselves will be exalted" (Luke 18:14). Then and there, Mike knew. As a Mormon priesthood leader, he was the Pharisee. The spiritual earthquake gained power.

Mike realized that according to the Bible, it was not his righteousness that would carry him through the veil, only Christ's righteousness. It was not his temple recommend that would make him worthy, but his understanding that he was a sinner pleading with God to be merciful, as the tax collector did. Mike's knowledge of the Masonic-like names, signs, and tokens that he knew from the Mormon temple endowment ceremony would not usher him beyond the veil of death into the presence of God. He would pass into God's presence because Christ nailed his sins and the law to the cross and washed him clean with his blood, and because Mike humbly accepted Jesus as his Savior.

Even with all that the Holy Spirit was teaching him from the Bible about grace and the insufficiency of his own righteousness, Michael still believed that the Book of Mormon was true and that Joseph Smith was a prophet of God. The foundation of the Mormon Church was cracking, but God needed to shatter it to pieces. Like me, Mike had all those years of false doctrine in his brain. That doctrine was hard to demolish. But our God is a loving God. He was about to get out the sledgehammer.

The Truth about Polygamy

When Mike joined the Mormon Church, he accepted the missionaries' explanation for why early Mormons practiced polygamy: there were more women than men in the church's early years. Besides, Old Testament prophets in the Bible practiced it. Then he put polygamy on a shelf and never thought much about it again, until we moved to Utah. He was thinking about it more and more lately. He told me, "This might seem strange for a man to state, but the whole concept of polygamy bugs me. It is degrading both to women and to men."

Numerous incidents in Utah brought the principle of polygamy to light. Mike spoke with an LDS business associate about the man's remarriage after his divorce. He was grinning at Mike, saying he was now sealed to two women. This rang a bell. Mike had not thought about plural wives for a while. This man had been sealed to his first wife in the temple and had gotten a civil divorce but not a temple divorce. So he and his first wife were still sealed in the temple. He was now remarried (sealed in the temple) to his second wife. Therefore, according to the Doctrine and Covenants, he was sealed to two wives and will have both after death in heaven. Mike felt sick. This seemed wrong.

Not long after this conversation, Mike met another man who was sealed to his first two wives, now dead, and was also sealed to his third wife. He told Mike that he believed he would have all three wives in the next life. This was 2006, not 1885!

Mike discovered that the practice of sealing a man to additional wives, if the previous wives were gone through death or divorce, was not unusual. Of course, the missionaries never taught us this concept before we were baptized. The method used by modern LDS missionaries with their potential converts includes three brief lessons and then baptism into the Mormon Church.[44] Polygamy is taught later, in priesthood lessons. But it never registered with Mike until now that this was how it played out. He was talking with people who expected to live it.

As Mike spoke with Mormons in Utah, he asked, "But didn't polygamy stop in the Mormon Church in 1890, as per the manifesto from God?" This "revelation" to the prophet is recorded in the Doctrine and Covenants as Official Declaration – 1.

"Well," he was told, "polygamy is not observed today with living wives, but spiritual plurality of wives is observed. It's an eternal principle. A man can be sealed to more than one wife in the temple, and he will have them in the next life."

With some research into Mormon Church history, Mike learned that polygamy began soon after Joseph Smith organized the church in 1830. The Republican Party formed in 1854 with a platform against the evils of slavery *and* polygamy (both in Utah at the time). President Abraham Lincoln detested the practice of polygamy, and Congress made polygamy illegal in the United States and her territories with the Morrill Anti-Bigamy Act of 1862. President Ulysses S. Grant later pressured the Mormons in October of 1871 when he arrested hundreds for breaking the law. Addressing polygamy, President Rutherford B. Hayes stated on December 6, 1880, "The sanctity of marriage and the family relation are the cornerstone of our American society and civilization."[45]

Utah's statehood was withheld until the U.S. government believed that polygamy had ceased in Mormonism. Polygamy officially ended in 1890 because of that pressure, although Mormons continued polygamy clandestinely for a long time. Under further pressure, Mormon polygamists fled to Mexico and Canada to continue the practice. Statehood was finally granted to Utah in 1896.

Mormonism still teaches in the scriptures (D&C 132) that plurality of wives is an eternal commandment from God. Church leaders teach that it will be reinstated during the millennium. Wow! None of this is or was taught in the Mormon missionary lessons.

Next, Mike met another business associate who liked to talk about religion. When the subject of Joseph Smith came up, Mike asked him what he thought about polygamy. This man spoke of Joseph Smith with great passion and stated that Smith was a prophet of God. He believed that the Book of Mormon was true and that all of Smith's revelations were from God, including the revelation of plural marriage found in D&C 132.

Mike replied that he was uncomfortable with Smith's teachings on polygamy. The man defended Joseph Smith and polygamy vehemently. Disagreement aside, Mike and this man became friends over the next few months. One day, Mike met his wife and some of his children. The next time Mike saw him, he was with a different woman. Mike wondered if he had gotten a divorce, so later he asked who she was. The man answered, "She is my second wife. My first and third wives were at home with the children." Michael was shocked but didn't say a thing. This was 2006, and here he was, face-to-face with a polygamist. Now Mike had not only met men who intended to be polygamists in the hereafter; he knew somebody who was one right now—following Joseph Smith's D&C 132 revelation. The earthquake registered even higher on the Richter scale.

Lies and More Lies

One night, Mike and I went to visit an older couple in our ward, wonderful people we loved a great deal. While in their home, Michael was drawn to a family portrait of the woman's grandfather with his several wives and children. He was an attorney who had lived in Salt Lake City circa 1900, she explained. He was good friends with top leadership of the Mormon Church, including the prophets Wilford Woodruff (1889–1898) and Joseph F. Smith (1901–1918).

We learned that LDS leaders had asked this man many times over the years—after the 1890 Manifesto—to practice polygamy, but he said no. Nevertheless, with increasing insistence from them, given his important church calling, he finally said yes. He married a total of five wives, as Mike recalls, the second through fifth after 1900.

"Wait a second," Mike said to the elderly couple, "the practice of polygamy ended after 1890, didn't it?" The older gentleman, with love in his voice, told us it ceased as far as the general public and U.S. government knew, but in reality, church leaders sealed couples in plural marriage long after. The last polygamist prophet, Heber J. Grant, died in 1945. Some polygamists who returned to the United States during the Mexican Revolution continued the practice into the 1950s and some were considered active Mormons who held temple recommends.

Our friend told us her grandfather was very upset with the prophet Joseph F. Smith when he lied to Congress, stating that the Mormon Church had stopped the practice of plural marriage when it had not. She told us her grandfather said that it was not right for a prophet of God to lie. She said this whole family history was in writing and the family had planned to publish it. However, when it was reviewed by a Mormon apostle, he told them that the story was not for public consumption. It was only for family. When the apostle of the Lord spoke, they had no option but to obey.

Did God Ordain Polygamy?

Mike was confused about polygamy. Did God command Joseph Smith to practice it, as Mike had been taught all these years? He was also taught that God commanded Abraham, Isaac, Jacob, Moses, David, and Solomon to practice it. Well, this was pretty good company to be associated with. Mike hated the idea of polygamy, but it must be okay with God if he asked these men to do it. Who was he to tell God what to do?

Through his Bible reading, Mike was learning to trust God's Word. He thought, *I will just reread the Bible and get proof that polygamy is justified.* This seemed a simple task. He was positive that an angel had told Sarah to give Hagar to Abraham as a second wife, or at least an angel had told Abraham. He would just read this story and find it. After an intense study of Genesis chapters 11 through 25, he found no commandment given to Abraham to practice polygamy. *This must not be translated correctly,* he thought, still caught in Mormon anti-biblical thought. Mike read about Isaac, Jacob, Moses, David, and Solomon. Nowhere did God tell these men to practice polygamy. It was not in the Word of God.

Where did I read about God giving Abraham the authority to practice polygamy? I know I read it somewhere ... Then he found it, but not in the Bible. It's in Mormon scripture D&C 132:1: "I, the Lord [Mormon Jesus], justified my servants Abraham, Isaac, Jacob ... as touching the principle and doctrine of their having many wives and concubines." And D&C 132:37: "Abraham received concubines and they bore him children; and it was accounted unto him for righteousness." D&C 132:65: "I [Mormon Jesus] commanded Abraham to take Hagar to wife."

The Bible gives no divine authorization for the practice of

polygamy. In contrast, the Mormon scriptures do. Joseph Smith supposedly received direct revelation from Jesus Christ himself that polygamy is an eternal doctrine of the Mormon Church commanded by God. Which is right, the Bible or Mormon scripture? They can't both be correct. They're polar opposites.

Step by Step

At Christmas in 2006, I removed my temple garments, stopped attending LDS services and activities, and quit tithing. In January of 2007, Mike decided to present his simple question about polygamy to God in the temple. As redeem-the-dead committee co-chair, Mike was still attending the temple on a regular basis. He had been taught that the most sacred place he could go to have his deepest prayers answered was the celestial room there. So he completed an endowment session for someone who was dead and passed through the veil into the celestial room by giving the proper Masonic-like names, signs, and tokens for the person he was representing by proxy. Dressed in his peculiar temple garb, with what he called his "baker's hat," he entered the posh celestial room and sat alone on a couch on the far side. The doctrine of polygamy was driving him crazy. He needed to know the truth, to have peace.

He prayed to the God he knew at that time. He asked a simple question and expected no answer. "Is polygamy an eternal principle?" Gratefully, God is no respecter of persons. Even though Mike was praying to a Mormon god who had a physical body and had worked his way to godhood, in the fullness of his grace the *true* God of Abraham, Isaac, and Jacob answered his prayer. As Mike sat with eyes closed, it was as if someone standing behind him whispered in his right ear, "No, it is of man; it is not of me." Nothing like this had ever happened to Mike before.

If polygamy was not from God, then Joseph Smith's revelation was not true. If that was not true, then Joseph Smith was not a prophet of God. Further, the priesthood keys given to Mormon Church prophets, described in D&C 132, were corrupt. This fraudulent priesthood taught the corrupt doctrine of polygamy in the name of Christ. Mike realized, *I hold this priesthood, and so does the current leadership of the Mormon Church. How can the Mormon Church, restored by Joseph Smith with his fraudulent priesthood, not also be corrupt today? Mormonism's own teachings stand as a witness that it is false.* With this indisputable answer from God — in the temple, of all places — the foundation of the Mormon Church crumbled and its false doctrines collapsed like the house of cards they'd always been. "God have mercy on me for what I believed for so many years and for what I taught my children," Michael prayed.

To get Michael's attention, God did not use as many dreams or health problems or extraordinary circumstances as he had used with me. Instead God took this gentle soul by the hand, leading him step by step — through intensive reading of Scripture and reason, then a whispered answer to prayer — to a saving knowledge of him.

For a while, Michael was quite angry that he'd been deceived. That Sunday, when the ward began to sing, "Praise to the man who communed with Jehovah," Mike could not even mouth the words.

CHAPTER 19

A LOT
TO GIVE UP

ψ

*Dear friends, do not be surprised at the fiery ordeal
that has come on you to test you, as though something
strange were happening to you.*

—1 PETER 4:12

After Michael received that answer to his prayer about polygamy, the few times he was inside the temple again, his radar was scoping. Soon enough, he knew he'd never again set foot in a Mormon temple, at least as a patron. When I read the passage from 1 Corinthians that March night in 2007 and knew I could not stay at BYU, Mike too accepted that we had to move on.

Even so, we'd all spent a lot of years in the temple. So many emotional ties to the temple and all things Mormon—smells, sights, sounds, feelings, traditions, people! The Mormon Church is false, yes, but it had been a profound part of our lives. I could not imagine leaving my colleagues or my students, my home, my neighbors, or Utah. Plus, I'd spent all those years developing a professional reputation, an LDS social network, and rank, tenure, and a good salary at BYU.

Leaving, for Mike, would mean leaving his business, his networks, his mountain home, and his priesthood reputation. He'd invested thirty years in his Mormon callings. He feared that his loss of priesthood would mean losing clients in Utah — along with respect, friends, and status. It was also hard for him to envision my giving up the tenured position at BYU. He'd watched me put so much blood, sweat, and tears into it. He mourned the loss of subsidized college educations for his three youngest children at BYU, an excellent private college.

He loathed the thought of leaving the hiking, the national parks, the mountains, and the red rock country. We loved watching the seasons march up and down the mountains, breathing the mountain air, eating meals on the deck with magnificent views, and enjoying the health of outdoor living. We had intended to retire in Happy Valley. It seemed a lot to give up.

Worst of all, he, like me, had to swallow that he was wrong all those years.

We were such baby Christians. We'd been puppets on a Mormon Church string for thirty years; life was fairly predictable. Now our life belonged to God, and everything seemed up for grabs. Even so, we were hoping for a painless way to take up our crosses and move forward. Although we'd made the decision to leave the Mormon Church, we both wanted to know *for certain* that the BYU door was closed.

"Just Like the Devil"

We had a new Christian friend who personally knew one of the twelve apostles of the Mormon Church. Our friend graciously volunteered to ask this apostle, without naming any names, if a tenured professor who became born again in Jesus and embraced evangelical Christianity could remain at BYU. The answer came in an email from our Christian friend in early June of 2007:

He [the apostle] is candid and it looks like there are no options. My prayer for you is to know the Lord's wisdom now. Personally, I agree with you, the matter of your own spiritual integrity is critical and I could not live out my faith quietly or privately either. We are to be a witness of truth for him. So, are you ready to move forward? You are in my prayers and thoughts much these days as I know it will be hard. But Lynn, remember the Lord will never and has never asked anything of us that he will not give us the strength to do. As well, the Lord's blessings are greater than the sacrifices we are asked to make. How can I help? What can I do? I am praying for you and Michael and for your family. God is good, know that you are now in his hands, and what a great place to be!

Our friend then delivered the LDS apostle's reply. The apostle suggested there would be near-impenetrable barriers in this situation — they had dealt with it before — and only the board of trustees (including the prophet, his counselors, and six of the twelve apostles) could execute a final determination. However, the apostle was unaware of any instance in which a BYU professor accepted biblical Christianity, no longer believed in Mormonism, and was allowed to remain at BYU, even if that person agreed not to share his or her newfound faith at work. He noted that the LDS Church financially supports the university. I had not yet earnestly considered giving up membership in the church; Mike was still attending. But now I knew that when I did, the BYU door apparently would be slammed shut.

The apostle seemed to recognize that someone who was born again and no longer accepted Mormonism probably could not remain a Mormon. Even though in recent years Mormonism has sought acceptance among evangelicals, most Mormons consider evangelical Christianity to be anti-Mormon.

The Bible *does* contradict Mormon doctrine. If Mike and I wished to remain biblical Christians, either we would have to ask to have our names removed from the LDS rolls, or a Mormon Church disciplinary court could excommunicate us. We accepted that we were now apostates, but because I was still an employee of BYU (I took a one-year leave of absence), we waited until the following March (2008) to request that our names officially be removed from the rolls.

Sometime later, I learned that if Matt had entered his senior year at the Y and professed biblical Christianity, he would not have been allowed to graduate from BYU. According to Mormonism, if we once knew the truth (accepted Mormonism) and turned from it (denied the Holy Ghost), we could be doomed to outer darkness with Satan and his minions.[46] Even Hitler, who was never Mormon, was relegated to the lower telestial kingdom (third degree of glory) but not outer darkness (hell) below. Yet Brigham Young said of apostates, "They will become gray-haired, wrinkled, and black, just like the Devil."[47]

Joseph's Story

The next season for us held great loss for our family and the band. God did not abandon us in our trials, but it did get tough. Joseph's story in particular encapsulates all the types of losses each of us felt keenly — losses of identity and status and support, and worst of all, loss of precious relationships.

When Joseph, Micah's friend who'd heard his testimony that day, returned home to Utah in June of 2006 after his mission to Florida, he'd already begun to develop a personal relationship with Jesus. Once home, he spent all day, every day with the fiancée who had waited for him, making plans to be sealed in the Bountiful Temple. Joseph didn't believe in the temple anymore, but he let her plan a wedding there to please others.

On July 1, he flew back to Florida, where he intended to work and join the band. He wanted to use his musical talents to show others a reason to choose Jesus. His fiancée was to follow a week later. She was the one person he was scared to death of losing by following the biblical Christ. So at first, he ignored what God thought about their marriage. Then, after feeling convicted, he got brave and asked. God's answer was clear: "No, Joseph."

When Joseph called his fiancée the next morning to break it off, one day before her flight to Florida, she was angry and told him he was being brainwashed. Her mom called Joseph crying and bearing her testimony of the Mormon gospel. Then his ex-fiancée called again to yell at him. When he didn't answer her repeated calls, she texted incessantly and called him names. He finally called her to say he would never call again. That was one of the hardest things Joseph ever had to do, because of how much he loved her and wanted her to understand his new faith. But she just couldn't.

His own parents didn't know yet that he had questions of faith. Before his mission, his parents had gotten divorced, and his mom was now remarried. As much as Joseph wanted everything to be the way it was before he found Jesus, he knew God's will. One day, he took a deep breath and sent his parents an email outlining his new beliefs. In response, his father called, and he told his dad on the phone that he no longer believed in the Mormon Church, only in the biblical Jesus.

At first, his dad blamed his faith conversion on Joseph's inability to deal with his parents' divorce. He said Joseph didn't want to come home to face the changes in his family. Then Joseph's dad called Joseph's mom, who called him the next night. She was calm and wanted to understand. But a few days later, he received emails from his mother and stepdad telling him to come home to Utah immediately. They had called his former mission president, who advised them to get Joseph out of Florida and back to Utah. Joseph's stepfather made accusations against Joseph similar to those of Micah's stake president. Then he demanded that Joseph reimburse him for the money he had donated to help pay for his mission.

Throughout the next year, Joseph's parents made it clear that they did not see the band as God's work, that they believed he was throwing his life away, and that they were disappointed in his choices. Were their reactions typical toward an apostate son? Naturally, different parents react in different ways. The only way Joseph was able to abide this painful rejection was with the strength and grace God gave him through his Word, his Holy Spirit, and the fellowship and love of people around him. Joseph gave up a fiancée, his LDS friends, and a close relationship with his parents. He also gained the disdain of most of his twenty-one siblings from the combined families—most, but not all.

Despite the dissonance, Joseph reached out to his siblings with the gospel of grace. One sister, Michelle, accepted his invitation to discover the Jesus of the Bible, and after a short visit to the hotel to learn more, she moved to Florida to begin a new life in Christ and to support the ministry full-time. Eventually Michelle dated and, in 2009, married band member Steve Kay. They have formed a family with Jesus as the chief cornerstone.

Joseph now thinks of himself like the Joseph who went down into Egypt, instead of Joseph Smith, and prays for that glorious reunion with the rest of his family that the Joseph of the Bible knew.

Purging the Old

Meanwhile Katie was asking God what was next for her. Should she go to college with the drama scholarship she'd been offered? Should she work? Should she support the band and ministry in

Florida? That was where her heart was. Pondering her future, she read the story of Saul's conversion in the New Testament. Saul (the apostle Paul) was told, "Now get up and go into the city, and you will be told what you must do" (Acts 9:6). Katie took this as her answer. Get up and go to Winter Garden, and you will be told what to do next.

So Katie decided to head to Florida with us. Just before we left Utah, she gave me a new journal. Mormons keep them religiously, and my seventh—the biblical number of completion—was filled. She said it was time for a new chapter.

And she was right. Before we left Utah, I engaged in a kind of purging. I got rid of everything Mormon. Michael finally removed his temple garments. I cut the markings out of our garments as I'd been taught to do to respectfully dispose of them. I gave away temple pictures, copies of the Book of Mormon, and LDS teaching materials. I packed up everything from my BYU office. I even hauled furniture to Deseret Industries, a Mormon version of Goodwill. I felt a need to vomit the old life as God helped us begin a new one unencumbered.

God had told us in one of our early morning answers to prayer to leave Utah by July 21—pretty specific. So in July 2007, Mike, Katie, and I packed up what we could get into two cars and made the three-day trip to Florida. Michael and I dropped Katie off at the hotel in Winter Garden, where she would work for a time and discover what was next. We would live three and a half hours south of the kids. I was apprehensive but, like Katie, excited to learn what God had in store for us.

Mike and I arrived in Fort Myers on July 24. Back in Utah, it was Pioneer Day, the day that Brigham Young and the first wagons of Mormon pioneers rolled into the Salt Lake Valley in 1847. This was the day I began liberation from the traditions of the LDS saints.

We moved in with my father (who was extremely excited about what was happening to our family), planning to live there until we could find our own place. Just after arriving, I prayed, "What should be my priorities?" God answered clearly, "Find a house and get to know Joseph. Then attend to your job."

Three days later, we were back in Winter Garden for an Adam's Road concert. The following weekend, we went again to take Joseph and Katie to dinner, to get to know him. We became so familiar with the seven-hour round trip, we could make it in our sleep.

Letting Go

Less than a month after we arrived in Florida, Joseph called Mike (back in Utah for a couple of weeks on business) to ask for our permission to ask Katie to marry him. He'd been with Adam's Road for fourteen months and was solid in Jesus. When the Spirit told me to get to know Joseph, I had no clue a marriage proposal was in the works. Although the two had been communicating for months by phone and text and had met several times, we never expected their relationship to solidify so quickly. In addition, Katie had never been boy-crazy, and I expected she would marry late. But God continued to surprise me.

The very next night, during an outdoor concert on a wooden platform in a field near a church, Joseph called Katie onstage to sing with him and to give her testimony. After she did, he got down on his knees and proposed to her. Katie looked stunned but thoroughly delighted. At that moment, she knew why God had brought her to Florida. When she chose to say yes to Joseph, she married into her life mission—supporting the band and the ministry for the glory of the Lord. God had a plan and a timing all along; she was the clay in the Potter's hand.

The speed of this courtship did take us by surprise. Each old assumption and expectation in my life was requiring reexamination. I would need to know my Bible well and trust God implicitly from now on as I let go and adjusted. But from what we knew of Joey, Katie was marrying a sweet, forthright, gentle, sensitive young man of faith.

They set the date for October 14, only two months away. I had a lot to do — adjust to a new job, find a new home, fly to Utah to load the moving van, move into a new home, and make arrangements for the wedding. The day I told Katie I'd drive up to help with the invitations, our moving van arrived early, and Mike wasn't back from Utah yet. I called Katie and we both had a good cry, but we're both tough and we each did what we had to do.

Shifting Sands

In less than a month, Mike and I had gone from having Katie's high school friends hanging out at our home to the deathly quiet of just us old folks. Since Mike was back in Utah a second time in the weeks after Katie's engagement (How *would* this work, with him living in Florida but having business in Utah?), I went to work during the day and hung out at the workout room in my dad's gated community at night. As I walked on the treadmill, pedaled the exercise bike, and lifted weights all alone, I listened intently to Vernon McGee and other Bible teachers on local Christian radio, Kingdom FM. Eventually, my workouts got shorter and shorter and my evening Scripture study and fervent prayer sitting at the weightlifting bench got more intense. In transition, I felt disoriented and lonely, but my brother was in the middle of a divorce he didn't ask for, and my LDS friend's daughter was cutting (self-mutilating). God placed me in the middle of both of their lives almost daily, a blessing and a distraction for me.

Mike came back from Utah and secured his business license in Florida. We still were not certain God would keep us there, but

Mike wanted a house, since most of his work would be online from home. I suppose we wanted one bit of worldly stability in the shifting sands of change.

We found a house, but it was in a gated community. As a multiculturalist, in the past I would never have agreed to buy a home in such a neighborhood. At the time, however, I was paranoid of the Mormon Church. I really was. Thirty years of Mormonism had so inbred me with fear of believing anything contrary to it that I was terrified they would find me, even though I didn't know exactly what its representatives would do. I imagined them monitoring phone conversations and computers.

In 2012, in the BBC documentary *The Mormon Candidate*, Elder Holland of the twelve apostles admitted on camera that the Mormon Church has a strengthening-church-members committee. That committee is alleged to hire former CIA and FBI agents to defend the church against "any insidious influence."[48] We had not spoken out yet, but I think we knew even in 2007 that we could not avoid doing so. I feared retribution.

Even if the Mormon Church didn't target us in a negative way, their persistent efforts to reach us spooked and annoyed us. My Mormon visiting teachers, the pair of women assigned to watch over me from the closest LDS ward building, located me at Dad's house and would sneak behind the gate into the closed community to leave notes at his door when I was at work. "Welcome! Church is at ..." Someone on campus with the same last name as one of the visiting teachers dropped by to welcome me and to tell me he'd read my vitae and that we had much in common. Although we had never shown up at a Mormon Church since moving to Florida, the local stake clerk (scurrying serf) was emailing me regularly through my BYU email, which was active for another several months. I was relieved when the email address expired.

I did not yet understand that one of the church's strongholds, from which I was still trying to extricate myself, was control through fear. I dreaded wearing the label of Mormon Church apostate. This fear had been bred into me over thirty years. I feared the shunning of church members who surely would not be as friendly if they knew what I believed. My new biblical knowledge was placing me in an awkward and uncomfortable position.

I felt lost and unsure of myself. At work, I didn't know what to say, what to wear, how to act. I had been in the Mormon bubble so long, the culture of the outside world was a complete puzzle to me and made me emotionally feeble. After I started sharing with a colleague at work some of my struggles and how Jesus sustained me, she stepped out and went to church for the first time since she was a girl. Now that I was in Jesus, was he working through me, using me? I'd need to get over my fear so he could.

The End of Myself

The professor I'd replaced for the one-year appointment opted to return, and the only professorial job posted close to my field that year was at the assistant professor level. If I returned to BYU, a research university, I would be only a year from full professor, yet if I stayed here, I would start all over again. I *did* need the chastening. My pride ran deep. Mormonism had fed its insatiable appetite all those years, and pride continues to be a thorn in my side. I applied for the assistant job and was hired full-time.

Given so many changes and challenges in my life, I wasn't sleeping well. My health deteriorated. I developed an ugly psoriasis. I believe God allowed all this to humble me. I needed humbling, and I needed to turn from professional rewards to the will of God, and from making idols of my children to deepening my relationship with him.

Mike experienced changes too. I noticed that he kept feeding our slim and trim cat Manny until he became portly and sleepy, as if Mike were trying to soothe his own soul by giving the cat comfort food. One Sunday afternoon, I drove him to the emergency room when he suffered with very high blood pressure. His business dwindled. With the economy the worst it had been in fifty years, it was nearly impossible for him to switch his business to Florida. Thank God, I had work. But I was accustomed to controlling my own life. Trusting God and not knowing what was coming next was a bit unnerving.

Whenever I was at the end of myself, though, feeling discouraged and lost, God showed up and encouraged me to hang on. *These must be the trials that James, the brother of Jesus, talked about as producing perseverance and maturity,* I thought. In return for obedience, God gave me the time to study the gospel, to think, and to write. Although I mourned the distance from our kids and grandkids, I rejoiced at their developing relationships and ministry and was grateful that most of them lived only three and a half hours away. We also felt blessed with the means to buy airline tickets to see Josh in Salt Lake.

And one more sign of God's grace: Soon after I started my new permanent job in Florida, I was offered additional contract work above and beyond my salary. It was worth—you guessed it—the *exact* amount of the check I'd been asked to write to Micah. A Christian friend suggested that God took the money I'd earned in service to the false god of Mormonism, cleansed it, redeemed it, and gave it back.

Eventually, Mike's business picked up in Utah, and he was able to work from Florida over the internet. I continued to swing between downright despair with so many changes at once and unfettered elation at this personal God.

Then one sleepless, anxious Friday night in early September 2007, I was reading the Bible and praying about all the blessings, the turmoil, and the changes. Although I'd given my life to Christ the previous fall, I now had an overwhelming desire to make a public profession of my faith in the biblical Jesus by being rebaptized. Michael agreed; he wanted it too. We wanted to trust God—no more fear.

So thirty hours later, we both received baptism on Sunday morning in the same glorious park where Joseph and Steve had been rebaptized. When I went down into the water, I had a vision of Scrooge's business partner, Marley, bound by all those chains. As I came up, I felt my own chains drop. I was light. When Mike went down and came up, a stream of sunlight broke through the clouds directly over his head. Micah was wearing one broad smile. Three days later, Katie was rebaptized at the same deep, clear spring. Mike and I were there, along with Micah and Alicia and baby Jacob, Steve and his then girlfriend Michelle (Katie's roommate and Joseph's only sibling to accept the biblical Jesus), and Katie's fiancée Joseph—all of us part of a new family in Jesus. Matt and Nicole were back at the hotel working.

Resignations

I had been on leave from BYU up to this point, so I officially resigned from my position there in January of 2008. Then, when that had been processed by BYU, we both resigned from the Church of Jesus Christ of Latter-day Saints. In honor of John 3:16, Mike and I composed our letters of resignation from the Mormon Church on March 16, 2008. It had been seventeen months since I first surrendered my life to Jesus, and seven months since Mike took off his temple garments and quit attending the Mormon Church.

We had bought a small home in Florida but still owned our home in Utah. When we left, we made a halfhearted effort to sell the Utah home by putting it on Craig's List, but we'd given up since we had good renters during that winter and home values were down. On March 17, 2008, the day after we wrote our resignations, a couple from California drove by our Utah home and saw the For Sale by Owner sign still up in the front yard, visible again now that the snow had melted. Our neighborhood was pretty isolated. Rarely did anyone who didn't live there drive through it.

The Californians called my husband's cell number on the sign, the renters let them in to see the house, and a couple of days later, they offered a decent amount for our Utah home. Cash buyers with the economy barely cranking — a miracle, and another example of God's provision and guidance! The question about whether God would take us back to Utah was settled. He had closed that door — for now.

Mike had our resignation letters notarized, flew to Utah, and took them directly to the church headquarters on Temple Square. The day was cloudy. The receptionist in the church office building asserted for some time that they could not possibly accept the letters there. It was a local matter, and we would have to deliver them to our bishop in Florida. Mike insisted that he knew the letters eventually ended up somewhere in the office building, and pressed her. Finally, she relented and directed him to an office down the hall to the right. This next receptionist knew exactly what they were and took them routinely. Mike had her sign them and indicate that they were received by the hands of the Mormon Church at 11:10 a.m. Mountain Standard Time on April 11, 2008. A few minutes later, after exiting the building into sunlight, he called me in Florida, and I could hear in his voice that his burden had lifted.

Although the letters had requested that the church remove our names without contacting us except for a letter confirming the removal, on June 11, 2008, a Florida bishop whose church was near my father's house called to talk about our resignation. Mike engaged him in conversation for ninety minutes, asking questions the bishop could not answer and teaching him facts he did not seem to know. The bishop said he did not need to talk with me and would send the letters up the ladder. In early September of 2008, we received an official letter from the LDS Church, dated August 11, 2008, informing us that our names were being (not had been) removed from the church rolls.

Inappropriately, the LDS Church continued to invite us to ward activities via mail for months afterward. The church had our new address from our resignation letters, so now another bishop closer to our home had family records. Katie had never lived with us in southwest Florida and didn't resign with us, but her records were with ours. She received visiting teaching letters and invitations to church until late 2010 at our home, even after I wrote to Relief Society to tell them she did not live with us in southwest Florida and never had. I concluded by saying, "Please do not contact us." Someone was checking off her visiting teaching duty by mailing letters because Katie was on her list. They meant well, but I wondered if we'd ever be completely free of the Mormon Church.

CHAPTER 20

BINDING AND
HEALING

⚜

Blessed is the one whom God corrects; so do not despise
the discipline of the Almighty. For he wounds, but he
also binds up; he injures, but his hands also heal.

—JOB 5:17–18

A new Christian friend described our family's journey like this:
We were a group of people scattered to the four winds by
a horrific spiritual war in the land—everyone off in their own
corner of the conflict, experiencing the same war but in different
ways. Then, when the main hostilities died down and the dust
and smoke cleared, most everyone managed to find a ship to get
across the ocean, away from the smoldering homeland, but not
the same ship and not necessarily to the same port. One by one,
we managed to find each other again in the new country, some
quickly, others not so quickly, all with different war stories and
traumas, covered with different battle scars and injuries, bleeding
in different places.

We each rejoiced at learning that the others had survived the war, but rebuilding a life in a new country and new culture was not easy. We were free, there was great hope and great opportunity in the new land, but everything and everyone had changed. It was natural to mourn the things we missed about our "peaceful" days in the old country — even while we recognized that the new land was far better than where we'd been.

In Florida, Michael and I found a Christian church that followed the biblical Christ, we joined numerous Bible studies (for men, for women, for couples), and we resumed some appearance of normalcy. But nothing was the same. Our hunger for God's Word did not lessen. We continued to read, study, and discuss the Word every morning, at night in bed together, and any other time we could sneak it in throughout the day. After Jesus, we were not and never would be the same. Everything was new — our standard of truth, our thoughts, our values, our behavior (Mike and I observed changes in each other), and our relationships.

And to my infinite joy and relief, the family relationship wound I had envisioned as a foot wide and eight fleshy inches deep began to heal.

A Healing Balm

First, my original family was healed, and my relationship with Dad strengthened. My Christian father, eighty-two in 2007 when we came to live near him, embraced our Christian faith with effusive gratitude. Then, four months after we arrived, he blacked out, fell off a tall ladder onto pavement, and was airlifted to the hospital unconscious. I'd been 2,500 helpless miles away in Utah when my mom died. Now I was right by my dad's side when he woke up. He came home to stay with us for a few days. Although he'd broken bones in his face, he was back to golfing within a couple of months.

My baby sister in Indianapolis was also thrilled. In 2009, the band toured through Indianapolis, and that week Katie and I stayed with Cindy and her husband, John, and their seven children, all homeschooled. After a crisis in their lives some years ago, Cindy and John had become very strong Christians. One day they were in the pool as I sat on the side. We were talking when I heard the sentiment rise in her voice. She began to cry. "I'm so glad God brought you to know Jesus even when I did nothing—except pray." My mom and dad had prayed, my sister had prayed, and Alicia and Micah had prayed. As time went on, we learned of others. Prayer works. I slid into the pool and we embraced, any past hurts caused by religious differences melting away.

In May of 2011, I flew with Dad to visit my only brother, who lived in Texas. As a new Christian, I'd prayed with Jim through his divorce, and he was now remarried to a strong Christian and patiently loving his adult daughters. Then my father and I went to the home of my middle sister, Sue, and her husband, Scott, in New Mexico. Their two children, polite and pleasant, took us in and showered us with love. My sister and her husband are now church attenders, and she has the unconditional love and gentle ways of our mother. In August of 2011, Dad and I flew to Wisconsin to see his sisters and my cousins. Many heard the story of what God had done in our lives, and the Dancer of grace applied a healing balm in all of these places.

More Harmonies

We also continued to revel in God's healing touch on our immediate family. The wedding of Katie and Joey in fall 2007 was a huge testimony of God's ability to take what was broken and bind it together again. Since her first night at the Edgewater, Katie has never had another episode of night terrors. She seemed to grow up overnight and exude an inner beauty. Joseph, a hopeless romantic, adores her.

The wedding, once again outdoors at Kelly Park, was lovely

in its simplicity. The morning dawned cool and overcast, a blessing for Florida in October. The band set up white chairs, a trellis, and a white runway near the crystal-clear water of the spring where we'd been baptized. Striding down the runway on her father's arm, Katie was radiant in her white veil and simple white halter dress. She was so full of joy; Joseph, no less so. The bridesmaids—Alicia, Nicole, and Michelle—were striking in their simple burgundy dresses. Joseph selected his brother, the band members, and Josh as groomsmen.

During the ceremony, Katie and Joseph sang intertwining harmonies to each other, a song the band composed called "By Your Grace," which appeared on their album *Adam's Road*. (Katie will occasionally record with the band.)

Micah, now a justice of the peace, married them. He stood between them in a brown striped shirt and tie, his now-longer dark hair in soft curls. Micah choked up as he told the guests how amazed he was that God would join two people he loved more than any in the whole world. Tears fell gently for me as I held on to my Michael. Another miracle—Micah's best friend marrying his beloved sister.

The reception was back at the Edgewater Hotel, in the first-floor lobby with the large stone fireplace. As the bride and groom rested on a bench outside the hotel before the reception, a family we knew from our Alpine, Utah, neighborhood—who had come to know the biblical Jesus before we did—pulled into the parking lot and stepped out of the car to a reunion of God-sized proportions. To our delight, they had flown to Florida to celebrate our family's inclusion in the body of Christ.

A Synagogue of Satan

Two weeks after the wedding, I was scheduled to attend a multicultural conference to present research I had completed at BYU.

Therefore my conference badge said BYU, although I had moved on. A man approached me brazenly in the hallway, introduced himself as a Palestinian, gave my BYU badge a wave of his hand, and said, "I lived in Arizona and met some Mormons. They told me they are Jews, something about adoption. Can you explain?"

Wow. That question knocked me off balance. I answered slowly, "Well, Mormons *are* told in their patriarchal blessings what tribe of Israel they are from and whether the blood of that tribe flows in their veins or they are adopted in." I was supposedly from the tribe of Manasseh, and Michael from Ephraim. Mormons believe that in these latter days, they are gathering the lost ten tribes of Israel, although, as I learned later from an archeologist in Israel, the ten tribes are not actually lost.

One afternoon later that week, while listening to Moody Radio, I heard someone read verses from Revelation that caught my attention. I quickly got my already disintegrating, well-worn paperback Bible and flipped to Revelation 2:9: "I know your afflictions and your poverty—yet you are rich! I know about the slander of those who say they are Jews and are not, but are a synagogue of Satan." *The slander of those who say they are Jews and are not? Does this point to the Mormon Church? Who else thinks they are Jews but are not—and instead are a synagogue of Satan?*

I read on and found Revelation 3:9: "I will make those who are of the synagogue of Satan, who claim to be Jews though they are not, but are liars—I will make them come and fall down at your feet and acknowledge that I have loved you." I shared all this with Mike, and his eyes widened in alarm. Perhaps this church we felt afraid of, suspected of control, and wanted freedom from really *was* dangerous spiritually—was, as the Bible put it, a synagogue of Satan.

In April 2008, the FBI stormed into the polygamist compound of Warren Jeffs (leader of the Fundamentalist Latter-Day Saints, or FLDS), in Texas, and removed more than four hundred children. FLDS are not technically part of the Mormon Church today, but they follow the original teachings of its founder, Joseph Smith, teachings still in the Doctrine and Covenants as section 132. As I watched the polygamist women speak to the media, I saw that each wore the same pastel pioneer clothes, had the same outdated hairdo, and said the same words. Their uniformity was eerily familiar.

Then it hit me. I realized that my BYU students—in fact, many Mormons—had that same clean-cut but foggy, detached appearance. They dressed alike within the prescribed honor code, talked alike using the same cultural phrases, and thought alike according to the same religious mandates. I still felt like such an anomaly in the world outside of Mormonism that I asked my mentor at work, "Do I look like a polygamist to you? Do I dress like one?" More and more, I was glad we had walked away, but the adjustment to Jesus' love, grace, and acceptance took his healing hand.

Another Family Celebration

God continued his binding and healing touch upon our family. Josh came for Christmas the first year we were in Florida. Soon after returning to Utah, he met his future wife, Mandy, also from Salt Lake. Mandy's a tall, talented, beautiful blond, a kind soul. At the time that they met, she was a single mom who'd been supporting herself and her respectful, good-natured son for almost a decade. Mandy had given up faith in Mormonism back in high school, but, as with all of the in-law families, some of her family is still strong in the Mormon Church.

Micah married them on an island beach near our home in Fort Myers, a sunset wedding with white chairs and trellis—grandchildren exploring the sand—and an intimate family dinner afterward. (Josh and Mandy have graced the family with a whimsical daughter and a joy-filled son.) Because the band family runs the Edgewater

Hotel 24/7 and at least part of the family must be there 365 days a year, the Florida weddings were blessings that gathered the Wilder family together for a few memorable hours. (Some members of the band family stayed behind to care for the hotel guests.)

One person who had always been at our family celebrations was absent this time. Michael's beloved older sister, whom he'd baptized into the Mormon Church, was still active there. That was one tenuous relationship that we had to entrust to God's care now that we had opposing faiths.

Public Profession

In August of 2008, a year after we moved to Florida, Adam's Road traveled to Utah for a few concerts. While in Utah, they were on the *Heart of the Matter* Salt Lake TV show with Shawn McCraney, a show where "Mormonism meets biblical Christianity face-to-face," as Shawn says. In addition, the *Salt Lake Tribune* wrote an article on the band, and their ministry began to be known in that desert land. Mike and I loved our Mormon people so much, we felt their pain when the band began to teach them the truth. We knew how brutal it was. I began praying in earnest that God would bring the Mormon people to know the Jesus of the Bible.

Shawn McCraney invited me to come on the TV show to explain to viewers why a BYU professor had left the Mormon Church. On January 20, 2009, the same date that three years prior we'd received that life-changing phone call from Micah and his priesthood leaders, I did. I agreed for one reason. I felt I needed to tell the many BYU students who knew me, and our numerous Mormon friends and neighbors, that I had found the truth — Mormonism is dubious, and the Jesus in the Bible is worth investigating.

That public profession opened the floodgates. Although no active Mormon would be caught dead watching the show, by the next day, I began to hear from former students and others.

First, I got emails from friends and past BYU students who were genuinely shocked. I received a very kind email from a former colleague at BYU who said that a few students had asked about the accuracy of the *Salt Lake Tribune* article that referenced my withdrawal from the LDS Church. The colleague suggested that those in my former department would have the students contact me on their own if they had questions, or they would tell them they don't know anything about it. This person concluded by writing, "Bottom line is we simply respect you, miss you, and wish you the very best." Some days I missed that Mormon Jesus niceness.

From a former student I received another sincere email. The student wanted to confirm that I had indeed left the Mormon Church and wanted to ask why. This student said that I had been someone who had helped them find peace in the gospel and believe in things that were hard for them. I had strengthened their testimony of the Mormon Church. This person asked me to help them understand why I would leave, so they would not feel abandoned. That was a tough word to hear. Like I said before, I loved my BYU students. Of course I wrote back with all the bulldozing enthusiasm of someone with new faith in Jesus, but I'm sure it was too much to hear. Over the years, I've gotten better at hearing a person's heart first and sharing my answers according to his or her personal concerns, one question at a time.

The responses to my public testimony have not always been kind. I've been accused of being on drugs, being stupid, and lying. Some internet posts have included vile cursing and sexual allegations. Mike and I nearly gave up our sanity, until we got used to these attacks. Thank God for his recurring love. Jesus said, "If the world hates you, keep in mind that it hated me first" (John 15:18).

"Mingling" with Scripture

Sadder than the vitriol that I've avoided printing, however, is the deafness and blindness that shackle so many Mormons, as I had been. As some of the comments posted on a YouTube clip from that episode of the *Heart of the Matter* demonstrated, the deafness and blindness are results of a lack of *knowledge*—not knowing the Bible and not understanding clear doctrinal differences with Mormonism. After watching the clip, one comment said that I was confused and didn't understand Mormonism, that I must have been inactive for thirty years, that I didn't seem to understand that Mormons don't follow Old Testament law, because Mormons do not refrain from eating lobster or pig. (Mormons, however, *do* build temples and *do* rely on laws and ordinances in order to earn the favor to live with God and Jesus after this life.)

Another post found it odd that Christians actually make ministries out of converting Mormons and declare victory whenever they convert one, seeming to ignore the fact that Mormon missionaries celebrate, too, whenever they earn converts from Christianity.

Another comment called my story a sad one—very sad—and wondered why I wouldn't have read the New Testament at least once in the thirty years I was a Mormon. After all, Mormons cover the New Testament and quote from it. (What Mormonism does with the New Testament I call cherry-picking—selecting verses that corroborate Mormon doctrine and ignoring or demonizing [call them mistranslated] others that don't.)

One comment was particularly interesting to me. It mentioned Micah and me, then referred readers back to the fireside chat held by President Benson in the 1980s in which the prophet warned all families to remove the mother from the workplace and place her back in the home. The comment pointed out that Benson had warned that mothers who forsook their children for "money or worldly acclaim" would reap the consequences in later years. This writer's implication was that because I had not been the primary nurturer in our home, I was now reaping what I had sown. I was bothered by this because, even though I was never a perfect mom, for sure, still I had been the primary nurturer.

Another comment questioned my saying that Mormonism presents a different Christ, one who teaches that works are necessary for salvation. This person noted that there are many laws right there in the Sermon on the Mount and that we have to obey them. The comment suggested that if I can't live the commandments, then, of course, I should go ahead and misinterpret Paul in order to weasel out of doing works. Several other comments agreed that one leaves the Mormon Church and becomes a Christian to avoid doing the works required and having to live by all the rules. One said that it is always easier to ride a bike downhill than up, and concluded that their preference was to follow a living prophet as opposed to the "philosophies of men, mingled with scripture."

This repeats a phrase from the LDS temple endowment ceremony contrasting the truth of the living prophet with "the philosophies of men mingled with scripture," or the lies of Satan taught in biblical Christianity. (Remember the Christian minister in Satan's employ we had seen at one time in — now removed from — the temple ceremony?) The individual who posted this likely has no idea how true that statement "mingled with scripture" is when applied to Mormonism, given the philosophies of Mormon prophets, seers, and revelators that mingle with scriptural cherry-picking. The charge here is that as an apostate and a Christian, I follow Satan's philosophies of men mingled with scripture.

Why Mormons Say Mormons Leave the Church

Typically, LDS Church members have a three-pronged mantra about why anyone leaves the church. One either has committed a big sin, can't live by the church standards, or was offended.

In December of 2009, a video critical of me, called *Adam's Road: The Pride and Fall of Lynn Wilder*, appeared on YouTube, accusing me of pride and a selfish desire to protect Micah from the consequences of his own choices. I have readily admitted to being prideful, but I was a faithful, temple recommend Mormon who lived by church standards for thirty years. As for protecting Micah, I do not know how my leaving the church twenty-six months after he was sent home from his mission could accomplish that. And while I was indeed offended by one or two individuals' treatment of Micah and Josh, I did not leave the church for that reason.

Did I leave because I couldn't live by the standards? No, I'd held a temple recommend declaring my worthiness from 1978 to 2008. We resigned two months after it expired. Did I commit any big sins? As a Mormon, I placed sins in a kind of hierarchy of bad to worse. I was not aware that any sin, small or large, kept me from worthiness. Except for apostasy to Mormon teaching, I did not commit any sins considered big to a Mormon. I have been completely open about why I left. I left the Mormon Church because of doctrinal conflicts between the Bible and Mormon doctrine and because I found the real Jesus.

Jesus is worth all of this. Following him requires everything. He said in Luke 9:62, "No one who puts a hand to the plow and looks back is fit for service in the kingdom of God." In Mormonism, Mike and I covenanted in the temple to give everything for the building up of the *organization* of the Mormon Church. In return, we expected blessings. Now, we have pledged everything to follow Jesus. The Bible promises God's indwelling, his love, and his insights — but also trials, rejection, and persecution. Now that we are born again, our lives belong to Jesus, and that means losing the old and taking up our crosses and following him.

With gentle caresses, Jesus bound and healed the open

wounds that Micah, Alicia, Matt, Nicole, Joseph, Katie, Jay, Steve, Michelle, Erik, Josh, Mandy, Mike, and I carried—not only the wounds within ourselves but also the relational wounds among us. Hardly a week passes now that we do not hear from others whom Jesus has called out of the LDS Church and who are going through the wounding and binding-and-healing process themselves. I've heard amazing stories of God's grace in people's lives. Yet there was one more important relational healing for which I still hoped.

Three Treasured Words

When we moved to Florida in 2007, we invited our children's families to our new home that first Christmas, and everyone came—except Micah and his family. We wondered, *If he couldn't make it on Christmas Day, since he and Alicia stayed back with others to run the hotel while Matt and Katie and their spouses were here, then why not another time during the holiday season?* Again, we assumed that he and Alicia had rejected us. Of course, each time something like this happened, Micah had good reasons for his behavior, but Mike and I misinterpreted these absences as personal rejection. We were still pretty self-centered. Does the sun rise in the morning? No, that is our perception. The earth actually spins. Our point of view was faulty.

On that dreadful evening back in January 2006 when, after Micah, Mike, and I left the stake president's office, Mike encouraged Micah to continue reading the Book of Mormon and wearing his temple garments, Micah felt he would not likely be the one to convert his parents. He later told me, "I did not feel rejected by you, just that Katie and Matt were open to hearing about the biblical Jesus, and they would eventually help teach you."

He flew to Florida, and he and Alicia were immediately consumed, at the ages of twenty-one and nineteen, with managing a three-story hotel with its restaurants, its lessees, its maintenance, and its employees. As they came to know the biblical God, they trusted him to gather the band and ministry. They prayed for their parents but, as Micah's email indicated, were quite overwhelmed with their own lives at first.

"When we went back to Utah in May for our wedding reception there," Alicia said, "we noticed some slight movement in you and Mr. Mike when, on the ride to the airport, you asked us about what you had read in the Bible. When I returned in December for Jacob's baby shower, we had real hope."

God used our false sense of rejection to break us so we were at the end of ourselves, hungry for Jesus' grace, which he freely gave. And even after our perception was corrected and we and Micah shared the same faith, we still needed fresh infusions of God's grace and love to heal wounds both old and new. Life now is a continuing process of grace infusion.

Josh, Matt, Micah, and Katie and their spouses—all of us— had residual feelings from the family disruptions. We had to redefine ourselves, both individually in relation to the new God of grace and as a family outside the scripted, prescribed life in the Mormon bubble. Plus, Michael and I found ourselves making adjustments in our triangular marriage relationship with Christ. Three of the kids and their spouses had a ministry family also to consider. We all had a broader family in Jesus. Of all of us, I was the basket case in this family evolution.

The first time Micah visited our home in southwest Florida was when Adam's Road came on the bus because the guys had a two-week string of concerts in the area in late January and early February of 2010. My grandson Jacob, now almost three, traveled with the band. Back home, Jacob had a little brother, Ben, who had Alicia's red hair, and a third brother, Timothy, on the way.

I was so excited to have Jacob with us. He slept at the house. The others slept in the bus, which was parked at a church five

minutes from our home. Each day, Mike shuttled the band members to the house to shower, prepare for concerts, practice, hang
out, and eat. I went to work during the day and came home to feed
and enjoy my quiver full of blessings. The band sat around the
long dining room table we had secured just in case we needed it.

Micah's twenty-fifth birthday fell during that week. We (the
five band members, the bus driver, their sweet grandmotherly
cook Jane, their communications administrator and booking agent
Stefan, who has another remarkable story of leaving Mormonism
for Jesus, Jacob, Mike, and I) had a meal of spare ribs with all the
trimmings and cake and ice cream. We sang the traditional Wilder
off-key birthday song and took lots of pictures—just like old
times—for Facebook and to send to the wives back at the hotel.

On the last concert day, the guys opted not to stay to watch
the Super Bowl, wanting to get home to their families. When the
bus pulled away, Micah texted me these three words: "I love you."
As God was healing me, I was now able to *hear* those treasured
words and believe that God loved me. Of course, I cried and
thanked Jesus. At the same time, I realized it was finally less and
less about me and my feelings and more about Jesus.

Given the prodigal daughter that I was, the reunion with
loved ones was exceedingly sweet, because we had all been lost
in a horrific spiritual war, but now we were found—safe in the
arms of our Father. And he was celebrating, dancing and singing
over us (Zeph. 3:17). The grace we gave to each other as a family
came not from us but from Jesus—the never-ending source of
grace, healing, and forgiveness for every family.

CHAPTER 21

UNVEILING GRACE

⚜

Even to this day when Moses is read, a veil covers their
hearts. But whenever anyone turns to the Lord, the veil
is taken away.

— 2 CORINTHIANS 3:15 – 16

A mere six years after the Berlin Wall fell, my Christian father
and I, still LDS at that time, journeyed into former West
Germany and then former East Germany. After twenty years of
doing genealogy—it was one thing he and I agreed on and did
together—the two of us wanted to find our relatives.

In Friedrichsdorf, I attended the Frankfurt Temple. Public
restrooms were scarce and my father, who would have to wait for
me for two hours in the rental car, needed one while I was gone.
There was one right inside the door of the temple before you
entered the temple proper, but the woman at the desk refused
my father entrance since he was not a Mormon and did not hold
a temple recommend. When I returned to the car, he was angry.
"Your church doesn't even think I'm worthy to use their restrooms." I apologized.

The contrast between West and East was stark! West Germany

was freshly painted, clean, and colorful. There we saw stocky little old ladies sweeping the streets in front of their window boxes full of bright blossoms. People were friendly. Public transportation was plentiful. Material goods and services were reasonably priced and readily available.

Former East Germany gave us hair-raising, spine-chilling shivers. Once, we were stopped in traffic at a dead standstill for hours, afraid for our safety. The miniscule, poorly constructed, blocky cars reminded me of the Flintstone mobile. The buildings were a bland gray of crumbling plaster and graffitied sameness, unkempt and dirty. Trash was everywhere. People were rude. Goods and services were hard to find and way too expensive. We hightailed it out of there. It occurred to me that West and East were a visual representation of light and darkness, a blatant contrast between the presence of Christ and his freedom in people's lives, and the complete absence of him and of hope. Jesus. No Jesus. Real Messiah. False Messiah.

A Dancing King

It's nearly time to unveil the Dancer of grace. But first, let's look at the most joyous dancer in all of Scripture who loved the Lord: King David. Can you see him twirling and leaping among those singing and playing musical instruments, in praise of the One he knew intimately, as the ark arrived in the City of David? His wife Michal, Saul's daughter, expressed disgust afterward because he danced with such wild abandon; apparently, she felt he was not properly dressed, and perhaps he lost part of his clothes in the dance (2 Sam. 6). She judged, "Undignified!" But David was a man with his eyes on the Lord, with no care for what others thought. To have a focus like David!

Oh, it's true that David messed up. He was responsible for foul immorality — lying, adultery, and murder. David was tormented with remorse, though, and the prophet Nathan told him the Lord removed his sin (Ps. 51; 2 Sam.12:13). Just like that, gone. But in the skewed-Old-Testament, works-based world of Mormon scripture, the Mormon Jesus says, "David hath fallen from his exaltation" (D&C 132:39). This means that because of David's sins, even though he asked for forgiveness, God punished him forever by allowing him neither to live with God nor to have his wives and concubines with him in the next life. In direct contrast, the Bible says David was forgiven (the forgiven do live with God in the next life).

So what Mormon scripture says and what the Bible says are polar opposites. At least one of these eternal results for David has to be a lie. Would the real Jesus please stand up? Even the most recent past LDS prophet, Gordon B. Hinckley, admitted that Mormons do not follow the same Jesus that Christians do: "The traditional Christ of whom they [Christians] speak is not the Christ of whom I speak."[49]

The biblical Jesus we now believe in *did not* and *does not* deliver a newfangled, updated, improved message only to Joseph Smith and his priesthood successors. Jesus' message hasn't changed and never will. He is big enough, intelligent enough, and strong enough to get it right the first time, for all time, and his words are in the Bible. He is God, for Pete's sake! But if the Jesus of the Bible is the true Jesus, why did it take so long for me to see it?

Rending the Temple Veil

Just what *is* the veil that covers the face of grace? What is it that kept us from seeing Jesus for who he is? From 2 Corinthians 3:14, "Their minds were made dull, for to this day the same veil remains when the old covenant is read. It has not been removed, because only in Christ is it taken away." The veil is the old covenant, the law given to Moses and the people of Israel. It was my immersion in the old covenant, or the Mormon version of the Old Testament law, that kept me blind. The real purpose of the Old Testament law — our schoolmaster — was not to get us to heaven, because it can't (Gal. 2:16–21; 5:4; Rom. 6:14). The purpose was to show us that we have sins and need the Savior (Gal. 3:23–25; Rom. 3:20). It was given to humble us, not to puff us up. Only Jesus' atonement on the cross, no work of our own, relieves us of sins, if we believe him.

The Mormon version of the old law includes temples, which seem like a judicious Old Testament biblical concept. God gave his people only one temple, in Jerusalem. In contrast, LDS temples are proliferating, 141 of them at last count. What the Jews did in the temple and what the Mormons do in their many temples are in no way similar. Jews gave tithes to support the priests, yes, but also to demonstrate their thankfulness to God and reliance upon him for their sustenance. The Mormons tithe to support their church organization and as a prerequisite to attend the temple, where they receive the saving ordinances (baptism, confirmation, ordination to the Melchizedek priesthood [for men], the temple endowment, and the marriage sealing). Performed by the authority of the LDS priesthood, these ordinances are essential to LDS exaltation. With each ordinance, the godly few temple-worthy Mormons enter into solemn covenants with the Mormon Lord. The result is that they learn how to be elevated to the highest rung of heaven, where they can achieve godhood and live with the Father and the Son and have plural wives (or be one). They pay and work their way through the Mormon Jesus' representatives to exaltation in the celestial kingdom.

The purpose of the Jewish temple was not to exalt one to godhood but to demonstrate that one needs a Savior. At the Jewish temple, Jews offered animal sacrifices to demonstrate sorrow for their sins and to seek God's forgiveness. Jewish temple attend-

ees placed their hands on the unblemished lamb to transfer their
sins to it. In exchange, they received the righteousness of the
lamb sacrificed. All of this is a likeness of the Messiah, Jesus, the
perfect sacrificial Lamb. The sacrifices conducted in the Jewish
temple were a representation of Jesus' sacrifice on the cross (Rom.
8:3–4). That's why Paul says the old law has passed away—temples included (2 Cor. 6:16; 1 Peter 2:5; Acts 7:48; Jer. 7:4). Jesus
fulfilled the law (Heb. 7–10).

At the moment of Jesus' death, when he atoned for our sins on
the cross, the Jewish temple veil was rent from top to bottom to
give us direct access to God. In the Mormon Church, the temple
veil is still up. Worthy church members must progress through a
literal white veil by giving the signs and tokens and handshakes
of the Mormon priesthood to access God. While working in the
temple, Michael and Micah both have played the role of God
behind the veil. I was a temple worker who helped the women
give the signs and tokens that allowed them to pass through the
veil and enter God's presence. This Mormon version of an Old
Testament system of laws and ordinances kept me veiled from the
real Jesus.

In performing LDS temple work, I was in subjugation to
Joseph Smith and his god, since Mormon temples were their
invention. Jesus himself warns in Matthew 24:26, "If anyone tells
you, 'There he is, out in the wilderness [desert, in the King James
Version],' do not go out; or, 'Here he is, in the inner rooms,' do
not believe it." We were once told a story of Christ appearing in
the inner rooms of the Salt Lake Temple.[50] And Brigham Young
said of Brother Joseph, "Every man and woman must have the
certificate of Joseph Smith, Junior, as a passport to their entrance
into the mansion where God and Christ are"[51] and "if we live
so that Joseph will justify us ... we will pass into the celestial
kingdom."[52] Even today in order to join the Mormon Church,

the baptismal interview requires one to accept that the gospel of Jesus Christ has been restored through the Prophet Joseph.[53] I no longer want to go where Joseph Smith is the gatekeeper!

Who blinded me? Second Corinthians 4:3–4 explains, "Even if our gospel is veiled, it is veiled to those who are perishing. The god of this age has blinded the minds of unbelievers, so that they cannot see the light of the gospel that displays the glory of Christ, who is the image of God." It was the god of this world whose demons had visited me and who had watched over me before I knew Jesus.

The truth was, at times the Dancer of grace did intercede on my behalf, but I erroneously gave credit to the Mormon Lord. I've thought a lot about why my life in the Mormon Church seemed so peaceful. I believe that the god of this world had me exactly where he wanted me. He soothed me with the thought that as long as I served the Mormon Jesus, life would be without trials and persecutions—the best were blessed. "Yea, blessed are they whose feet stand upon the land of Zion, who have obeyed my gospel; for they shall receive for their reward the good things of the earth, and it shall bring forth in its strength" (D&C 59:3). All was well in Zion, as the LDS hymn said.[54] I bought it hook, line, and sinker.

Thank God he allowed the trials that took me into the Word and unveiled the true Messiah. Jesus explains through Paul the *unveiling* that occurs when one turns to the Lord Jesus Christ: "Even to this day when Moses is read, a veil covers their hearts. But whenever anyone turns to the Lord, the veil is taken away. Now the Lord is the Spirit, and where the Spirit of the Lord is, there is freedom. And we all, who with unveiled faces contemplate the Lord's glory, are being transformed into his image with ever-increasing glory, which comes from the Lord, who is the Spirit" (2 Cor. 3:15–18).

For a long time, a veil covered my heart. Caught up in the rules and regulations of the Mormon gospel, I was—like many religious leaders in Jesus' time—unable to see the real Jesus. Yes, as a Mormon I read the New Testament, but always through the veil of Mormonism. Only when I earnestly sought the true Jesus while reading the New Testament was the veil taken away and was I fully able to contemplate his glory.

The Word as Sledgehammer

Did you notice? Mike and I came to know Jesus, to be converted, changed, and healed, only when we read and soaked in the Word of God—where the Dancer of grace unveiled to us the real and living and powerful Jesus.

In the very beginning, Alicia tried to discuss with us new biblical concepts. God chose this sweet and tender young woman to do the initial difficult first steps of offering a new Jesus to a well-meaning but prideful couple. She was the very example of his love. The blood I followed, though—blood coursing through the veins of a sinful man, Joseph Smith—washed me in lies, resulting in hardness, blindness, and stubbornness. Why couldn't I just listen to Alicia? She was the perfect messenger of grace. But Mormonism places parents as gods to be mentors for their children, so my mindset was that I was supposed to teach her. In addition, I was rock-hard with pride and completely unaware of the valuable pearl she offered.

Micah too was the perfect messenger of grace. Given the many years we'd grown up together as a family, plus his loving service to us before his mission, we trusted him implicitly. Why couldn't we just read the New Testament when he asked us to, when he was still on his mission? Then by the time he was sent home, we might have known the truth too and defended him. But we were trapped in the whirlwind desert life of Mormon expectations. We did not know that we were spiritually dead and that we desperately needed the infused lifeblood of Jesus. But he knew.

Erik, the former Mormon and now Christian hotel owner in Florida, sometimes called us to talk about the problems with Joseph Smith, LDS Church history, and the Mormon Church, but that approach did not work either. Instead we vigorously defended the Mormon Church. His bold witness to us seemed harsh. The truth was brutal. I envisioned Erik as a lion slashing fresh wounds into my belly. Then one day I stumbled on this passage in the Bible: "Let a righteous man strike me—it is a kindness; let him rebuke me—that is oil on my head. My head will not refuse it" (Ps. 141:5).

All three of them had tried to teach us with three personal approaches, but we had not accepted the rebuke. We would not turn. The enemy of our souls, the god of this world, blinded us. "Just read the New Testament," Micah had been saying all along.

Finally, because of the painful family disruption after Micah was sent home—specifically, what I perceived as his rejection of us—Michael and I did pick up the Bible to hear what Jesus had to say. We searched Jesus' words and the words of his disciples, starving for answers about what—really—was true. In the turmoil, we yearned for love.

As thoughtful Matt and determined Nicole sat with us on the weekends, all of us Scripture-chaining in earnest through the Word of God, we met a new Jesus. Pastor Jim and Katie and our Christian friends each had a part. God used his Word as a sledgehammer, shattering our blindness little by little, like the thick Berlin Wall.

The Holy Spirit and Counterfeits

Of course, the real Dancer of grace is the Holy Spirit, a member of the triune God. I would not have come to truth without him. It was likely he who prompted my prayer back in kindergarten to make music for God, then raised up the musicians forty-eight years later. Probably it was he who told me to marry my Michael—a godsend beyond words—who traveled this road beside me and never gave up on me. The Holy Spirit watched as we danced into and then out of the Mormon Church, and blessed us with four awesome children. Among them was one who would discover truth first.

The Dancer saved us from the flue fire and the bee sting and only God knows how many other disasters. He knew that one day we'd accept Jesus, and he would use our voices in the grand synchronization of his eternal master plan. Maybe he permitted the auto accidents that forced me to lie still and think. Perhaps he sent me back to school because someday Mormons would listen to the story of what God has done in the life of a former high priest husband and BYU professor wife. Maybe he moved us to Mormon country and to BYU to set up relationships and events that have birthed this story of his grace.

Josh and Mandy, while maintaining great respect for LDS family and coworkers, recently relinquished their membership in the Mormon Church. God can expunge the record of any-one's wrongs, whether the Mormons keep them or not. The Holy Spirit of grace perhaps allowed Josh to be excommunicated to help open our eyes about Mormonism's decree of unforgiveness, which stands opposed to Jesus' gospel of grace.

Or maybe it wasn't the Holy Spirit of God in each of these instances. After getting to know the Word, I give a stern caution about "spiritual" experiences, even though I have shared many such experiences in this book. Sometimes it is easy to discern the origin of an experience. Obviously, my two visits from demons were not positive experiences, and I clearly recognized them as such. But I also had many spiritual experiences that, while seem-ingly positive in nature and in memory, were *not* from the Spirit of God.

For example, I now believe that the electricity I felt coursing through my body when the LDS patriarch laid his hands on my head and gave me my patriarchal blessing *was not* from the Spirit of God. The Bible is clear that any method of communication with any spirit other than the Spirit of God comes from an evil source (Deut. 18:10–11; 1 Kings 22:21–22). I have learned to test the spirits (1 John 4:1; Rev. 2:2) by using reason (Isa. 1:18) and the Word of God (Acts 17:11).

As another example, I often experienced what felt like tingles of spiritual ecstasy while walking the campus of BYU, during BYU Tuesday morning devotionals, in a temple, at church conferences, or in the presence of a general authority. Now I would put those experiences under the category of "false spiritual goose bumps." The Bible says the heart is deceitful above all things (Jer. 17:9). I no longer trust my feelings. My own sentimental judgments have been pretty ignorant in the past. I now test feelings against a truth source that I *do* trust—the Bible.

Many spirits work to influence us, and not all of them influence us for good. Perhaps some of my experiences came from false spirits, like my impression to support Josh's excommunication or to hold my tongue at Micah's inquisition, or the chills I felt up my spine during fast-and-testimony meetings. Before Jesus, we did not know that we needed to test a spirit against the Word of Truth. If it does not reconcile—and Mormonism does not—reject it as a false spirit. First John 4:1 says, "Dear friends, do not believe every spirit, but test the spirits to see whether they are from God, because many false prophets have gone out into the world." The more we know God's Word, the better we can discern.

For the Good

Likely, all of these experiences didn't come from the Spirit of God, but once I accepted Jesus, he worked for my good, as he promises in Romans 8:28: "In all things God works for the good of those who love him, who have been called according to his purpose."

That's exactly what God did for Matt and Nicole, worked a difficult situation for good for his purpose. Having a child was a big decision for them because of the health risks involved for Nicole. However, the Lord gently let them know in 2009 that they would be having a child. Nicole prodded Matt a couple of times to consider the possibility, as God laid it heavily on her heart. Matt was not ready to consider having a child, but shortly after Nicole approached him about it, the Lord confirmed it by sending him two powerful dreams, on two separate occasions, that woke him up with a spiritual intensity: first, he saw a newborn with Nicole, and second, a five-year-old girl. The experiences were so real and intimate, and they gave him a deep and abiding love toward his future daughter.

Months later, with the news that Nicole was expecting, came joy and anticipation. The first doctor they saw warned it was a high-risk pregnancy and subtly suggested it may be prudent to have an abortion. He feared Nicole's life was at risk. They found a new doctor and put faith in God that he would work everything out. Nicole gave birth to a charming healthy girl, but there were complications for Nicole as she suffered a blood clot after she was home from the hospital and had to return. But baby Tessa was not allowed in with her. Matt and his mother-in-law sat in the parking garage with the newborn and took turns visiting Nicole. Nevertheless, this experience was a faith-builder for the new parents, demonstrating that God was in control and was personally invested in the details of their lives. They thank the Lord Jesus for bringing Tessa into their lives and for saving Nicole's life. They are awash in the blessings of the Holy Spirit.

Mormonism calls its spirit the "Holy Ghost." It's not the same as the eternal, omnipresent, omnipotent, Holy Spirit of Truth from the Bible. The LDS Holy Ghost is described in the church manual for new members, *Gospel Principles*, as "a spirit that has the form and likeness of a man (D&C 130:22). He can be in only one place at one time, but his influence can be everywhere at the same time."[55] The Holy Ghost of Mormonism can be in only one place, but the Holy Spirit of the Bible is all places at once (Ps. 139:7–10). The Doctrine and Covenants says, "The idea that the Father and the Son dwell in a man's heart is an old sectarian notion, and is false" (D&C 130:3). The Bible says that the Holy Spirit of Truth "lives in you" (1 Cor. 3:16 NIV 1984). As these conflicting passages demonstrate, they're not the same spirit.

There is one more "spiritual" incident I will mention. In 1981, when Josh was little, very early one morning I dreamed that terrorists in camouflage clothes and black headscarves, carrying AK47s, went from house to house in this country, finding scriptures and burning them in the streets. A few of us hid in a barn at dusk, watching their silhouettes. That dream affected me for hours. I determined as I got up that I would learn my scriptures so well that if they were removed from me, God could still speak to me through what my mind remembered (John 14:26).

Back then, I thought I needed to know my Mormon scriptures. Now I know I need to know the Bible that well (Heb. 8:10). Just a dream? A message from God or from Satan? Either way, God used it for good. Now I know what source to trust for truth, what words against which to test anything that claims to be truth. Not my feelings. Only the Word of God, where the rightful Holy Spirit resides.

Backward Theology

In 2012, Michael and I traveled to the land of Israel and into the West Bank. There we saw the ruins of Shechem, Samaria, Dan, the City of David, Jerusalem, and the walls of Jericho. We saw pottery, swords, utensils, coins, furniture, clothing, homes, scrolls, columns, streets, and ancient synagogues and "high places." The mountains, valleys, bodies of water, and geography of the Bible are accurate. More than five thousand existing manuscripts have been found throughout Europe, Asia, and Africa that corroborate the historicity and accuracy of the Bible.

In contrast, Joseph Smith "translated" the Book of Mormon from one set of "gold plates," and those plates no longer exist where one can see them. The geography of the Book of Mormon has not been located, at least the Mormon Church has no official position. There is no DNA evidence that ties Book of Mormon descendants with Israelites as the Book of Mormon teaches. Historical, physical, and geographical evidence does not exist. Mormons are asked by their leaders to believe the authenticity of the Book of Mormon by faith, not by scientific evidence.

Geographically, Utah has several similarities with Israel, the land of the real Jesus, but Utah is the opposite. In Israel from north to south, springs from the mountains feed the Sea of Galilee, a freshwater lake, from which flows the Jordan River. The Jordan River ends at the Dead Sea, a dead salt sea.

In Utah from south to north, springs from the mountains feed Utah Lake, a freshwater lake, out of which flows the Jordan River. The Jordan River in Utah ends at the Great Salt Lake, a dead salt sea. It seems like Israel, but on closer examination, it's got everything backward. In the same way, Mormonism might seem like Christianity, but on closer examination, it's not the same. Not at all.

Our story has highlighted a number of inconsistencies between Mormon scripture and biblical Scripture. Mormonism says that the fullness of truth, saving ordinances, and prophecy reside in Joseph Smith and his living successors—in the Mormon Church. But the Bible says that Jesus is the end of the Law for all who believe (Rom. 10:4); love fulfills the Law (Rom. 13:8–10);

truth and prophecy come from Jesus and reside in the Word (Heb. 1:1–3). Mormonism says that we can become gods (D&C 130:20, 37). But the Bible says, "Before me no god was formed, nor will there be one after me" (Isa. 43:10).

Mormonism says that two sins that cannot be forgiven are murder anytime and adultery the second time (D&C 42:18–19, 25–26). But the Bible says that after David asked forgiveness for murder and continued adultery, the prophet Nathan said, "The LORD has taken away your sin" (2 Sam. 12:13). Moses and Paul also committed murder and were forgiven (Rom. 3:23–24). Mormonism says that the dead sometimes come back as angels or as spirits to guide us. But the Bible says, "Let no one be found among you ... who is a medium or spiritualist [like the Mormon patriarch] or who consults the dead [as Mormons seek to do when they baptize the dead]" (Deut. 18:10–11). (For a comprehensive comparison of Mormon scriptures and beliefs with what Jesus and his disciples said in the Bible, see appendix 2.)

Now, a Christian might still ask, "What's the big deal? We're all in the body of Christ. You choose to be Baptist one day and Assembly of God or Nazarene the next. No one condemns you for moving around as you progress in knowledge and in your relationship with Jesus." Leaving Mormonism and coming to faith in the biblical Jesus is *nothing* like moving from one part of the body of Christ to another! The Mormon Church is *not in* the body of Christ, because Mormonism teaches doctrine that is contrary to what Jesus himself taught.

Mormonism wraps itself in the cloak of Christianity, using and twisting Christian words. Mormon doctrine sounds terribly Christian, but it's not. Religious words such as *grace, salvation,* and *atonement* have different meanings for Christians and Mormons. (See the glossary for the Mormon meanings of religious words.) With its official name, Mormonism declares itself a "church of Jesus Christ."

With its focus on church community, family, hard work, tithing, and missions, it presents itself as just another Christian denomination. And its clean-cut, hardworking, high-achieving members seem to proclaim its goodness and rightness. But as the Bible points out, counterfeit spirits pose to deceive and can even cloak themselves with an aura of goodness and light. "And no wonder, for Satan himself masquerades as an angel of light" (2 Cor. 11:14).

Mormons are ensconced in a false Christ and the culture built on his foundational false prophet, Joseph Smith, and his successors. The lies this fabricated system promotes set up in a person what the Bible calls "strongholds" (2 Cor. 10:4) — deceptions that become part of a belief system that is untrue and allows Satan to have influence. The deceptions include everything from the principle of eternal plural marriage (birthing lust) to the idea that God marked Cain with a dark skin (birthing racism).

Mormonism's strongholds also include allegiance to a man-made religion run by a few privileged priesthood brethren, instead of allegiance to the real Jesus. Another stronghold is the belief that God's own Word is not reliable, and instead we must trust the Mormon scriptures and prophets and apostles for truth. An additional stronghold is the belief that salvation is dependent on personal works and the approval of men in authority. Salvation is never guaranteed in Mormonism, unless one is righteous enough to have his calling and election made sure.[56] Members work to attain exaltation and never know if they've done enough.

In short, the juxtaposition of the Mormon Church's media campaign slogan "I'm a Mormon" with the declaration "I am *yours*" makes differences evident.

Loving Mormons

How we have love for the LDS members who are caught in this web of deception and futile works! Those who have a heart for the Mormon people, please learn about Mormonism. Reach out to the wonderful Christian ministries listed in appendix 1, who understand Mormonism and can help answer questions and teach how to lovingly witness truth to a Mormon. Read the resources on their websites and blogs and watch their YouTube videos. My first suggestion is always to pray that God will loose LDS members and set them free, will show them truth, and will reveal himself—the biggie God—to them. I've seen many miracles come after prayer. Prayer works. In fact, God is already drawing in and working with many dear Mormon souls to show them the truth.

My second suggestion is to listen and to gently challenge. Hear the hearts of Mormon friends and family, listen for concerns, ask them to explain different aspects of their faith, and ask them questions respectfully. Choose questions that might cause them to wonder, to scratch their heads, to reason, and to research. For some, typing "Joseph Smith" into Google could open a whole new world. Learning historical facts about polygamy, racism, false prophecies, the Mountain Meadows Massacre, blood atonement, Egyptian papyri, and other realities from Mormon Church history might begin the journey. We implore LDS church members questioning their faith and LDS heritage to consider the *real* Jesus if they are angry and feeling betrayed. This Jesus is *so* worth the relationship.

It can take a long time to sort out lies, absorb truth, and find solid ground. The ground under my feet took nearly *five years* to stabilize. Remember as you talk, that words may have different meanings to a Mormon and to a Christian.

Ultimately, it is the work of the Dancer of grace to draw someone to truth, but along the way, we can certainly plant seeds from the Word that never return void. In my case, accepting truth took the persistent sledgehammer of the Word, the work of the Spirit, and a lot of trials.

At one point during the binding-and-healing process, Mike and I were burdened with the thirty years we had spent teaching our children what was not true, and the time we had wasted in useless endeavors like genealogy, temple work, and studying and teaching scripture that didn't come from God. We felt such sorrow for all the lost years. It was heaviness for me.

I apologized to Micah for having immersed him in lies all of his life. His gentle answer to me was, "Mom, don't you realize that God planned this whole journey for our family? He took Dad and you and all of us into Mormonism so we would learn to love the people. Then he brought us out so we could reach back and help them find the truth." No more profound truth could have been spoken. Maybe that dream Mike had about defending the Mormon people would now require us to do just that—guard them from their false faith.

It's All about Jesus

Psalm 90 says a man's life is threescore and ten. Mike and I don't have all that many years left, but what we have left we dedicate to God's great purpose of redeeming people. We've seen God redeem the money we've given away. Now we watch for him to redeem the time we've lost, bringing it back a hundredfold as he promises. We don't want life to be about us anymore. We want it to be about Jesus and his exquisitely orchestrated work.

I find it miraculous how God has worked in each of our lives. First, the Dancer called, unveiling grace little by little, even while we took a long detour following the false god of Mormonism. Then we gave our lives to the biblical Christ. Then, for several years, he took us to the wilderness as we worked through Kübler-Ross's stages of grief and were birthed to new life. We studied the Word, and he bound the relational hurts, healed them, and gave us grace to bear testimony of who he is and what he can do. It has all been his plan. His timing. His calling. His preparation. His work. And it will be his harvest.

Most remarkable is the transformation that a personal relationship with Jesus and knowledge of him through the Word has brought all of us. My mind has stopped racing and constantly judging and is at peace. I am more willing to see myself as imperfect, and to relax and allow God to change me. I don't worry as much about what others think. No longer do I need to control people or money or my schedule. I have surrendered these things to God's will. I'm not as likely to fight against my circumstances, instead trying to understand what I can from them and use them to draw closer to Jesus. I seek authenticity now — no more "behind the back, under the table" relationships. I've stopped expecting people to meet my needs. I turn to Jesus. I am beginning to have a sense of who I am in Jesus. I still teach at a university, yet God's work is growing.

The changes in my husband of thirty-eight years have been nothing less than miraculous too. This transformed man is an attentive spouse. He laughs easily, loves generously, and listens with his whole body. He is calmer in his characteristically chaotic line of work, more accepting, and less irritated by difficulties at work. Michael is generous with his money. He seems more alive, happier. Once quieter, now he persistently talks about Jesus, the Word, and his faith. He and Dave Mitchell have a Christian radio show out of Miami each week (1080 the Answer) that he is always excited about. Mike talks on the phone with men who are questioning their Mormon faith. It appears he is stepping up into a leadership role that is different from what he did and how he did it in Mormonism. He's more humble, more willing to listen, more dependent on the Spirit for direction, and more energized. He's getting to know the Bible well and loves to discuss it. He allows God to take him away from his own full-time work and into God's work. At the completion of this book, our beloved cat, Manny, died. We held each other and cried.

The children in ministry, the Adam's Road families, are hard-working and sold out to Jesus. They take bed-and-breakfast reservations, feed guests breakfast, maintain the property, and clean the rooms. The women homeschool the kids. The ministry works with people who are questioning Mormonism, mails out CDs and books for free, books venues, travels, gives concerts, speaks at churches and Christian schools and colleges, and bears testimony of what Jesus can do. They work themselves to a satisfying exhaustion with the business and the ministry, and they do it all for Jesus.

Jesus is not some mystical figure one conjures up through meditation. Jesus is real. I think now I can grasp how someone like Iranian pastor Youcef Nadarkhani is willing to endure persecution, prison, and the threat of death for the name of Jesus. I understand why some trapped in the rubble of the World Trade Center exclaimed the name of Jesus with their dying breath, and why Dietrich Bonhoeffer, the German pastor who opposed the Nazi regime, gave his life for Jesus.

Where will that tender Jesus of Katie's dream, the one who bent down and gently plied her with his blood, lead me? In the few short years since surrendering my will to Jesus, everything has changed. "Therefore, since we have such a hope, we are very bold" (2 Cor. 3:12). I will declare Jesus lives and loves with my dying breath.

As a final testimony, I use Paul's words from 1 Timothy 1:15–17: "Christ Jesus came into the world to save sinners—of whom I am the worst. But for that very reason I was shown mercy so that in me, the worst of sinners, Christ Jesus might display his immense patience as an example for those who would believe in him and receive eternal life. Now to the King eternal, immortal, invisible, the only God, be honor and glory for ever and ever. Amen."

EPILOGUE

Since Mike and I came to know Jesus, we have been blessed with seven grandchildren who fill our lives with untold joy. In Winter Garden, Florida, Micah and Alicia have three active sons who love Jesus. Matt and Nicole have one articulate two-year-old daughter who is full of life. Meanwhile, to our delight when visiting Joseph and Kate, we share their two rooms of living space with three cats and a snake. Disney, twenty minutes away from the hotel, is Mr. Mike's favorite activity. Holidays at the historic Edgewater are magical.

In Utah, Josh and Mandy have three children. Mandy brought a wonderful now-fourteen-year-old son to their union, and she and Josh have a dancing and whimsical three-year-old daughter and a smiling, chubby one-year-old son. Mandy is a joy to us — so much so, Mike hired her to work with him. They're on the phone nearly daily across states, so we talk to their children often too. God provided Josh and Mandy's family with a home in Utah with plenty of room for Grandma and Grandpa to stay whenever we can and for Adam's Road to rest when they are ministering to people in Utah.

The Adam's Road band and ministry matures, increasingly reaching more Christians and Mormons with the Word of God. Pastor Shaw's sons, Jonathan and Dominick, and Katie Wilder Warren sometimes record with the band. Many have come to know the biblical Jesus through both the Adam's Road ministry and the ministry that Michael and I started, Ex-Mormon Christians United for Jesus. Each person we talk to becomes like family to us, part of God's chosen family. After Michael and I were on *The John Ankerberg TV Show* for a six-week series on Mormonism in early 2012 with the co-founder of Utah Lighthouse Ministry, Sandra Tanner, we wrote a book called *Seven Reasons We Left Mormonism*, which was promoted by John Ankerberg's ministry and is available on Amazon. A quick two-hour read, it gives the basic differences between biblical doctrine and Mormon doctrine.[57]

What makes our ministry unique is that we were very active LDS and I was tenured faculty at BYU. We know church doctrines and culture inside and out. Since Michael and I had a difficult transition out of Mormonism, we are sensitive to truth-seeking individuals who worry about the reactions of their Mormon spouses, families, and friends.

I tell God I could die tomorrow and be perfectly content to see his face. I thank him daily that he allowed us to know the truth before we died. Our prayer now is that others, especially our dear Mormon people, will know the joy we know in Jesus.

ACKNOWLEDGMENTS

With sincere appreciation to God, I acknowledge the individuals who agreed to tell their stories.

First, I thank Jesus for my husband of thirty-eight years, Michael, who traveled this dynamic journey beside me — always beside me — and who compiled the doctrinal comparison for appendix 2. I acknowledge our oldest son, Josh, for his courage to tell his story so that others will not be afraid to seek the truth, and his beautiful bride, Mandy, for allowing her life to be revealed. I express thanks to God for the extraordinary musical and spiritual gifts of our second son, Matt, which have blessed my life immeasurably, and for the devotion of his invincible wife, Nicole, who lives a life of servitude to Jesus. To our third son, Micah, and his indomitable wife, Alicia, the ones who bravely stepped out to meet Jesus first and to dedicate their lives to serving him, I will be eternally grateful for their daring strong faith. And, to our steadfast, blessed daughter, Kate, and her spirited husband, Joseph, I express love and appreciation to God for their enthusiasm to minister to others in the name of Jesus.

Warmest regards to my Savior for the entire Adam's Road band and ministry: Micah Wilder, Matt Wilder, Joseph Warren, Steve Kay, Jay Graham, as well as their administrator and booking agent Stefan Dennis and his sagacious wife, Sarah, and their bus driver, Erik, and his mother, Jane.

I am thankful God sent Scott Johnson, who generously gave feedback for the manuscript and allowed us to share the title of his documentary *Unveiling Grace*, as well as Tom Jones, who adeptly compiled the glossary.

Special appreciation to Jesus for the pastors who have offered us solid biblical teaching. Heartfelt thanks to the Shaw family and for the prayers of my parents and others, including the Barretts of Yorktown and my Christian siblings.

Working with the professional and gracious individuals at Zondervan has been a God-given pleasure, including Sandra Vander Zicht, Tom Dean, Brian Phipps, Cindy Wilson, and Joyce Ondersma. I am indebted to Jesus for my freelance writing coach, Lori Vanden Bosch, without whom the book would not have been birthed. And kudos to Elissa Cohen from HarperCollins and the capable women of McClure/Muntsinger Public Relations. Finally, I thank God for John Ankerberg and Latayne Scott, who believed in us and acted as instruments in God's hands.

APPENDIX 1

CHRISTIAN MINISTRIES WITH INFORMATION ON MORMONISM

Note: websites, phone numbers, and addresses were accurate at the time of printing.

Adam's Road Musical Ministry
Micah Wilder
99 West Plant Street
Winter Garden, FL 34787
(407) 654-8833
info@adamsroadband.com
www.adamsroadband.com

Alathea Ministries
Heart of the Matter TV show
Shawn McCraney
4760 Highland Drive, Suite 515
Salt Lake City, UT 84117
(888) 868-4686
shawn@hotm.tv
www.hotm.tv

**Ankerberg Theological Research
  Institute**
Dr. John Ankerberg
P.O. Box 8977
Chattanooga, TN 37414
(800) 805-3030
www.ankerberg.com

**Christian Apologetics and Research
  Ministry**
Matt Slick

P.O. Box 1353
Nampa, ID 83651
www.carm.org

Christian Research and Counsel
Randy Gavin
randy@crcmin.org
Tom Jones (founding missionary)
P.O. Box 270
Palmyra, NY 14522
(727) 667-4112
tom@crcmin.org
www.crcmin.org

Concerned Christians
Andy Poland
525 E. Broadway Road
Mesa, AZ 85204
(480) 833-2537
andy@concernedchristians.org
www.concernedchristians.com

Courageous Christians
Rob Sivulka
rob@courageouschristians
  united.org
www.mormoninfo.org

Evidence Ministries
Keith Walker
P.O. Box 690371
San Antonio, TX 78269
gracenotworks@ephesians2.net
www.evidenceministries.org

**Ex-Mormon Christians United
for Jesus**
Next Step radio show, 1080 AM
The Answer
Michael and Lynn Wilder
michael@unveilingmormonism.com
lynn@unveilingmormonism.com
(239) 989-7102
www.unveilingmormonism.com

HIS Ministries International
Dennis and Rauni Higley
2890 E. Willow Bend Drive
Sandy, UT 84093
(801) 943-5011
hismin@xmission.com
www.hismin.com

Institute for Religious Research
Roger Hansen and Joel B. Groat
1340 Monroe Avenue N.W.
Grand Rapids, MI 49505
(616) 451-4562
www.IRR.org

Janis Hutchinson
author, *Out of the Cults and into the Church*
1318 37th Street, Unit 1506
Everett, WA 98201
(425) 783-0476
janishutchinson@frontier.com
www.janishutchinson.com
www.janishutchinson.blogspot.com

Latayne Scott
author, *The Mormon Mirage*
http://latayne.com
www.exmormonscholarstestify.org

Main Street Church
Jim Catlin
48 N. Main Street
Brigham City, UT 84302

www.mscbc.org
Scott Johnson
www.sacredgrovesonline.org

Mormonism Research Ministry
Viewpoint on Mormonism radio show
Bill McKeever
P.O. Box 1746
Draper, UT 84020-1746
(801) 572-2153
contact@mrm.org
www.mrm.org

Next Step Outreach
Next Step radio show
Dave Mitchell
13463 78th Place North
West Palm Beach, FL 33412
http://davemitchellsblog.blogspot.com
www.nextstepoutreach.org

Oasis Books
Brad Scheelke and Eli Brayley
25 Center Street
Logan, UT 84321
(435) 753-8697

A Shield and Refuge Ministry
Polygamy: What Love Is This? TV show
Doris Hanson
P.O. Box 651292
Salt Lake City, UT 84165
www.shieldandrefuge.org

Sourceflix / Living Hope Ministries
Joel Kramer
P.O. Box 606
Brigham City, UT 84302
Our address in Israel is:
4 Avigayil #5
Jerusalem 93551
Israel

Sword, Cross, and Crown Ministry
Larry and Shawna Lindsey
515 Mathis Cove Road
Birchwood, TN 37308
swordandcross70@gmail.com
www.swordcrossandcrown.org

Transitions
John Morehead and Ken Mulholland
358 S. 700 E., Box 356
Salt Lake City, UT 84102
(801) 643-6983
info@ldstransitions.com
www.ldstransitions.com
http://ldstransitions.wordpress.com
www.wiics.org

Tri-Grace Ministries
Daniel (Chip) Thompson
96 E. Center Street
Ephraim, UT 84627
www.TriGrace.org

Truth Broadcasting Network
Russ East
Station Manager
KUTR-AM 820
3701 Harrison Blvd.
Ogden, UT 84403

Truth in Love Ministry
Mark Cares and Dave Malnes

2830 E. Umatilla Drive
Nampa, ID 83686
(877) 887-3436
www.tilm.org
www.markcares.wordpress.com
www.latterdaysaintwoman.wordpress.com

**Utah Lighthouse Ministry
& Bookstore**
Sandra Tanner
1358 S. West Temple
Salt Lake City, UT 84115
(801) 485-8894
www.utlm.org

**Salt Lake City Messenger
(semiannual newsletter)**
P.O. Box 1884
Salt Lake City, UT 84110

Watchman Fellowship, Inc.
James Walker
P.O. Box 13340
Arlington, TX 76094
(817) 277-0023
www.watchman.org

QUICK DOCTRINAL COMPARISON OF MORMONISM AND THE BIBLE

MORMONISM TEACHES	THE BIBLE TEACHES
Bible Is Not Infallible (it is sometimes translated incorrectly)	**Bible Is the Infallible Word of God**
• "We believe the Bible to be the word of God as far as it is translated correctly; we also believe the Book of Mormon to be the Word of God" (8th Article of Faith).	• "We also have the prophetic message as something completely reliable, and you will do well to pay attention to it, as to a light shining in a dark place" (2 Peter 1:19).
• "First: The prophet is the only man who speaks for the Lord in everything. Second: The living prophet is more vital to us than the standard works [including the Bible]. Third: The living prophet is more important to us than a dead prophet" (Ezra Taft Benson was a member of the quorum of the twelve apostles of the Church of Jesus Christ of Latter-day Saints when this devotional address was given at Brigham Young University on February 26, 1980).	• Jesus said, "Heaven and earth will pass away, but my words will never pass away" (Matt. 24:35).
	• Jesus said, "If you hold to my teaching, you are really my disciples. Then you will know the truth, and the truth will set you free" (John 8:31–32).
	• God said, "My word ... will not return to me empty" (Isa. 55:11).
	• "The LORD Almighty, the God of Israel, says: 'Do not let the prophets and diviners among you deceive you. Do not listen to the dreams you encourage them to have. They are prophesying lies to you in my name. I have not sent them'" (Jer. 29:8–9; see also Rev. 22:18).

MORMONISM TEACHES	THE BIBLE TEACHES
The Mormon Church Is the Only True Church	**The Church Consists of the Body of Believers**
• "And also those to whom these commandments were given, might have power to lay the foundation of this church, and to bring it forth out of obscurity and out of darkness, the only true and living church upon the face of the whole earth, with which I, the Lord, am well pleased, speaking unto the church collectively and not individually" (D&C 1:30). Here, allegedly, Christ himself gives Joseph Smith and the other early church leaders power to lay the foundation of the only church with which he is well pleased. • "I was answered that I must join none of them [Christian churches], for they were all wrong; and the Personage [Jesus] who addressed me said that all their creeds were an abomination in his sight; that those professors were all corrupt ..." (Joseph Smith—History 1:19).	• "Just as each of us has one body with many members, and these members do not all have the same function, so in Christ we, though many, form one body, and each member belongs to all the others. We have different gifts, according to the grace given to each of us" (Rom. 12:4–6). • "Make every effort to keep the unity of the Spirit through the bond of peace. There is one body and one Spirit, just as you were called to one hope when you were called; one Lord, one faith, one baptism; one God and Father of all, who is over all and through all and in all. But to each one of us grace has been given as Christ apportioned it" (Eph. 4:3–7). • Jesus said, "I tell you that you are Peter, and on this rock I will build my church, and the gates of Hades will not overcome it" (Matt. 16:18). • Also see: Matt. 18:19–20; Mark 3:24–25; 1 Cor. 1:10–12; 12:11–14; Eph. 1:22–23 (cf. Col. 1:24); 5:25–26.
God the Father Has a Body of Flesh and Bones	**God Is Spirit**
• "The Father has a body of flesh and bones as tangible as man's" (D&C 130:22). • "God himself was once as we are now, and is an exalted man, and sits enthroned in yonder heavens!... I am going to tell you how God came to be God. We have	• "To the King eternal, immortal, invisible, the only God, be honor and glory for ever and ever" (1 Tim. 1:17). • "God is spirit, and his worshipers must worship in the Spirit and in truth" (John 4:24). • "The Son is the image of the invisible God, the firstborn over all creation" (Col. 1:15).

MORMONISM TEACHES	THE BIBLE TEACHES
imagined and supposed that God was God from all eternity. I will refute that idea, and take away the veil, so that you may see ... he was once a man like us ... and you have got to learn how to be Gods yourselves" (*Teachings of the Prophet Joseph Smith*, 345 – 46).	• "No one has ever seen God, but the one and only Son, who is himself God and is in closest relationship with the Father, has made him known" (John 1:18). • "'Who can hide in secret places so that I cannot see them?' declares the LORD. 'Do not I fill heaven and earth?'" (Jer. 23:24).

Plurality of Gods — Do Not Accept the Triune God — Man Works His Way to Godhood

There Is One God

MORMONISM TEACHES

- 'Then they shall be gods, because they have no end ... then shall they be above all, because all things are subject unto them. Then shall they be gods ... and the angels are subject unto them" (D&C 132:20).
- 'They have entered into their exaltation, according to the promises, and sit upon thrones, and are not angels but are gods" (D&C 132:37).
- "Let us go down. And they went down at the beginning, and they, that is the Gods, organized and formed the heavens and the earth" (see Abraham 4:1 – 31; 5:1 – 21).
- "I have always declared God to be a distinct personage, Jesus Christ a separate and distinct personage from God the Father, and the Holy Ghost a distinct personage or spirit, and these three constitute three distinct personages and three Gods" (*Teachings of the Prophet Joseph Smith*, 370).

THE BIBLE TEACHES

- "'You are my witnesses,' declares the LORD, 'and my servant whom I have chosen, so that you may know and believe me and understand that I am he. Before me no god was formed, nor will there be one after me'" (Isa. 43:10).
- "This is what the LORD says — Israel's King and Redeemer, the LORD Almighty: I am the first and I am the last; apart from me there is no God.... Do not tremble, do not be afraid. Did I not proclaim this and foretell it long ago? You are my witnesses. Is there any God besides me? No, there is no other Rock [God]; I know not one" (Isa. 44:6, 8).
- Also see: James 2:19; Deut. 6:4; Neh. 9:6 (cf. Hos. 13:4); Isa. 45:21 – 22.

God Is Not a Man

- "I am God, and not a man — the Holy One among you" (Hos. 11:9).
- "In the pride of your heart you say, 'I am a god; I sit on the throne of a god in the heart of the seas.' But you are a mere mortal and not a god, though you think you are as wise as a god" (Ezek. 28:2).
- See also: Num. 23:19; Ps. 102:26 – 27.

MORMONISM TEACHES	THE BIBLE TEACHES
	Triune God
• "If an acceptance of the Trinity makes one a Christian, then of course Latter-day Saints are not Christians, for they believe the doctrine of the Trinity as expressed in modern Protestant and Catholic theology is the product of the reconciliation of Christian theology with Greek philosophy" (BYU Professor Robert L. Millet, *A Different Jesus? The Christ of the Latter-day Saints*, 171).	• "For us there is but one God" (1 Cor. 8:6; John 10:27–30).
	• The Triune God has existed since the beginning. "I the LORD do not change" (Mal. 3:6).
	• "Jesus Christ is the same yesterday and today and forever" (Heb. 13:8; see also James 1:17).
• "In bearing testimony of Jesus Christ, President [LDS Prophet] Hinckley spoke of those outside the Church who say Latter-day Saints 'do not believe in the traditional Christ.' 'No, I don't. The traditional Christ of whom they speak is not the Christ of whom I speak. For the Christ of whom I speak has been revealed in this the Dispensation of the Fullness of Times. He, together with His Father, appeared to the boy Joseph Smith in the year 1820, and when Joseph left the grove that day, he knew more of the nature of God than all the learned ministers of the gospel of the ages'" (*Deseret News, Church News* [June 20, 1998], 7).	• "In your relationships with one another, have the same mindset as Christ Jesus: Who, being in very nature God, did not consider equality with God something to be used to his own advantage; rather, he made himself nothing by taking the very nature of a servant, being made in human likeness. And being found in appearance as a man, he humbled himself by becoming obedient to death—even death on a cross!" (Phil. 2:5–8).
	• "In the beginning was the Word" (John 1:1–18).
	Additional Verses about the Nature of God
	• Gen. 1:26–27; Ps. 139:1–6; Acts 2:23; Matt. 19:26; 28:19; Job 42:2; Luke 24:39; John 17:10; Col. 1:16; Heb. 1:3, 10–12; Rom. 1:22–23.
Christ's Atonement Did Not Cover All Sins	**Christ Atoned for All Sins**
• "Thou shall not kill; and he that kills shall not have forgiveness in this world nor in the world to come" (D&C 42:18–19).	• "Then David said to Nathan, 'I have sinned against the LORD.' Nathan replied, 'The LORD has taken away your sin'" (2 Sam. 12:13).

MORMONISM TEACHES	THE BIBLE TEACHES
• "Thou shalt not commit adultery.... But if he doeth it again, he shall not be forgiven" (D&C 42:25–26). • "He [David] hath fallen from his exaltation, and received his portion; and he shall not inherit them out of the world, for I gave them unto another, saith the LORD" (D&C 132:39).	• "In him [Jesus Christ] we have redemption through his blood, the forgiveness of sins, in accordance with the riches of God's grace" (Eph. 1:7). • "All have sinned and fall short of the glory of God, and all are justified freely by his grace through the redemption that came by Christ Jesus" (Rom. 3:23–24).
Eternal Life Requires Grace Plus Works • Salvation = resurrection is a free gift *plus.* • Exaltation = system of laws, ordinances, correct behavior. It is works based. • "All mankind may be saved, by obedience to the laws and ordinances of the Gospel" (3rd Article of Faith). • "We know that it is by grace that we are saved, after all we can do" (2 Nephi 25:23). • "My faith is, when we have done all we can, then the Lord is under obligation, and will not disappoint the faithful; he will perform the rest" (*Discourses of Brigham Young*, 155). • "The true gospel requires works" (*The Teachings of Lorenzo Snow* [former LDS prophet], 16). • "The fallacy that Jesus has done for us, and live as we may, if on our deathbed, we only believe, we shall be saved in his glorious presence is most pernicious" (David O. McKay [former LDS prophet], *Gospel Ideals*, 8).	**Eternal Life Is a Free Gift of God** • "The law was given through Moses; grace and truth came through Jesus Christ" (John 1:17). • "We believe it is through the grace of our Lord Jesus that we are saved" (Acts 15:11). • "Sin shall no longer be your master, because you are not under the law, but under grace" (Rom. 6:14). • "To the one who works, wages are not credited as a gift but as an obligation. However, to the one who does not work but trusts God who justifies the ungodly, their faith is credited as righteousness" (Rom. 4:4–5). • "If by grace, then it cannot be based on works; if it were, grace would no longer be grace" (Rom. 11:6). • We are saved by grace and not by works; it is a free gift of God (Eph. 2:1–9, author's summary). • "I do not set aside the grace of God, for if righteousness could be gained through the law, Christ died for nothing!" (Gal. 2:21).

MORMONISM TEACHES	THE BIBLE TEACHES
• "One of the most fallacious doctrines originated by Satan and propounded by man is that man is saved alone by the grace of God; that belief in Jesus Christ alone is all that is needed for salvation" (Spencer W. Kimball [former LDS prophet], *The Miracle of Forgiveness*, 208).	• "He has saved us and called us to a holy life—not because of anything we have done but because of his own purpose and grace" (2 Tim. 1:9). • See also: Rom. 5:15–21; 6:23; Gal. 2:16; 5:4; Eph. 1:7; 4:7; Titus 3:4–7; Acts 20:24; Rom. 5:2; 2 Cor. 12:9–10; John 3:16–17.
Eternal Life (Life with Jesus and Heavenly Father) Is Dependent on Secret Temple Ordinances • "In order to obtain the highest, a man must enter into this order of the priesthood [meaning the new and everlasting covenant of marriage in the temple]" (D&C 131:2). • This marriage (temple sealing) is one of many ordinances that take place in temples. Events (ordinances) that take place in the Mormon temples cannot be spoken of in detail outside the temple. • One of the requirements to get into the temple is that a person must pay a tithe to the Mormon Church. • " . . . a day for the tithing of my people; for he that is tithed shall not be burned at his [Christ's] coming" (D&C 64:23).	**Gospel Is Not Secret; It Is Openly Proclaimed** • Jesus said, "Do not be afraid of them, for there is nothing concealed that will not be disclosed, or hidden that will not be made known. What I tell you in the dark, speak in the daylight; what is whispered in your ear, proclaim from the roofs" (Matt. 10:26–27). • "This is the verdict: Light has come into the world, but people loved darkness instead of light because their deeds were evil" (John 3:19). • "Have nothing to do with the fruitless deeds of darkness, but rather expose them. It is shameful even to mention what the disobedient do in secret" (Eph. 5:11–12). • Jesus said, "I have spoken openly to the world. . . . I said nothing in secret" (John 18:20). • "Whatever is hidden is meant to be disclosed, and whatever is concealed is meant to be brought out into the open. If anyone has ears to hear, let them hear" (Mark 4:22–23; see also Luke 11:33). • "Do not trust in deceptive words and say, 'This is the temple of the LORD, the temple of the LORD, the temple of the LORD!'" (Jer. 7:4).

MORMONISM TEACHES	THE BIBLE TEACHES
No Cross on Mormon Buildings; Angel Moroni on Top of the Mormon Temples	**Boast in the Cross**
• "For us, the cross is the symbol of the dying Christ" (Former LDS Prophet/President Gordon B. Hinckley, "The Symbol of Our Faith," *Ensign* [April 2005], 3).	• "Whoever does not take up their cross and follow me is not worthy of me" (Matt. 10:38; see also Luke 9:23; 14:27).
• "His [Jesus Christ's] great suffering was before he ever was placed upon the cross. It was in the Garden of Gethsemane that the blood oozed from the pores of his body ... 'that I might not drink the bitter cup, and shrink.' That was not when he was on the cross; that was in the garden" (tenth president Joseph Fielding Smith, Doctrines of Salvation 1:130).	• "The message of the cross is foolishness to those who are perishing, but to us who are being saved it is the power of God" (1 Cor. 1:18).
	• "I have been crucified with Christ and I no longer live, but Christ lives in me" (Gal. 2:20).
• "It was in Gethsemane, on the slopes of the Mount of Olives, that Jesus made his perfect atonement by the shedding of his blood—more so than on the cross" (BYU professor Robert J. Matthews, "A Bible! A Bible!" *Ensign* [January 1987], 282).	• "May I never boast except in the cross of our Lord Jesus Christ, through which the world has been crucified to me, and I to the world" (Gal. 6:14).
	• "Being found in appearance as a man, he humbled himself by becoming obedient to death—even death on a cross! Therefore God exalted him to the highest place and gave him the name that is above every name" (Phil. 2:8–9).
• "Why should we bow down before a cross or use it as a symbol? Because our Savior died on the cross, the wearing of crosses is to most Latter-day Saints in very poor taste and inconsistent to our worship" (tenth president Joseph Fielding Smith, "The Wearing of the Cross," *Answers to Gospel Questions*, 4:17).	• "As I have often told you before and now tell you again even with tears, many live as enemies of the cross of Christ" (Phil. 3:18).
	• "God was pleased to have all his fullness dwell in him ... by making peace through his blood, shed on the cross" (Col. 1:19–20).
	• " ... having canceled the charge of our legal indebtedness, which stood against us and condemned us; he has taken it away, nailing it to the cross" (Col. 2:14).
	• "For the joy set before him he endured the cross" (Heb. 12:2).
	• See also: Matt. 16:24; Mark 8:34; Luke 9:23; Eph. 2:16.

MORMONISM TEACHES	THE BIBLE TEACHES
Polygamy Is an Eternal Principle	**Polygamy Not Commanded by God**
• " As pertaining to the law of the priesthood—if any man espouse a virgin, and desire to espouse another … then is he justified; he cannot commit adultery for they are given unto him. • "And if he have ten virgins given unto him by this law, he cannot commit adultery, for they are given unto him; therefore is he justified" (D&C 132:61–62; see entire section of D&C 132). • "If any man have a wife … he teaches unto her the law of my priesthood … then shall she believe and administer unto him, or she shall be destroyed, saith the Lord your God; for I will destroy her" (D&C 132:64).	• A husband and wife are united, and the two will "become one flesh" (Gen. 2:22–24, author's summary). • "An elder must be blameless, faithful to his wife" (Titus 1:6; see also 1 Tim. 3:2, 12). • "He must not take many wives, or his heart will be led astray" (Deut. 17:17). • "'Haven't you read,' he [Jesus] replied, 'that at the beginning the Creator "made them male and female" [Gen. 1:27], and said, "For this reason a man will leave his father and mother and be united to his wife, and the two will become one flesh" [Gen. 2:24]? So they are no longer two, but one flesh. Therefore what God has joined together, let no one separate'" (Matt. 19:4–6). • "Since sexual immorality is occurring, each man should have sexual relations with his own wife, and each woman with her own husband" (1 Cor. 7:2).
Christ's Church Went into Apostasy	**Christ's Church Did Not Go into Apostasy**
• "After the deaths of the Savior and his apostles, men corrupted the principles of the gospel and made unauthorized changes in church organization and priesthood ordinances. Because of this widespread apostasy, the Lord withdrew the authority of the priesthood from the earth. This apostasy lasted until Heavenly Father and his beloved Son appeared to Joseph Smith in 1820 and initiated the restoration of the fullness of the gospel.	• "Surely I am with you always, to the very end of the age" (Matt. 28:20). • "Don't let anyone deceive you in any way, for that day will not come until the rebellion occurs and the man of lawlessness is revealed, the man doomed to destruction" (2 Thess. 2:3). • Jesus said, "Heaven and earth will pass away, but my words will never pass away" (Matt. 24:35). • "To him [God] be glory in the church and in Christ Jesus throughout all generations, for ever and ever!" (Eph. 3:21).

MORMONISM TEACHES	THE BIBLE TEACHES
"During the Great Apostasy, people were without divine direction from living prophets. Many churches were established, but they did not have priesthood power to lead people to the true knowledge of God the Father and Jesus Christ. Parts of the holy scriptures were corrupted or lost, and no one had the authority to confer the gift of the Holy Ghost or perform other priesthood ordinances. "We now live in a time when the gospel of Jesus Christ has been restored. But unlike the church in times past, the Church of Jesus Christ of Latter-day Saints will not be overcome by general apostasy. The scriptures teach that the church will never again be destroyed (see D&C 138:44; Daniel 2:44)." (Source: official Mormon Church website [www.lds.org], under "Teachings" and then "Gospel Topics" and then "Apostasy.")	• "At that time many will turn away from the faith and will betray and hate each other, and many false prophets will appear and deceive many people.... But the one who stands firm to the end will be saved" (Matt. 24:10–11, 13). • Seeds that fall on rock have no root and when tested fall away (Luke 8:11–15, the parable of the sower, author's summary). • "The Spirit clearly says that in later times some will abandon the faith and follow deceiving spirits and things taught by demons" (1 Tim. 4:1). • "The time will come when people will not put up with sound doctrine. Instead, to suit their own desires, they will gather around them a great number of teachers to say what their itching ears want to hear. They will turn their ears away from the truth and turn aside to myths" (2 Tim. 4:3–4). • Jesus said, "Truly I tell you, until heaven and earth disappear, not the smallest letter, not the least stroke of a pen, will by any means disappear from the Law until everything is accomplished" (Matt. 5:18).
Baptism for the Dead— Temple Saving Ordinance • "Let me assure you that these are principles in relation to the dead and the living that cannot be lightly passed over, as pertaining to our salvation. For their salvation [baptism for the dead] is necessary and essential to our salvation" (D&C 128:15).	**Do No Work for the Dead** • "If there is no resurrection [some people did not believe in the resurrection], what will those do who are baptized for the dead [if the living are baptized but do not believe in the resurrection, they are spiritually dead]? If the dead are not raised at all, why are people baptized for them?" (1 Cor. 15:29).

MORMONISM TEACHES	THE BIBLE TEACHES
• "The dead who repent will be redeemed, through obedience to the ordinances of the house [temple] of God. And after they have paid the penalty of their transgressions, and are washed clean, shall receive a reward according to their works, for they are heirs of salvation" (D&C 138:58–59). • " ... the baptism for the dead; for Malachi says, last chapter, verses 5th and 6th: 'Behold, I will send you Elijah the prophet ... smite the earth with a curse.' ... and behold what is that subject? It is the baptism for the dead. For we without them [the dead] cannot be made perfect; neither can they without us be made perfect" (D&C 128:17–18). • Joseph Smith said, "Those saints who neglect it [salvation for the dead as temple work] in behalf of their deceased relatives, do it at the peril of their own salvation ... The greatest responsibility in this world that God has placed upon us is to seek after our dead" (*Teachings of the Prophet Joseph Smith*, 193, 356). • "The dead will be after you, they will seek after you as they have after us in St. George" (Wilford Woodruff [former LDS prophet], *Journal of Discourses* 19:229).	• "Let no one be found among you who ... practices divination or sorcery, interprets omens, engages in witchcraft, or casts spells, or who is a medium or spiritist or who consults the dead. Anyone who does these things is detestable to the LORD" (Deut. 18:10–12). • "Jesus told him, 'Follow me, and let the dead bury their own dead'" (Matt. 8:22). • The dead won't be sent back to warn about the hereafter, nor can the living save the dead (Luke 16:30–31, the parable of the rich man and Lazarus, author's summary). • "He is not the God of the dead, but of the living, for to him all are alive" (Luke 20:38; see also Heb. 6:1–3). • "Avoid foolish controversies and genealogies" (Titus 3:9; see also 1 Tim. 1:3–4). • "The disciples asked him, 'Why then do the teachers of the law say that Elijah must come first [Mal. 4:5–6]?' Jesus replied, 'To be sure, Elijah comes and will restore all things. But I tell you, Elijah has already come, and they did not recognize him, but have done to him everything they wished. In the same way the Son of Man is going to suffer at their hands.' Then the disciples understood that he was talking to them about John the Baptist" (Matt. 17:10–13).

MORMONISM TEACHES	THE BIBLE TEACHES
Mormon Church Maintains 141 Temples	**No Temple Needed Today**

MORMONISM TEACHES

Mormon Church Maintains 141 Temples

- "Temple ordinances, covenants, endowments and sealing enable individuals to be reconciled with the Lord and families to be sealed beyond the veil of death. Obedience to temple covenants qualifies us for eternal life—the greatest gift of God to man" (Russell M. Nelson, "Eternal Life Comes from Obedience to Temple Ordinances," *Church News* [April 7, 2001], 10).
- "Behold, I reveal unto you a new and an everlasting covenant; and if ye abide not that covenant, then are ye damned; for no one can reject this covenant and be permitted to enter into my glory" (D&C 132:4).

Temple Covenant Law of Consecration

- "You and each of you covenant and promise before God, angels, and these witnesses at this altar, that you do accept the Law of Consecration as contained in this [the officiator holds up a copy of the Doctrine and Covenants], the Book of Doctrine and Covenants, in that you do consecrate yourselves, your time, talents, and everything with which the Lord has blessed you, or with which he may bless you, to the Church of Jesus Christ of Latter-day Saints, for the building up of the Kingdom of God on the earth and for the establishment of Zion. Each of you bow your head and say 'yes.'"

THE BIBLE TEACHES

No Temple Needed Today

- Jesus said, "I tell you that something greater than the temple is here" (Matt. 12:6).
- Temple veil torn from top to bottom at the death of Christ on the cross (Matt. 27:51; Mark 15:38; Luke 23:45, author's summary).
- True worshipers worship in spirit and truth (John 4:20–24, author's summary).
- "Don't you know that you yourselves are God's temple and that God's Spirit dwells in your midst?" (1 Cor. 3:16).
- "Do you not know that your bodies are temples of the Holy Spirit, who is in you?" (1 Cor. 6:19).
- "We are the temple of the living God" (2 Cor. 6:16).
- " . . . built on the foundation of the apostles and prophets, with Christ Jesus himself as the chief cornerstone. In him the whole building is joined together and rises to become a holy temple in the Lord. And in him you too are being built together to become a dwelling in which God lives by his Spirit" (Eph. 2:20–22).
- Jesus said, "Where two or three gather in my name, there am I with them" (Matt. 18:20).
- See also: 1 Kings 8:27; 2 Chron. 2:6; 6:18; Isa. 66:1; Rev. 21:22; Acts 7:48; 17:24; 1 Peter 2:4–5; Heb. 9:11–12.

GLOSSARY

Aaronic priesthood: The Aaronic priesthood is the lesser (Melchizedek is the greater) priesthood in the Mormon Church. The Aaronic priesthood is typically conferred on young men when they turn twelve and on new male members who have just joined the church. The offices of the Aaronic priesthood, in order, are deacon (ages 12–13), teacher (ages 14–15), priest (ages 16–17), and bishop (similar to a pastor). From the LDS Church website: "With the authorization of the presiding priesthood leader (usually the bishop or branch president), deacons pass the sacrament. They help the bishop or branch president watch over Church members by giving service and assisting with temporal matters such as gathering fast offerings. Teachers may perform all the duties of deacons, and they also receive other opportunities to serve. They prepare the sacramental bread and water and serve as home teachers. Priests may perform all the duties of deacons and teachers. With the authorization of the presiding priesthood leader, they may also bless the sacrament, baptize, and ordain others to the offices of priest, teacher, and deacon."[58]

apostate: A person who once had a testimony of the "one true church" and then leaves it, or someone who ignores the teachings. From the church website: "Members of the Church vary in their levels of participation or belief. Latter-day Saints who have seriously contravened or ignored cardinal Church teachings (publicly or privately) are considered apostates, whether or not they have officially left the Church or affiliated with another religion."[59]

apostle: This is an office in the higher Melchizedek priesthood. There are generally fifteen apostles in the Mormon Church: the members of the quorum of the twelve apostles, plus the three members of the first presidency (the prophet and his two counselors).

atonement: A current member of the twelve apostles explained how the atonement works in Mormonism: "Because of the Atonement of Jesus Christ, all mankind, even as many as will, shall be redeemed. The Savior began shedding His blood for all mankind, not on the cross but in the Garden of Gethsemane. There He took upon Himself the weight of the sins of all who would ever live. Under that heavy load, He bled at every pore."[60]

The following is the third Article of Faith from the LDS book of scripture called the Doctrine and Covenants: "We believe that through the Atonement of Christ, all mankind may be saved, by obedience to the laws and ordinances of the Gospel." Mormonism teaches that because of the atonement, every person who ever lived on the earth will be bodily resurrected and then assigned to one of the three kingdoms of heaven or to outer darkness, based on a judgment of their works. In order to be exalted to the highest degree of heaven, one must obey the laws and ordinances of the Mormon gospel and endure to the end.

baptism for the dead: Baptism is essential for salvation, according to Mormonism. Therefore baptism for the dead is performed in case the dead person who did not have the opportunity to accept the Mormon gospel during his earthly life is willing to accept it from spirit prison after the earthly life.

bishop/bishopric: The bishop is called to preside over the ward (congregation). He is roughly equivalent to a pastor but is a lay leader who volunteers his time without pay. He and the two counselors he chooses to serve with him form the three-member bishopric.

born under the covenant: Children born to parents whose marriage has been sealed in a special ritual in a Mormon temple for time and all eternity.

celestial life: Life in the upper of three levels of Mormon heaven, where God and Christ dwell throughout eternity.

Doctrine and Covenants (D&C): One of the four standard works of LDS scripture, the D&C is a collection of revelations said to be from the Mormon Christ to the Mormon prophets.

discussions: Refers to the LDS missionary proselytizing lessons. There are six lessons altogether, usually one each week. The church currently uses the manual *Preach My Gospel* to guide the missionaries' presentations.

endowment: A ritual in an LDS temple wherein the participant watches a series of live skits or a video portraying the Mormon version of creation and learns a series of handshakes and incantations that must be remembered in order for the participant to pass through the veil to the celestial kingdom where God the Father and Jesus Christ dwell.

eternal life: In LDS theology, eternal life is said to be the kind of life God lives. Only people who reach the upper of three levels in the celestial kingdom (the third level of heaven) with their eternally sealed families are considered to have eternal life. Again from the official LDS Church website: "Eternal life, or exaltation, is to live in God's presence and to continue as families (see D&C 131:1–4). However, to inherit eternal life requires our 'obedience to the laws and ordinances of the Gospel'" (Articles of Faith 1:3).[61]

eternal progression: The process, from eternity, without beginning, to eternity, without end, of working one's way to godhood procreating physical and someday spirit children who have the potential to become gods. The goal of faithful Mormons is to live a good life and attend the temple so as to eventually become a god or the wife of a god.

exaltation: Synonymous with eternal life and godhood. Exaltation is above and beyond salvation. Personal works make exaltation possible.

family home evening: Mormon families are encouraged to spend Monday evenings together praying and singing, reading their scriptures, teaching the gospel to one another, and doing other activities that build family unity.

first presidency: The LDS Church president and his two assistants, called the first counselor and second counselor.

general authorities: The first presidency, quorum of the twelve apostles, presidency of the seventy, quorums of the seventy, and the presiding bishopric. See title definitions separately in this glossary.

God the Father: He was once a man like us. He has a father, unlike the God of the Bible, who has always been God (Ps. 90:2; Deut. 33:27).[62] He is one of many gods, whereas the God of the Bible is the only God who has ever existed or will ever exist (Isa. 43:10).[63] He has a body of flesh and bones as tangible as man's (Doctrine and Covenants 130:22). But the God of the Bible is a spirit. A spirit does not have flesh and bones (John 4:24; Col. 1:15; Luke 24:39).

godhood: This literally means becoming exalted to a station in life wherein a person has all the qualities and power that the God of the Bible (or one of his wives) has, including the ability to have children throughout eternity who will have the same relationship with that person as we have to our God (or Heavenly Mother).[64]

grace: From the official Mormon Church website: "It is through the grace of the Lord Jesus, made possible by his atoning sacrifice, that mankind will be raised in immortality, every person receiving his body from the grave in a condition of everlasting life. It is likewise through the grace of the Lord that individuals, through faith in the atonement of Jesus Christ and repentance of their sins, receive strength and assistance to do good works that they otherwise would not be able to maintain if left to their own means. This grace is an enabling power that allows men and women to lay hold on eternal life and exaltation after they have expended their own best efforts."

"Divine grace is needed by every soul in consequence of the fall of Adam and also because of man's weaknesses and shortcomings.

However, grace cannot suffice without total effort on the part of the recipient. Hence the explanation, 'It is by grace that we are saved, after all we can do' (2 Nephi 25:23)."[65]

Grace, according to Mormonism, but unlike the Christian view of grace, must be accompanied by works to be efficacious for salvation. One passage in the Book of Mormon says it best: "If ye shall deny yourselves of all ungodliness, and love God with all your might, mind and strength, then is his grace sufficient for you" (Moroni 10:32). See also "salvation."

Heavenly Father: Mormons use "Heavenly Father" as the personal name of one of the three gods in their godhead, even though his name, according to doctrine taught in the LDS temple, is Elohim.

Jesus Christ: He is God's first spirit child, thus was not always God, unlike the Jesus Christ of the Bible, who has always been God, the beginning and the end, the Almighty (John 1:1; Ps. 90:2; Rev. 1:8).[66] In Mormonism, he is the spirit brother of Lucifer (Satan, the Devil), not the creator of everything in heaven and earth, including Lucifer, as in the Bible (Col. 1:16–17).[67]

laying on of hands: In the Bible, there are examples of sometimes laying hands on people while commissioning them to service. But in the LDS Church, it is an essential step in performing priesthood duties. A person must receive the gift of the Holy Ghost through the laying on of hands when he or she is declared a member of the LDS Church. To heal the sick, Mormon elders lay hands on them and anoint them with oil.

mission call: An invitation from the LDS prophet to serve a two-year mission. The prospective missionary submits application forms to request the invitation. The prophet decides where he or she will serve. The age for a male LDS missionary was recently lowered from nineteen to eighteen.

Mormon gospel: All the laws and ordinances (rituals) necessary to gain eternal life and progress to godhood, according to Mormonism.

patriarchal blessing: "Patriarchal blessings are given to worthy members of the Church by ordained patriarchs. Patriarchal blessings include a declaration of a person's lineage in the house of Israel and contain personal counsel from the Lord. As a person studies his or her patriarchal blessing and follows the counsel it contains, it will provide guidance, comfort, and protection."[68]

presidency of the seventy: "Consists of seven members of the First or Second Quorum of the Seventy who are called by the First Presidency and are given authority to preside over the Quorums of the Seventy. Most presidencies in the Church have a presidency of three: a president and two counselors. However, in accordance with scripture, all are presidents in the Presidency of the Seventy — none are counselors: 'And it is according to the vision showing the order of the Seventy, that they should have seven presidents to preside over them, chosen out of the number of the seventy; and the seventh president of these presidents is to preside over the six' (D&C 107:93–94)."[69]

presiding bishopric: The presiding bishop and his two counselors, the presidency of the Aaronic priesthood, serve under the direction of the first presidency to administer the temporal affairs of the church.

priesthood keys: "The Prophet Joseph Smith taught 'the fundamental principles, government, and doctrine of the Church are vested in the keys of the kingdom.' Those keys refer to the right to preside over priesthood authority in the name of the Lord Jesus Christ. Keys carry the right to preside over a local organization of the Church, such as a stake, a ward or branch, a mission or district, a priesthood quorum, or a temple. Keys are conferred by the laying on of hands by one who holds proper authority and whose authority is known to the Church. All the keys of the kingdom of God on earth are held by members of the First Presidency and members of the Quorum of the Twelve Apostles. The President of the Church — the senior Apostle — presides over the entire Church and is the only person on earth who exercises all the keys in their fullness. He delegates authority by conferring or authorizing the conferral of keys upon other bearers of the priesthood in their specific offices and callings. Priesthood is the authority of God delegated to man to minister for the salvation of men. 'The power of directing these labors constitutes the keys of the Priesthood.' We distinguish between holding the priesthood and holding keys of the priesthood. When an individual is given keys, he does not receive additional priesthood. What he has is the right to direct the work of the priesthood."[70]

quorum of the twelve apostles: "Apostles are special witnesses of Jesus Christ, called to teach and testify of Him throughout the world. They travel frequently, addressing and encouraging large congregations of members and interested nonmembers, as well as meeting with local leaders. These men are considered to hold the same position as the original twelve apostles. They are also considered prophets, although only the president can receive revelation for the whole church."[71]

quorums of the seventy: "There are currently [in the year 2012] eight Quorums of the Seventy. Each quorum may have up to 70 members. Members of Quorums of the Seventy are often referred to simply as 'Seventies.' Seventies are called to proclaim the gospel and build up the Church. They work under the direction of the Quorum of the Twelve Apostles and the Presidency of the Seventy. Some Seventies are assigned to headquarters administrative functions, but most live and work within a specific geographic region of the Church. Like the Apostles, they also travel frequently to visit and teach congregations of the Church."[72]

sacrament: The specific name of the Mormon version of the Lord's Supper. The two elements, today, are leavened bread and water. In the early days of the LDS Church, Mormons made their own wine for the sacrament. Their scriptures still say wine is for the sacrament; however, Joseph Smith later said it did not matter if wine or water was served. Here is the sacramental prayer from D&C 20:79: "O God, the Eternal Father, we ask thee in the name of thy Son, Jesus Christ, to bless and sanctify this wine to the souls of all those who drink of it."

Sacred Grove: The foundational historic site of the LDS Church where the Father and the Son supposedly appeared to Joseph Smith when he was fourteen years old. The Sacred Grove was located on the Smith farm in Manchester, New York (near Palmyra).

salvation: According to the official Mormon Church website, there are two kinds of salvation:

"Salvation from Physical Death. All people eventually die. But through the Atonement and Resurrection of Jesus Christ, all people will be resurrected — saved from physical death. Paul testified, 'As in Adam all die, even so in Christ shall all be made alive' (1 Cor. 15:22). In this sense, everyone is saved, regardless of choices made during this life. This [bodily resurrection] is a free gift from the Savior to all human beings.

"Salvation from Sin. To be cleansed from sin through the Savior's Atonement, an individual must exercise faith in Jesus Christ, repent, be baptized, and receive the gift of the Holy Ghost (see Acts 2:37 – 38). Those who have been baptized and have received the Holy Ghost through the proper priesthood authority have been conditionally saved from sin. In this sense, salvation is conditional, depending on an individual's continuing in faithfulness, or enduring to the end in keeping the commandments of God (see 2 Peter 2:20 – 22)."[73]

seminary: LDS seminary does not include the college-level courses that the Christian world thinks of when they hear this word. These are Mormon classes in LDS theology for LDS youth during their four years of high school. In a geographic area with a large LDS population, the youth typically attend these classes in a seminary building located next to the public high school. In areas where the LDS population is sparse, seminary is held in the early morning before high school or once a week, with a week's worth of homework assigned.

sons of perdition: People who were members of the LDS Church and then left "the truth," becoming apostate.

stake: A stake is a regional ecclesiastical area the equivalent of a Catholic diocese. A stake president is the equivalent of a Catholic bishop and is responsible for from five to twelve wards (local congregations).

stake presidency: The stake president and two assistants, the first counselor and the second counselor, preside over a stake, or area with several wards (congregations).

temple: A Mormon temple is not the place where LDS conduct Sunday worship services. Rather it is a place reserved for certain sacred and secret rituals (first for LDS members and then for their kindred dead) that must be experienced in order to inherit eternal life and become a god or his eternal wife. Only the most faithful Mormons who have a special pass, called a temple recommend, are permitted entrance into a temple.

temple garb: Mormons are not permitted to show or speak of their temple clothes outside the temple. And because it is offensive to our LDS friends for us to show them, let's just say that, in addition to the temple garments donned after the washing and anointing ritual, special all-white attire (except for the green fig-leaf apron) is worn when going through the other sacred (also secret, as commanded in the endowment ritual itself) rituals. There's a baptism suit, for example, and a somewhat Masonic outfit worn during the endowment ceremony that includes a peculiar flat-top hat with a gathered headband for the men, a white veil for the women, and a green fig-leaf-pattern apron.

temple garments: Special undergarments, short sleeved and to the knees, that a Mormon puts on after the washing and anointing ritual in the temple. They are to be worn both day and night and are said to be a constant reminder of those covenants and a "shield and protection" against evil. They have Masonic symbols (including a compass and a square) over the nipples, navel, and right knee.

temple recommend: A special pass to the temple issued only to worthy persons. Bishops and stake presidents interview church members to make sure they are maintaining a worthy lifestyle before they are given a temple recommend. The requirements include attending meetings, tithing, sustaining (supporting) church leadership, avoiding associations with apostates, and keeping certain health laws (see "Word of Wisdom"). Members must reapply each year, which includes repeating the interviews.

Temple Square: The campus in Salt Lake City that contains the famous landmark Mormon Temple, the Mormon Tabernacle, and a visitor's center.

ward: A local Mormon congregation. Sometimes "ward" is also used to refer to the building for church meetings.

washings and anointings: Symbolic rituals performed first for oneself and, on subsequent visits to the temple, for the dead.

Word of Wisdom: "The Word of Wisdom is a law of health revealed by the Lord for the physical and spiritual benefit of His children. On February 27, 1833, as recorded in section 89 of the Doctrine and Covenants, the Lord revealed which foods are good for us to eat and which substances are not good for the human body. He also promised health, protection, knowledge, and wisdom to those who obey the Word of Wisdom."[74] The LDS Church is somewhat inconsistent on which parts of the health code (found in D&C 89) are required. For instance, D&C 89:12 13 says, "Yea, flesh also of beasts and of the fowls of the air, I, the Lord, have ordained for the use of man with thanksgiving; nevertheless they are to be used sparingly; And it is pleasing unto me that they should not be used, only in times of winter, or of cold, or famine." But Mormons eat as much meat as anyone else. Nevertheless, they must never drink tea, coffee, or alcohol or use tobacco products. Tenth Mormon prophet Joseph Fielding Smith once said, "Are you letting a cup of tea or a little tobacco stand in the road and bar you from the celestial kingdom of God, where you might otherwise have received a fullness of glory?"[75] The BYU Honor Code includes keeping the word of wisdom, as well as earning and retaining a temple recommend.

NOTES

1. Hymn 27, "Praise to the Man," *Hymns of the Church of Jesus Christ of Latter-day Saints* (1985). This hymn was written before 1872.
2. Announced at the Semiannual General Conference of the Church of Jesus Christ of Latter-day Saints on October 6, 2012, male Mormon missionaries may now be recommended to serve at the age of eighteen, female at the age of nineteen. See the official church website: *www.lds.org/church/news/follow-october-2012-general-conference -on-news-and-events?lang=eng.*
3. You can read my mother's story in Lynn K. Wilder and Rob Weidmann, "Hope for Children like Betsy," *Marriage and Families* (April 2002), 2–8.
4. Joseph Smith's First Vision from the LDS scripture Pearl of Great Price, Joseph Smith History, 15: "After I had retired to the place where I had previously designed to go, having looked around me, and finding myself alone, I kneeled down and began to offer up the desires of my heart to God. I had scarcely done so, when immediately I was seized upon by some power which entirely overcame me, and had such an astonishing influence over me as to bind my tongue so that I could not speak. Thick darkness gathered around me, and it seemed to me for a time as if I were doomed to sudden destruction."
5. *www.lds.org/ldsorg/v/index.jsp?locale=0&sourceId=17517c2fc20b8010VgnVCM1000004d8262 0a____&vgnextoid=bbd508f54922d010VgnVCM1000004d82620aRCRD.*
6. Book of Mormon, 3 Nephi 11:29: "For verily, verily I say unto you, he that hath the spirit of contention is not of me, but is of the devil, who is the father of contention, and he stirreth up the hearts of men to contend with anger, one with another."
7. From the official Mormon Church website: *https://www.lds.org/callings/relief-society /getting-started/introduction-to-relief-society?locale=eng.*
8. For more on the temple recommend questions, see Ex-Mormon Christians United for Jesus, "An Open Letter to Glenn Beck about His Mormon Faith," *www.exmormon christiansunited.com/an-open-letter-to-glenn-beck-about-his-mormon-faith/*, or see Michael and Lynn Wilder, *7 Reasons We Left Mormonism* (ATRI, 2012), *www.lightsource.com/ministry /ankerberg-show/download-buy/current-series-offers/7-reasons-we-left-mormonism.html.*

9. The Law of Consecration, The Mormon Temple Endowment Ceremony, http://mit.irr.org/mormon-temple-endowment-ceremony.

10. One of the church manuals quoted on the LDS website explains it like this: "To live in the highest part of the celestial kingdom is called exaltation or eternal life. To be able to live in this part of the celestial kingdom, people must have been married in the temple and must have kept the sacred promises they made in the temple. They will receive everything our Father in Heaven has and will become like Him. They will even be able to have spirit children and make new worlds for them to live on, and do all the things our Father in Heaven has done. People who are not married in the temple may live in other parts of the celestial kingdom, but they will not be exalted." See The Church of Jesus Christ of Latter-day Saints, Gospel Fundamentals (2002), 201, www.lds.org/ldsorg/v/index.jsp?locale=0&sourceId=12a3cb7a29c20110VgnVCM100000176f620a_____&vgnextoid=e1fa5f74db46c010VgnVCM1000004d82620aRCRD.

11. LeRoi C. Snow, "An Experience of My Father's," The Improvement Era (September 1933), www.lds.org/ldsorg/v/index.jsp?hideNav=1&locale=0&sourceId=bb9555faa5cab010VgnVCM1000004d82620a_____&vgnextoid=21bc9fbee98db010VgnVCM1000004d82620aRCRD.

12. From the official Mormon Church website: http://www.lds.org/ensign/1976/07/accepted-of-the-lord-the-doctrine-of-making-your-calling-and-election-sure?lang=eng&query=roy+w.+doxey.

13. Fireside address given by LDS prophet Ezra Taft Benson, "To the Mothers in Zion" (February 22, 1987), http://fc.byu.edu/jpages/ee/w_etb87.htm, and LDS Church education system student manual Marriage, p. 237, www.ldsces.org/inst_manuals/marriage35311000/Selections/Marriage35311000_38.pdf.

14. U.S. Census Bureau, 2012 Statistical Abstract, Births, Deaths, Marriages, and Divorces, www.census.gov/compendia/statab/2012/tables/12s0082.pdf.

15. U.S. News and World Report, Rankings and Reviews, Best Graduate Education Schools, http://grad-schools.usnews.rankingsandreviews.com/best-graduate-schools/top-education-schools/brigham-young-university-provo-mckay-06205.

16. Oddly, the Book of Mormon warns of saying "All is well": "Others will he pacify, and lull them away into carnal security, that they will say: All is well in Zion; yea, Zion prospereth, all is well—and thus the devil cheateth their souls, and leadeth them away carefully down to hell" (2 Nephi 28:21).

17. Hymn 30, "Come, Come, Ye Saints," Hymns of the Church of Jesus Christ of Latter-day Saints (1985).

18. Newell G. Bringhurst, Saints, Slaves, and Blacks: The Changing Place of Black People within Mormonism (Westport, Conn.: Greenwood Press, 1981).

19. Pearl of Great Price, Moses 5:25. This too is LDS scripture.

20. Thomas S. Monson, On the Lord's Errand: Memoirs of Thomas S. Monson (1985), 184.

21. John L. Lund, The Church and the Negro (John Lewis Lund, 1967), 13.

22. Ibid., 54.

23. Joseph Fielding Smith, *Doctrines of Salvation*, 1:61, 66.

24. Brigham Young, *Journal of Discourses* (October 9, 1859), 7:290–91.

25. John Taylor, *Journal of Discourses* (October 29, 1882), 23:336.

26. Lund, *The Church and the Negro*, 45.

27. Lynn Wilder, personal journal entry (February 23, 2006). The information for this book is largely from my numerous personal journals and from interviews with family members and Adam's Road band members in 2009 and 2012.

28. Adam's Road, "I Would Die for You" (2009–2013), *www.adamsroadband.com/i_would_die_for_you_lyrics1*.

29. Sara Israelsen-Hartley, "The Tragedy of the 'Kidnapped' Bride," *Deseret News Online*, November 29, 2007, *http://www.deseretnews.com/article/695231617/The-tragedy-of-the-kidnapped-bride.html?pg=all*.

30. Charles M. Larsen, *By His Own Hand upon Papyrus*, 1992.

31. The Honor Code Statement from the undergraduate catalog on BYU's website: "Students without a current [ecclesiastical] endorsement are not in good Honor Code standing and must discontinue enrollment. Students who are not in good Honor Code standing are not eligible for graduation, even if they have otherwise completed all necessary coursework. Excommunication, disfellowshipment, or disaffiliation from The Church of Jesus Christ of Latter-day Saints automatically results in the withdrawal of the student's ecclesiastical endorsement and the loss of good Honor Code standing. Disaffiliation is defined for purposes of this policy as removal of an individual's name from the official records of the Church" (*http://saas.byu.edu/catalog/2011-2012ucat/GeneralInfo/HonorCode.php#HCOfficeInvovement*).

32. Joseph Smith, *History of the Church* (May 26, 1844), 6:408–9.

33. Wilford C. Wood, vols. 1 and 2, *Joseph Smith Begins His Work* (Wilford C. Wood, 1958). These volumes include the 1830 edition of the Book of Mormon and the church's original Book of Commandments, the Doctrine and Covenants, the Lectures on Faith, and the Fourteen Articles of Faith. They were certified as authentic by a sworn statement from the current prophet, Thomas S. Monson.

34. *Discourses of Brigham Young*, comp. John A. Widtsoe, 458.

35. Ibid., 471.

36. This incident became an Adam's Road song and the name of their third album. Adam's Road, "Enemy of the Cross" (2010–2013), *www.adamsroadband.com/enemy_of_the_cross_lyrics*.

37. Henry and Richard Blackaby and Claude King, *Experiencing God: Knowing and Doing the Will of God* (Nashville: Lifeway Press, 2007).

38. Mike read these Scriptures originally in the King James Version published by the Church of Jesus Christ of Latter-day Saints (1979), but they are presented here in the New International Version (2011) for easier understanding.

39. The Church of Jesus Christ of Latter-day Saints, *Teachings of the Presidents of the Church: Spencer W. Kimball* (2006).
40. Ibid., 1, from Conference Report (April 1964), 94, and *Improvement Era* (June 1964), 496.
41. Ibid., 5, from Spencer W. Kimball, *Miracle of Forgiveness* (1969), 6.
42. Ibid., 5, from Edward L. Kimball, *Teachings of Spencer W. Kimball* (1982), 49–50.
43. Ibid., 6, from Spencer W. Kimball, *Miracle of Forgiveness* (1969), 6.
44. Church of Jesus Christ of Latter-day Saints, *Preach My Gospel: A Guide to Missionary Service* (2004).
45. American Minute with Bill Federer, "Various Presidents on Polygamy," *The Moral Liberal* (July 5, 2011), www.themoralliberal.com/2011/07/05/various-presidents-on-polygamy/.
46. Former LDS apostle Bruce R. McConkie, *Doctrinal New Testament Commentary* 3:75: "All apostates are turned over to the buffetings of Satan in one degree or another, with the full wrath of Satan reserved for those who are cast into outer darkness with him in that kingdom devoid of glory."
47. Brigham Young, *Journal of Discourses* (October 7, 1857), 5:332.
48. http://www.youtube.com/watch?v=i6O5sNyzb5M.
49. Gordon B. Hinckley, "Crown of the Gospel Is on Our Heads," *Church News* (June 20, 1998), 7.
50. As Mike and I were leaving the Salt Lake Temple celestial room (which represents the highest rung of heaven) with Micah, an elderly temple worker invited us into a back office that once belonged to temple president Lorenzo Snow. Near the Holy of Holies, the man whispered this story to us that, in 1898, Lorenzo Snow was in line to be the next Mormon Church prophet. As the current prophet lay dying, Lorenzo Snow was burdened by taking on the mantle of prophet, so he prayed. To his surprise, Jesus Christ himself appeared to him right there, standing three feet above the floor by the stairs exactly where we were standing. See LeRoi C. Snow, "An Experience of My Father's," *The Improvement Era* (September 1933), www.lds.org /ldsorg/v/index.jsp?hideNav=1&locale=0&sourceId=bb9555faa5cab010VgnVCM1000004d8262 0a____&vgnextoid=21bc9fbee98db010VgnVCM1000004d82620aRCRD.
51. Brigham Young, *Journal of Discourses* (October 9, 1859), 7:289.
52. Brigham Young, *Journal of Discourses* (March 8, 1857), 4:271.
53. Church of Jesus Christ of Latter-day Saints, *A Guide to Missionary Service: Preach My Gospel* (Salt Lake City: Church of Jesus Christ of Latter-day Saints, 2004), 206.
54. Hymn 30, *Hymns of the Church of Jesus Christ of Latter-day Saints* (1985).
55. Church of Jesus Christ of Latter-day Saints, *Gospel Principles* (1997), 37.
56. Personal description of a second anointing, www.exmormon.org/mormon/mormon508.htm. See also Roy W. Doxey (former dean emeritus of religious instruction at Brigham Young University and regional representative of the council of the twelve), "Accepted of the Lord: Making Your Calling and Election Sure," *Ensign* (July 1976), www.lds.org/ensign/1976/07/accepted-of-the-lord-the-doctrine-of-making-your-calling-and -election-sure?lang=eng.

NOTES

57. Michael Wilder and Dr. Lynn Wilder, *Seven Reasons We Left Mormonism*, available at our Ex-Mormon Christians United for Jesus website or on Amazon.com.

58. LDS Church website: *www.lds.org/topics/aaronic-priesthood?lang=eng*.

59. Encyclopedia of Mormonism (1992), 1:59, *www.lds.org/topics/apostate?lang=eng*.

60. Russell M. Nelson, "His Mission and Ministry," *New Era* (December 1999), 4, 6.

61. LDS Church website: *www.lds.org/topics/eternal-life?lang=eng*.

62. *Gospel Principles* (1997), 305; (2009), 279.

63. *Teachings of the Prophet Joseph Smith*, 370; *Search These Commandments* (a priesthood study guide) (1985), 152–53.

64. See chapter 47 in the Sunday school teaching manual for members, *Gospel Principles* (2011).

65. LDS Church website: *www.lds.org/scriptures/bd/grace?lang=eng*.

66. *Mormon Doctrine*, 129; *Gospel Principles* (1997), 11.

67. *Gospel Principles* (1997), 17–18; *Gospel Through the Ages*, 15.

68. LDS Church website: *www.lds.org/topics/patriarchal-blessings?lang=eng*.

69. LDS Church website: *www.lds.org/church/leaders/presidency-of-the-seventy?lang=eng*.

70. Elder Russell M. Nelson, "Keys of the Priesthood," *Ensign* (October 2005), *http://www.lds.org/ensign/2005/10/keys-of-the-priesthood?lang=eng*.

71. LDS Church website: *www.lds.org/topics/quorum-of-the-twelve-apostles?lang=eng*.

72. LDS Church website: *www.lds.org/church/leaders/quorums-of-the-seventy?lang=eng*.

73. LDS Church website: *www.lds.org/topics/salvation?lang=eng*.

74. LDS Church website: *https://www.lds.org/topics/word-of-wisdom?lang=eng*.

75. Joseph Fielding Smith, *Doctrines of Salvation* 2:16.

Share Your Thoughts

With the Author: Your comments will be forwarded to the author when you send them to *zauthor@zondervan.com*.

With Zondervan: Submit your review of this book by writing to *zreview@zondervan.com*.

Free Online Resources at
www.zondervan.com

Daily Bible Verses and Devotions: Enrich your life with daily Bible verses or devotions that help you start every morning focused on God. Visit www.zondervan.com/newsletters.

Free Email Publications: Sign up for newsletters on Christian living, academic resources, church ministry, fiction, children's resources, and more. Visit www.zondervan.com/newsletters.

Zondervan Bible Search: Find and compare Bible passages in a variety of translations at www.zondervanbiblesearch.com.

Other Benefits: Register to receive online benefits like coupons and special offers, or to participate in research.

Printed in the USA
CPSIA information can be obtained
at www.ICGtesting.com
LVHW090020060824
787165LV00004B/9